Intercultural Communication

To my students: past, present and future

Intercultural Communication
A Critical Introduction
Second Edition

Ingrid Piller

EDINBURGH
University Press

Edinburgh University Press is one of the leading university presses in the UK. We publish academic books and journals in our selected subject areas across the humanities and social sciences, combining cutting-edge scholarship with high editorial and production values to produce academic works of lasting importance. For more information visit our website: edinburghuniversitypress.com

© Ingrid Piller, 2017
Edinburgh University Press Ltd
The Tun – Holyrood Road
12(2f) Jackson's Entry, Edinburgh EH8 8PJ

Typeset in 11/13 Adobe Garamond by
Servis Filmsetting Ltd, Stockport, Cheshire

A CIP record for this book is available from the British Library

ISBN 978 1 4744 1290 2 (hardback)
ISBN 978 1 4744 1291 9 (paperback)
ISBN 978 1 4744 1292 6 (webready PDF)
ISBN 978-1-4744-1293-3 (epub)

The right of Ingrid Piller to be identified as the author of this work has been asserted in accordance with the Copyright, Designs and Patents Act 1988, and the Copyright and Related Rights Regulations 2003 (SI No. 2498).

Contents

Preface to the Second Edition

I have been teaching intercultural communication courses and workshops for almost two decades and have often been disappointed by the literature in the field. This is because textbooks in intercultural communication are rarely populated by people like my students or myself. I have lived in a number of countries for extended periods, I speak a number of languages and I have close relationships with people whose backgrounds and trajectories are very different from mine. The same is true of the students in my classes and the people around me, who hail from a wide variety of national, ethnic, linguistic, educational, class and gender backgrounds with many different trajectories, experiences and stories. My disappointment with much of the intercultural communication literature stems from the fact that 'real people' with all their differences hardly ever seem to figure in that literature. It stems from the fact that the object of enquiry often does not seem 'real': intercultural communication in real life is embedded in economic, social and cultural globalisation, and transnational mobility resulting from forced or voluntary migration for work, study or tourism. The main challenges of intercultural communication are the linguistic challenges of language learning, the discursive challenges of stereotyping, and the social challenges of inclusion and justice.

The first (2011) edition of this book had therefore been motivated by my desire to introduce the study of intercultural communication in a way that was relevant to and reflective of real life. This motivation continues to be the driving force behind this revised and expanded second edition. In our fast-changing world that is ever-more characterised by global flows, systems and networks, intercultural communication is a dynamic field and a lot has changed since the first edition of this book was published. Therefore, the second edition has been thoroughly revised and updated to take account of new developments in the field. In addition to updating and

CHAPTER I

Approaching Intercultural Communication

CHAPTER OBJECTIVES

This chapter will enable you to:

- Start thinking about intercultural communication in terms of one central research question: Who makes culture relevant to whom in which context for which purposes?
- Familiarise yourself with the terms cross-cultural communication, intercultural communication and inter-discourse communication, and identify how the terms are used with different, similar or overlapping meanings in different studies.
- Analyse culture-related texts for the uses, content, scope and status of culture.

INTERCULTURAL COMMUNICATION: WHAT IS IT?

'Intercultural communication' is one of those terms that everybody uses, and in many different and not necessarily compatible ways. Instead of starting with a definition, I will start with a description of three studies that come under the heading 'intercultural communication', and I will ask you to work out for yourself how the researchers who conducted and wrote these studies understand 'intercultural communication'.

Study 1 is an investigation of the ways in which British and Italian service staff of an airline respond to service failure (Lorenzoni and Lewis 2004). Service failure is another term for 'when something goes wrong' such as baggage being lost or a customer not being able to get on their flight due to overbooking. The researchers administered a questionnaire to thirty-seven British and thirty-nine Italian ground, telephone and cabin staff who worked for the same airline. Both British and Italian staff were very similar in their 'behavioural responses', that is, they reported that they would respond similarly to service failure. For instance, most participants claimed that they would try to change an arrangement if doing so was within company regulations. If it was impossible to change an arrangement, they indicated on the questionnaire that they would explain to the customer why this was so.

While British and Italian employees said they would behave in similar ways in response to a service failure, the two groups reported different attitudes towards customers affected by service failure. For example, Italian service staff reported that they sometimes bent the rules a bit for 'compassionate cases' but British workers did not.

In terms of intercultural communication, the researchers explain the similarities they found in the way the workers act as resulting from the same training that all employees of the airline receive, irrespective of where they are based; and they explain the differences they found in the workers' attitudes as resulting from British and Italian culture, and conclude that attitudes are more influenced by culture and not as amenable to training as behaviour.

Study 2 is concerned with the ways in which Korean immigrant shopkeepers in Los Angeles interact with their African-American customers (Bailey 2000). The researcher observed these interactions by visiting a number of retail shops owned by Korean immigrants. He installed a video camera in one such shop and recorded all interactions during a four-hour period, and he also interviewed the shopkeepers and customers. The researcher found that service encounters with Korean customers were very straightforward, and usually contained three communicative activities – greeting, business transaction, closing – as in this example between a Korean shopkeeper and a Korean customer.[1]

Customer: [enters store]
Cashier: Hello.
Customer: Hello. Cigarettes!
Cashier: You would like cigarettes? [reaches for cigarettes under counter] Here you are. [takes customer's money and hands her cigarettes]
Customer: [turns to leave]
Cashier: Good-bye.
Customer: Okay.

By contrast, interactions with African-American customers were more complex because these customers initiated additional communicative activities such as small talk about the weather, jokes about current affairs, or personal talk about their jobs and families. The Korean storekeepers never proactively introduced such additional communicative activities, they rarely reciprocated and often they did not even respond to such attempts at making the encounter more personal. When the researcher interviewed African-American customers about their views on these retail encounters, it emerged that they often felt ignored by the Korean shop-keepers and complained about their lack of involvement. Furthermore, they felt that this lack of involvement was due to racist attitudes on the part of Korean shopkeepers. By contrast, Korean shop-owners and cashiers considered their customers' attempts at personalising the encounter an imposition and a sign of bad manners, which they attributed to lack of education (or lack of 'good breeding', as they called it) on the part of the African Americans.

Even after years of doing business in African-American neighbourhoods and after years of shopping in Korean convenience stores, intercultural communication between shopkeepers and customers did not improve and they failed to accommodate to each other's ways of speaking. The researcher explains the persistence of divergent communicative styles with reference to the wider socio-historical context in which the two groups interact: there is a long history of racial tensions between immigrant shop-keepers and African Americans in some low-income Los Angeles neigh-bourhoods and against this background each interaction is turned into a new micro-enactment of prior conflicts.

Study 3 is concerned with the ways in which people who live in tourist destinations are being represented in travel writing (Galasiński and Jaworski 2003). The researchers collected travel narratives published in the travel section of a British broadsheet newspaper. They found that travel journalists used three distinct strategies to describe people who live in tourist destinations: to begin with, those people are referred to in very general terms, either as 'locals', as members of a national or ethnic group (for example, 'Russians', 'Dominicans'), or as members of a broad social group (for example, 'women', 'children'). These groups are then described as homogeneous and with clearly identifiable attributes; for example, 'Madeirans being a modest, undemonstrative, devoutly Catholic people.' A second strategy of representing people in tourist destinations was to single out one or more prototypical representatives that the journalist has observed or, more rarely, interacted with. In a story about a trip to China, for instance, a beggar was singled out for such an individual description: 'A beggar in cotton shoes, black felt hat and padded coat, approaches me. Suddenly, he pulls back his coat to reveal a right arm that is no more than a fingered flipper attached to the shoulder.' A third strategy was to

country-specific news and are part of the branding of a country. The institutional links to government seem to be limited but are ultimately unclear
for all the three websites I have chosen: China, Ecuador and Russia. All
three sites have a link to 'culture' on their home page.[2]

The culture page on China.com features a list of blog posts about topics
such as 'Chinese Calligraphy', 'Beijing Roast Duck', 'Chinese Cloth
Shoes', 'Traditional Chinese Dress Cheongsam' or 'Dragon Boat Festival'.
An image of a table laden with food also features prominently on the
page. By contrast, the culture page of Ecuador.com consists of a text page
headed 'Unlock the Treasures of Ecuadorian Culture.' The text, which is
only around 300 words in length, takes the reader on a quick spin through
'Ecuador's official language', 'music and dance festivals', 'Ecuadorians'
distinctive dress code', 'cuisine' and 'Christmas in Ecuador'. Finally, the
culture page on Russia.com is dominated by an image of three smiling
women in traditional dress reaching out to the viewer with a plate of pan-
cakes in a gesture of offering. The headline tells the reader that 'Russia has
a long and rich history.' The page then offers 'some basic understanding of
Russian culture' through links to four 'stories' about 'Russian traditions',
'Russian mentality', 'Russian irrational beliefs' and 'Holidays in Russia'.

Example 2 considers 'culture' in business travel advisories. In addition to practical advice and assistance, such sites often also provide some
'cultural advice'. They usually present the 'culture' of travel destinations
as one 'risk' that business travellers and their employers need to manage,
along with health or safety risks. An example comes from the site www.
riskconversation.com,[3] which is operated by the UK-headquartered and
US-owned multinational insurance provider Chubb. The site recom-
mends 'cultural sensitivity training' for business travellers so that they can
learn cultural 'dos and don'ts' and improve their 'cultural IQ'. The following examples are provided to show what a 'cultural IQ' might look like:

- In Brazil, locals thrive on meaningful interpersonal relationships. If,
  upon greeting your business partner, you immediately 'get down to
  business', most likely you have offended – and even lost – your host or
  local counterpart.
- Similarly, making comments in the Middle East about women's
  rights or telling jokes about an ethnic group may result in 'bad blood'
  between you and your client.
- Not removing your shoes when entering a business associate's home in
  India or China may result in a loss of confidence in your abilities and
  reputation – right from the get-go.

Example 3 comes from news reports about an international gay and lesbian
conference, which was banned in Ghana in 2006 (Forji 2006; 'Ghanaian

Gay Conference Banned' 2006). Part of the ban issued by the Ghanaian government read as follows:

> Ghanaians are unique people whose culture, morality and heritage totally abhor homosexual and lesbian practices and indeed any other form of unnatural sexual acts. [. . .] The government does not condone any such activity which violently offends the culture, morality and heritage of the entire people of Ghana.

These three examples relate to uses of 'culture' in three contexts where culture is oftentimes invoked in today's world: Example 1 comes from the context of tourism marketing, and country marketing more generally, where 'culture' is part of a country's assets. Example 2 is from the world of international business travel, where 'cultural difference' is one aspect of the challenges and difficulties that international companies and their employees might need to manage. Example 3 relates a governmental decision and thus belongs to the sphere of state control, where 'culture' is invoked in relation to citizenship. That means that a hegemonic notion of 'Ghanaian culture' is used to deny some members of society equal rights to those of the majority. While 'culture' is used to disenfranchise gays and lesbians in the example case, 'culture' is also often invoked against the equal rights of immigrants, indigenous minorities, religious minorities or women.

My initial focus on the uses of 'culture' in these examples is intended to set the tone for the rest of this book: as I said above, I regard it as the fundamental research question of the field of intercultural communication to ask who makes culture relevant to whom in which context for which purposes. However, the three examples are also instructive in relation to other definitional issues, namely content, scope and status.

Let's start with content: What is it that 'culture' comprises in the three examples? 'Culture as a national asset' is linked to what often has been called 'high culture': history, the arts and festivals. At the same time, there is also 'popular culture' such as folklore, belief systems and particularly cuisine. 'Culture as challenge' is mostly about interpersonal relationships and how these are communicated verbally (for instance, through engaging in or avoiding small talk) and non-verbally (for instance, through removing or not removing outside shoes when entering a home). Finally, 'culture as citizenship' is presented as consisting of practices that are widely seen as signifying a particular identity: sexual practices in our example. Other such practices which have widely been linked to 'culture' as a basis for discrimination are dress codes (think of debates surrounding the Muslim hijab) or ways of speaking (think of the endless debates about some immigrant group or other not learning 'our' language or not integrating into 'our' society in other ways).

These various contents of 'culture' include some people and exclude others: in Example 3, it is obvious that gay and lesbian people are being excluded from any claim to 'Ghanaian culture'. The exclusionary character of a 'high culture' understanding is also fairly obvious: if 'culture' is thought to reside in museums, theatres, concert halls and the like, it is limited to people who have the means to access these, that is the middle and upper classes who have the education to appreciate this kind of 'culture' and the financial means to do so. The exclusionary character of culture as interpersonal relationships may be less obvious at first glance. However, on closer inspection, it is embedded in the homogenising nature of statements such as those offered in Example 2: the advice to not mention women's rights in the Middle East, for instance, imagines the Middle Eastern interlocutor as male and, more specifically, as a misogynist male who is incapable of rationally discussing women's rights without his 'bad blood' being made to boil.

The exclusionary character of aspects of the content definition of culture brings me to the third definitional aspect, scope, because exclusion and inclusion – the identity work that 'culture' does – become apparent only relative to the scope of a definition of culture.

At first sight, it might seem that these diverse aspects of 'culture' – culled as they are from such a limited set of data – do not have much in common. But look more closely and they actually do: all three of them take the nation as the basic unit of culture. The scope of each underlying understanding of culture, that is, the cultural unit, is a nation in each example (with the exception of the Middle East, where a region is treated as a nation-like homogeneous unit). This is hardly surprising in any of the examples: in Example 1, the national .com websites are explicitly about a nation so obviously the nation would be the unit to which culture applies. Only if you consult corporate websites for contrast does the ubiquity of 'culture' on the nation .com sites become striking: 'culture' is a key aspect of marketing a nation, but it is a rare aspect of marketing any other entity from advertising agencies to zoos. The cultural tips in Example 2 also relate to countries. Again, this may seem 'natural' at first glance because international travel is typically conceived of as travel involving a country of origin and a destination country. However, on second sight, a country – and even more so a region such as the Middle East – is not a good unit when it comes to risk assessment because every country is large, complex and diverse. In the same way that security threats may differ from one part of a country to another, between urban and rural areas, or even across venues in one and the same neighbourhood, behavioural norms are not uniform across a country. Example 3, coming as it does from a state act, also invokes the culture of the nation as unit. Taking the nation or another large group based on social variables (for example, ethnicity or religion) as the unit of analysis in much of the intercultural communication literature is inevitably simplistic and has a number of theoretical and practical consequences, which will be discussed in detail in Chapter 4.

Last but not least, the status of 'culture' in all three examples is that of an entity and the existence of that entity is presupposed. When we encounter definite noun phrases such as 'Ecuadorian culture' or 'Russian mentality', we do not usually stop to think, 'Hey, wait a minute! Does such a thing as "Ecuadorian culture" or "Russian mentality" really exist?' This is because definite noun phrases such as this trigger a presupposition of existence. A presupposition is a proposition that remains constant under negation. For instance, Russia.com advises readers that it is a 'good idea to get some basic understanding of Russian culture before your visit'. You may disagree with that and negate the statement ('Getting some basic understanding of Russian culture before your visit is *not* a good idea.'). However, your critical effort in negating the overall statement does not go very far because it does not call into question the existence of 'Russian culture' (nor 'your visit', incidentally) because the status of 'Russian culture' as a real entity remains presupposed.

We would arrive at a different understanding of the status of 'culture' if we treated it as a verb: 'to do culture', or, more specifically, 'to do Chinese, Ecuadorian, Ghanaian or Russian culture'. Brian Street, an anthropologist of education, argued in a famous essay that 'culture is a verb' because 'culture is an active process of meaning making and contest over definition, including its own definition' (1993: 25).

If we treat culture as something people do, then its status changes from an entity to a process. The entity understanding of culture is essentialist: it treats culture as something people have or to which they belong. The process view of culture is constructionist: it treats culture as something people do, which they perform, and, crucially, compete over. These two understandings of the status of culture can both be found in the intercultural communication literature. Intercultural communication studies are a truly multidisciplinary undertaking and a university course on intercultural communication might be offered under the umbrella of any (or all) of the following disciplines, and probably some other ones, too: anthropology, business studies, communication, cultural studies, education, linguistics, management studies, languages, psychology or sociology. However, multidisciplinary does not mean interdisciplinary, and there is not necessarily much actual interaction – or should I call it 'intercultural communication'? – going on between the various stakeholders. One of the obstacles to a productive dialogue is precisely these two fundamentally incompatible understandings of the status of culture. The product understanding is best epitomised in the work of Geert Hofstede, who considers culture to be 'the software of the mind [. . .] our mental programming' (Hofstede, Hofstede and Minkov 2010). Hofstede has inspired an immense body of work in cross-cultural communication, and I will return to this work in more detail in Chapter 7.

By contrast, the view of culture espoused here and grounded in the anthropological and sociological traditions is that 'culture is not a real thing, but an abstract and purely analytical notion. It does not cause behaviour, but summarises an abstraction from it, and is thus neither normative nor predictive' (Baumann 1996: 11).

In sum, culture has many different meanings and is used in many different ways, which differ along the dimensions of use, content, scope and status. In this section, I have laid out the issues and illustrated them on the basis of three everyday examples. However, these different understandings of culture also have theoretical and practical consequences for research in intercultural communication, and these will be further explored throughout this book.

KEY POINTS

This chapter made the following key points:

- Culture is not something that exists outside of and precedes intercultural communication. Instead, intercultural communication is one domain where 'culture' as concerned with the specific – and different – ways of life of different national and ethnic groups is constructed.
- Culture is an ideological construct called into play by social actors to produce and reproduce social categories and boundaries, and it must be the central research aim of a critical approach to intercultural communication to understand the reasons, forms and consequences of calling cultural difference into play.

COUNTERPOINT

While culture is not something we have – a trait – but something we do – a performance – it is also something that is done to us when others perceive us and treat us as representatives of a particular culture. Being ascribed a particular culture may, for all intents and purposes, be the same where culture is made relevant. To make your notes systematic, you can use a grid which identifies the following aspects of each observation:

- Who is talking? Is the speaker or writer an identifiable individual or an institution? In which role do they speak or write?
- Who is the intended audience? Are there any overhearers? In case of an interaction, what are their reactions?
- What is the relevant context? For example, the relationship between the interactants, the time and place, the medium.
- What is the form? Record what was said or written as accurately as possible and consider the content, scope and status of culture.
- What is the purpose of bringing up culture?

NOTES

1. The transcript has been adapted from Bailey (2000: 94) and the interaction was originally conducted in Korean.
2. See http://english.china.com/chinese/culture/index.html; http://www.ecuador.com/culture/; and http://russia.com/interest/culture/. All URLs provided in this book were last accessed on 2 January 2017.
3. See http://riskconversation.com/blog/business/2014/10/14/cultural-sensitivity-training-for-business-travelers/

as 'having' a culture. Does that mean the essentialist and the constructionist view of culture are ultimately the same? Where do they differ? You
may wish to reflect on this question on the basis of your own experience:
How do you have culture(s)? How do you do culture(s)? How is/are
culture(s) done to you?

FURTHER READING

Scollon et al. (2012) provide an overview of the implications of the three
approaches to intercultural communication – as cross-cultural communication, as intercultural communication and as inter-discourse communication – for research in the field. Sarangi (2009) offers a concise yet
comprehensive overview of approaches to culture from the perspective of
intercultural communication. Blommaert (2005) is a good introduction to
the critical and ethnographic tradition in discourse analysis.

ACTIVITIES

Cross-cultural, intercultural or inter-discourse communication?
Look up one or more of the following studies and identify the underlying
definition of intercultural communication. If the study treats culture as
given, also identify the underlying definition of culture.

- Communicating a credible narrative in asylum interviews (Smith-Khan
  2017).
- Communicating suspects' rights in interpreted police interviews
  (Nakane 2007a).
- Discussing depression in a migrant context (Tilbury 2007).
- Joking in Australian English (Goddard 2009).
- Making sense of study abroad experiences (Tusting, Crawshaw and
  Callen 2002).
- Representations of indigenous people on postcards (Thurlow, Jaworski
  and Ylänne-McEwen 2005).
- Soft-skilling cultural difference in the Canadian labour market (Allan
  2016).

Everyday intercultural communication: reflect on your own experience
Individually or as a class blog, keep a journal throughout the duration of
your course about any texts – public or private, spoken, written or computer-mediated – you come across or any interactions you are involved in

CHAPTER 2

The Genealogy of Intercultural Communication

CHAPTER OBJECTIVES

This chapter will enable you to:

- Gain an overview of the historical and socio-economic contexts in which the contemporary concern with cultural difference, multiculturalism and intercultural communication is embedded.
- Critically engage with the ideologies and material interests informing specific understandings of culture, multiculturalism and intercultural communication.

'CULTURE'

Generations of Latin students have had to memorise the beginning of Caesar's account of the Gallic wars (59–51 BCE):

> All Gaul is divided into three parts, one of which the Belgae
> inhabit, the Aquitani another, those who in their own language are
> called Celts, in our Gauls, the third. All these differ from each other
> in language, customs and laws. (Caesar 2009 [ca. 50 BCE])

Compare Caesar's account of the Belgae, Aquitani and Gauls with the beginning of this modern text about the Kurds:

> A largely Sunni Muslim people with their own language and
> culture, most Kurds live in the generally contiguous areas of
> Turkey, Iraq, Iran, Armenia and Syria – a mountainous region of

southwest Asia generally known as Kurdistan. ('Who are the Kurds?' 1999)

What Caesar saw as important in describing a people or a tribe – or, to put it in more contemporary terms, an ethnic group – are, in the Latin original, *lingua, institutis, legibus* ('language, customs, laws'). There is no mention of culture where the contemporary text has 'language and culture' – a ubiquitous collocation in modern writing about ethnic groups. Conversely, reference to customs and laws is typically absent from modern accounts of ethnic groups. This is even more striking when one considers that 'customs' – which sometimes does appear in modern writing – may not be the most accurate translation of Latin *institutis*. As is obvious, Latin *institutis* is closely related to English 'institutions' and its precise meaning lies somewhere on the spectrum between English 'institutions' and 'customs'.

This example may serve as a springboard for two observations: first, something that Caesar regarded as of prime importance in describing an 'exotic' ethnic group to his fellow Romans, namely institutions and laws, is no longer salient in the genre of *description of an ethnic group*. Second, culture – which is so ubiquitous today that it can be considered an English keyword, as explained in Chapter 1 – was not even part of Caesar's vocabulary. While contemporary English *'culture'* does etymologically derive from Latin *cultura*, that Latin word was used to refer to human intervention in agriculture, the tending of natural growth, cultivation and husbandry (Kramsch 1998: 4).

How then did this way of talking about ethnic groups, specifically ethnic groups other than our own, in terms of culture arise? When and why did culture emerge as a central aspect of the social life of a group, and when did institutions disappear as a central aspect? How did we arrive at a situation where everyone from academics to business people to journalists to politicians seems to have something to say about cultural differences and intercultural communication? This enquiry into the history of *'culture'* is instructive because '[t]he history of the idea of culture is a record of our reactions, in thought and feeling, to the changed conditions of our common life. [. . .] Its basic element is its effort at total qualitative assessment' (R. Williams 1982: 295).

The key argument I will be putting forward here is that discourses of culture, cultural difference and intercultural communication arose in the historical context of the nineteenth and twentieth centuries as part of the processes of colonialism. The salience of intercultural communication in the present period is itself an aspect of globalisation, and, at the same time, it is a response to globalisation. Furthermore, discourses of culture, cultural difference and intercultural communication are an essential aspect of global inequality and they often serve to obscure power relationships and material differences.

Let's follow cultural theorists Raymond Williams (1983) and Tony Bennett (2005) to trace the history of the English word *'culture'* some more and explain its current ascendancy. *'Culture'* was first adopted into English from French and Latin in the fifteenth century in the agricultural meaning mentioned above ('husbandry and tending to natural growth'). From the early sixteenth century onwards this meaning was metaphorically extended to human growth, specifically aesthetic, spiritual and intellectual development. In the late nineteenth and early twentieth centuries a more abstract meaning developed from this one, referring to the works and practices of intellectual and artistic activity. However, the meaning most important for our purposes developed in the nineteenth century through influences from German. The equivalent German word, *Kultur*, had in the eighteenth century developed the meaning of 'historical self-development of humanity', which was seen as a linear process culminating in eighteenth-century European culture. As a counter-movement, the Romantic movement of the nineteenth century began to emphasise folk cultures or popular cultures. The German polymath Johann Gottfried Herder[1] (1744–1803) was the first to argue for the use of *Kulturen* in the plural with reference to 'the specific and variable cultures of different nations and periods, but also the specific and variable cultures of social and economic groups within a nation' (R. Williams 1983: 89).

It is thus against the background of European Romanticism that this new meaning of *'culture'* emerged in English, and became the central category in the new discipline of anthropology. It was a key assumption of early anthropology that cultures formed a cline and that each culture was located somewhere on a specific point on a general path of human development from savagery to civilisation. The comparative study of cultures was supposed to serve the purpose of illustrating various points on this cline. A frequently quoted example of this new meaning of *'culture'* in English comes from the book *Primitive Culture,* which was written by Edward B. Tylor (1832–1917), the first professor of anthropology at Oxford University, and first published in 1871. Tylor argued that 'cultures' could be scientifically measured by comparison with each other. His idea of scientific measurement was to set 'the educated world of Europe and America' as standard on the top end of a scale and 'savage tribes' on the bottom end and then arrange the world's national and ethnic groups in between on this gradient. Employing this method, he concluded: 'Few would dispute that the following races are arranged rightly in order of culture: Australian [Aboriginals], Tahitian, Aztec, Chinese, Italian' (Tylor 1920: 27).

Tylor's bigoted ideas of a global cultural hierarchy were not the ideas of a lone academic in his ivory tower but embedded in the broader socio-political context of the time. The emergence of anthropology as an academic discipline and the spread of a new central meaning of culture as 'a particular way of life, whether of a people, a period, a group, or humanity in general' (R. Williams 1983: 90) occurred in the context of the development of the modern nation state, the Industrial Revolution, nineteenth-century colonialism and its twentieth-century extension, globalisation. The academic concerns of Tylor need to be read in the context of a period where increased travel led to an increased awareness of different peoples and where the subjugation and exploitation of those peoples needed to be morally justified: their assumed cultural inferiority together with the assumption of a developmental path from savagery to civilisation provided the moral justification for colonialism. This form of exerting dominance over others by 'making statements about [them], authorizing views of [them], describing [them], by teaching [them], settling [their lands], ruling over [them]' has famously been termed 'Orientalism' by Edward Said (1978: 3). This new view of culture that emerged in the nineteenth century – of different peoples having different cultures and these cultures being hierarchically ordered, with European culture the most superior – was not restricted to academia and the emerging discipline of anthropology. On the contrary, it found expression in a myriad of popular discourses.

One such genre that contributed to the wide circulation of the idea of a global cultural hierarchy was through cultural displays in shows and exhibitions. During the ages of European exploration and colonial expansion, audiences in Europe and North America delighted in viewing the wonders of the 'new' world. Collecting and displaying 'exotic' specimens in zoos, botanical gardens and museums did not stop with animals, plants and cultural artefacts. 'Exotic' humans were put on display, too. For instance, in the 1830s a French merchant snatched the body of a young African man and stuffed it in the way animals are sometimes stuffed and prepared for display. The body was then shipped to Europe and displayed for almost two centuries in various museums. The body was removed from public display only in 2000, when the remains were repatriated to Botswana (Westermann 2016). In addition to dead people, live people were turned into spectacles for the Western gaze, too. For instance, in the collections of Heinrich Zille (1858–1929), an illustrator and photographer who documented the lives of Berlin's poor in the late nineteenth and early twentieth centuries, there is a series of photographs of an amusement park festival, a *Rummel* (Flügge 1984).[2] The photographs were intended to capture the perspectives of the common people who attended the festival.

As it so happens many of the spectacles on display for the amusement of Berlin's poor relate to *fremde Völker* ('foreign peoples'). Browsing through the photos, one notices an 'Indian Pavilion', one that displays 'Roses from the South' (that is, 'exotic' women), or another one that features 'Sioux-Indians from the Island of [illegible]'. In the displays, anthropological accuracy is obviously completely beside the point. While the name of the island, where the Sioux on display are supposed to come from, is illegible in the image, it does not matter because the basic mistake is the claim to island residence. Furthermore, the painted image of a 'Sioux' on the front of the tent that bears the inscription is of a black African person. The most haunting image in the collection is of a tent displaying *Die Original Australier* ('the original Australians'). In front of the tent, three Aboriginal- or South-Pacific-looking men stand on display. They are wearing long white robes in the manner of Christian monks or possibly traditional Arabs. The headdress of two of them includes some feathers and the third wears a headdress that includes the horns of cattle. Again, accuracy is completely beside the point: cattle are not native to Australia and so horns would most certainly not have been part of traditional Aboriginal dress. One cannot but wonder what the three costumed men who are being gawked at make of their position. Their facial expressions seem withdrawn and the viewer is left to wonder how these men from the Southern Hemisphere ended up as display objects in a Berlin amusement park in 1900; what they made of life in Wilhelmine Germany; and where these men who ended up as display specimens of 'Aboriginal culture' died.

In addition to displaying real bodies and people as specimens of the 'exotic' cultural other, books, newspapers and paintings equally contributed to the exoticisation of non-Europeans. The stalls photographed by Zille also display painted images of and short slogans about the featured group. Another vivid example of the textual display of foreign cultures and their inferiority comes from a poem by Scottish writer Robert Louis Stevenson (1850–1894). The poem is part of a collection of children's verses called *A Child's Garden of Verses* (Stevenson 1885). First published in 1885, the collection continues to be in circulation today and is widely considered 'a cherished classic' ('A Child's Garden of Verses' 2016). One of the poems in the collection is entitled 'Foreign Children' and positions non-European children as objects of a mixture of pity and amusement.

Little Indian, Sioux, or Crow, // Little frosty Eskimo, // Little Turk or Japanee, // Oh! don't you wish that you were me?

You have seen the scarlet trees // And the lions over seas; // You have eaten ostrich eggs, // And turned the turtle off their legs.

Such a life is very fine, // But it's not so nice as mine: // You must
often as you trod, // Have wearied NOT to be abroad.

You have curious things to eat, // I am fed on proper meat; // You
must dwell upon the foam, // But I am safe and live at home.

Little Indian, Sioux or Crow, // Little frosty Eskimo, // Little Turk
or Japanee, // Oh! don't you wish that you were me?

Whether this poem presents any actual facts about the culture of 'foreign
children' is completely beside the point. That there are no lions or ostriches
where the exemplars of 'foreign children' in the poem live is beside the
point. What the poem does – in the same way as the displays described
above – is to set the foreign other up as a weird spectacle. Ultimately,
the point of the poem is not even about the other but about the self: the
British children who read the poem – or have the poem read to them – can
feel reassured that they are safe, normal and proper – in contrast to all the
imagined inferior others out there.

The examples I have shared so far are over a century old and come from
the heyday of the idea of a global cultural hierarchy. However, we should
not therefore dismiss them as irrelevant. Traces of the orientalist view of
the cultural other can still be found in contemporary discourses. While
we may have lost the appetite for putting real humans – whether dead
or alive – on display, the proliferation of images of the cultural other as a
stereotypical spectacle continues unabated. Not only do texts such as the
'Foreign children' poem continue to circulate but new texts presenting
people as stereotypical representatives of a country and a weird spectacle
appear all the time. For instance, in 2016 the Australian supermarket chain
Woolworths ran a marketing campaign called 'World Explorers' aimed
at children. The campaign was a collectibles programme where shoppers
could collect card sets. The front of each card was dominated by a cartoon
character, who was clearly identified as a representative of a particular
country.[3] On the back of each card some 'facts' about the country were
printed and presented as if they were voiced by the cartoon character. The
character for Papua New Guinea, for instance, is a little girl in a colour-
ful 'exotic' dress; her skirt seems to be made of grass and on her head she
wears some sort of felt hat with feathers attached to it. The 'country fact'
the cartoon character shares about Papua New Guinea is as follows: 'The
Huli Wigmen, where I live, grow their hair long to make helmet-like wigs.
They often paint their faces yellow too.' In this description, Huli culture is
described as a timeless fixture unaffected by the logging, mining and pros-
pecting ventures that have profoundly changed all aspects of life in Papua
New Guinea's highlands in recent decades (Kirsch 1996).

According to the Woolworths campaign website, the purpose of the 'World Explorers' campaign was 'to educate kids about the world and different cultures'. Indeed, 'education' was also the purported aim of displaying 'exotic cultures' and their representatives during the earlier period described above. However, as I have shown above this was an 'education' not in facts, knowledge, understanding and empathy but an 'education' in orientalism, that is an education in a particular way of viewing the world where the foreign other is always defined by their national identity and destined to offer a stereotypical spectacle for the Western viewer. This spectacle of the 'weird but true' other may cause amusement, pity or disgust in the viewer but, above all, it is designed to bring home to the viewer their own essential difference from, if not superiority to, those exotic others.

This new meaning of culture which emerged in the nineteenth century was not only part of the justification of colonialism, it made colonialism as a civilising effort a moral obligation, the 'White man's burden'. Rudyard Kipling's poem of this title was published in a popular magazine in 1899 during the early phase of the Philippine–American War, when the USA tried to gain colonial control over the Philippines after having successfully deposed the Spanish. In this context, the poem was widely read as a justification of US colonialism in the Philippines.

Take up the White Man's burden, send forth the best ye breed. // Go bind your sons to exile, to serve your captives' need; // to wait in heavy harness, on fluttered folk and wild // your new-caught, sullen peoples, half-devil and half-child.

Take up the White Man's burden, in patience to abide, // to veil the threat of terror and check the show of pride; // by open speech and simple, an hundred times made plain // to seek another's profit, and work another's gain.

Take up the White Man's burden, the savage wars of peace. // Fill full the mouth of famine and bid the sickness cease; // and when your goal is nearest the end for others sought, // watch sloth and heathen folly bring all your hopes to nought.

Take up the White Man's burden, no tawdry rule of kings, // but toil of serf and sweeper, the tale of common things. // The ports ye shall not enter, the roads ye shall not tread, // go mark them with your living, and mark them with your dead.

Take up the White Man's burden and reap his old reward: // the blame of those ye better, the hate of those ye guard; the cry of hosts ye humour (Ah, slowly!) toward the light: // 'Why brought he us from bondage, our loved Egyptian night?'

Take up the White Man's burden, ye dare not stoop to less; nor call too loud on freedom to cloak your weariness; // by all ye cry or whisper, by all ye leave or do, // the silent, sullen peoples shall weigh your gods and you.

Take up the White Man's burden, have done with childish days; // the lightly proffered laurel, the easy, ungrudged praise. // Comes now, to search your manhood, through all the thankless years // cold, edged with dear-bought wisdom, the judgment of your peers!

Kipling's widely-read poem is yet another example of a larger body of discourse in which cultural difference and cultural superiority became central aspects of European and North American understandings of the wider world (McClintock 1995). The idea of the 'White Man's burden' became, in fact, so popular that it was even used in advertising. A soap ad from around 1900, for instance, shows a ship's captain, a middle-aged white male, in a crisp white uniform washing his hands, surrounded by images of ships on the high seas, at port being loaded with containers, and a naked submissive black person cowering before a white colonial official.[4] The impetus to better inferior cultures is the key positive association for the soap that is being marketed as the soap of choice of 'the cultured of all nations'. The body copy of the ad reads:

The first step towards lightening // The White Man's Burden // is through teaching the virtues of cleanliness. Pears' Soap // is a potent factor in brightening the dark corners of the earth as // civilization advances while amongst the cultured of all nations // it holds the highest place – it is the ideal toilet soap.

So far, I have outlined the origin of the broad meaning of culture upon which intercultural communication studies are based: 'the specific and variable cultures of different nations and periods'. When this meaning first emerged in the nineteenth and early twentieth centuries these cultures were most frequently seen as positioned at various points on a scale from savagery to civilisation. This evaluation of cultures as better or worse continues to this very day, as evidenced in the example of the 2016 'World Explorers' campaign. However, at the same time, another discourse has emerged which is also based on the conception of different cultures and cultural difference but which does not consider some cultures inferior or superior to each other. In this view, which is most commonly known as 'multiculturalism', cultural difference is seen as a form of diversity that is enriching and that is a cause for celebration.

'MULTICULTURALISM'

The non-evolutionary view of cultural difference also has its roots in anthropology, and is usually traced back to the work of Franz Boas (1858–1942). Like Tylor, Boas is one of the pioneers of anthropology and he is often described as 'the father of American anthropology'. Boas argued for the equal worth of all cultures and his work became an important foundation for 'criticisms of American society as a melting pot in which differences were to be extinguished' (Bennett 2005: 67). This celebration of cultural diversity is most commonly termed 'multiculturalism'.

According to the *Oxford English Dictionary* (*OED*) the adjective 'multicultural' predates the noun 'multiculturalism'. The *OED* has this definition of 'multicultural': 'Of or relating to a society consisting of a number of cultural groups, especially in which the distinctive cultural identity of each group is maintained.' The *OED*'s first citation of the adjective dates from 1935 in an academic paper in *The American Journal of Sociology*, where it had a distinctly negative flavour: 'The marginal man arises in a bi-cultural or multi-cultural situation.' The *OED*'s first citation for the noun 'multiculturalism' dates from 1957 in a reference to Switzerland, also in an academic journal. Both the adjective and the noun became widely used outside academia only from the 1970s onwards, in the beginning mostly in references to Australian and Canadian society where it referred to 'a social doctrine that distinguishes itself as a positive alternative for policies of assimilation, connoting a politics of recognition of the citizenship rights and cultural identities of ethnic minority groups' (Ang 2005: 226). Multiculturalism is based on the idea that 'human groups and cultures are clearly delineated as identifiable entities that coexist, while maintaining firm boundaries' (Benhabib 2002: 8). The ascendancy of multiculturalism in the final decades of the twentieth century is also documented by the fact that it does not have an entry in a collection of cultural and societal keywords from the early 1980s (R. Williams 1983) but it does in a similar collection of such keywords published twenty-two years later (Bennett, Grossberg and Morris 2005).

Positive connotations of cultural difference thus became widespread in the climate of political decolonisation, the civil rights movement, and other reform and protest movements of the 1960s. During that period ethnic diversity resulting from migration also became increasingly visible to the mainstream in North America and Western Europe. In many of these contexts 'multicultural' became a euphemism for 'multi-ethnic' or 'multiracial', 'indicating the extent to which debates on multiculturalism are predominantly concerned with the presence of non-white migrant communities in white, Western societies' (Ang 2005: 226).

Culture has been used as a euphemism for ethnicity and race both by majority groups in multi-ethnic societies as well as some minority groups. Many of the groups seeking recognition from the 1960s onwards – groups marginalised on the basis of race, ethnicity, gender or sexuality – turned to their 'culture' as a rallying point for their interests, in a move that came to be known as 'identity politics'. Identity politics – or 'politics of recognition' – is concerned with the liberation of a marginalised constituency whose 'members' do not rally around a particular ideology or party affiliation but around demands for the recognition of their cultural distinctiveness (Heyes 2002).

In order to put some meat on the bones of these terms, I will now exemplify them with a case study of Indians in North Carolina, USA (Subramanian 2000). I will first describe the historical and socio-economic background to Indian migration to North Carolina, before discussing how 'culture' has been deployed in this context and exploring the implications and consequences for multiculturalism.

North Carolina is inter alia known for Research Triangle Park (RTP), one of the largest centres of high-tech research and development in the world. RTP was founded in 1959 in the so-called triangle of Duke University, North Carolina State University and the University of North Carolina at Chapel Hill. In 2009, the year of its fiftieth anniversary, RTP was home to over 170 companies employing around 39,000 workers in research- and development-related jobs. Of these, eighty-three per cent worked for multinational companies such as IBM, GlaxoSmithKline, Cisco or Nortel in the fields of biotechnology, computing, chemicals, environmental sciences, IT, instrumentation, materials science, microelectronics, pharmaceuticals, public health, telecommunications and statistics ('Research Triangle Park' 2016). RTP was founded at the height of the Cold War, two years after the Soviet launch of Sputnik had thrown the USA into a technological and scientific panic. In order to staff RTP and similar research initiatives around the country, the US government chose to rely to a great degree upon immigrants and to a much lesser degree on local training. India became one of the major source countries of US researchers. Between 1966 and 1977 roughly 20,000 scientists, 40,000 engineers and 25,000 doctors from India migrated to the USA. This changed after immigration laws were tightened in 1976. The high numbers of Indian scientists that became part of this brain drain are a direct product of Indian state developmental planning in the post-Independence period, which aimed at increasing the number of scientists in the country and expanding the number of technical institutions in order to achieve economic self-sufficiency and poverty alleviation. Most of the students at technical institutions were drawn from the highest castes of Indian society. This background is essential to understanding Indian-American 'culture' because a 'key attribute [of Indian-American culture in North Carolina], one that has buttressed their claim to first-class citizenship, is professional class status' (Subramanian 2000: 106):

> Indians are currently one of the most affluent U.S. minority populations. They have emerged as a 'model minority' whose public profile fits neatly into the logic of American multiculturalism. They are 'hard-working,' they have their community institutions and practices, and they subscribe to a political conservatism that supports their material interests. Most importantly, they have attempted to define themselves in cultural terms that avoid any obvious racial referent. The coincidence of Indian professional migration to the U.S. and civil rights legislation that instituted a formal equality has permitted the ascendance of a politics of culture. [. . .] Now, 'culture,' with its constituent elements of region, language, and religion, has superseded race as the definitive characteristic of Indian immigrant identity. (Subramanian 2000: 107)

Class – both in the country of origin and the country of residence – is an important factor in the experience of North Carolina's Indian professionals. The second important factor is race. In the US context race is a key aspect of social structure and Reyes (2007) explains the positioning of Asian Americans within a tripartite model of identity discourses: Asian Americans may be positioned vis-à-vis African and European Americans as 'not real Americans', that is, as perpetual foreigners. Asian Americans may also be positioned as either a problem minority or a model minority – in the former case they are associated with African Americans, and in the latter with European Americans, that is, they are seen as honorary whites.

In these complex racial positionings, North Carolina's Indian professionals have successfully avoided being racially framed. In particular, this has meant that they have been able to avoid the problem minority discourse of being associated with African Americans or with Hispanic immigrants. In order to dissociate themselves from these and other more recent and less successful immigrant groups, they have wielded their unique 'cultural identity' through building a range of cultural institutions: these include religious institutions (for example, Hindu temples, Sikh gurdwaras, Muslim mosques), national organisations (for example,

India Heritage Society, Indian American Forum for Political Education, The Indus Entrepreneurs), regional language associations (at the time of her fieldwork in the late 1990s, Subramanian encountered twelve such language associations), and film and music festivals.

What does this case study tell us about multiculturalism and identity politics? To begin with, there is the obvious point that cultures meet and mingle in a specific historical, social and economic context. In the example, this context includes, for instance, the development aspirations of post-Independence India, the Cold War, the race politics of the USA and particularly the American South, and the boom in scientific research and development over the past decades. Thus, multiculturalism per se does not exist; it exists in a specific context. Second, there is the less obvious point that 'culture' does not precede context but is created by various socio-economic contexts, that is, there are no essential American and Indian 'cultures' that encounter each other to become 'multi-culture'. Instead this specific version of Indian-American 'culture' emerged in its specific context.

The invocation of culture has a number of consequences. First, the appeal to 'culture' is one way for Indians to gain acceptance as non-white persons in a society characterised by white privilege. Second, the mobilisation of 'culture', while partly enabled by the Civil Rights movement, also obscures the persistence of racial and class inequality, and the appeal to 'culture' includes a distancing from ethnic and class solidarity. Multiculturalism thus becomes a new way to secure class privilege. Third, 'culture' also provides a means to stake a claim for a share of the pie of global capitalism: these Indians, like other non-European societies and minority populations within the West, 'make their own claims on the history of capitalism by finding capitalist ethics within their own "cultural traditions." [. . .] they wield cultural difference as a necessary vehicle of social mobility and capitalist success' (Subramanian 2000: 113).

Discourses of multiculturalism are closely aligned to discourses of intercultural communication: they share a similar understanding of culture and they emerged at around the same time. However, while multiculturalism is mostly concerned with intra-national 'cultural diversity', the thrust of intercultural communication tends towards 'cultural diversity' on an international scale. It is towards the specific genealogy of intercultural communication that I will now turn.

'INTERCULTURAL COMMUNICATION'

In English, people started to talk about intercultural communication at around the same time that multiculturalism appeared. The *OED* has the first entry for 'intercultural' in a 1937 article in the journal *Theology*, and a second one from 1955 from the *Scientific American*. The first occurrence of the term in the corpus of *Historic Australian Newspapers* at the National Library of Australia is slightly earlier, from a 1931 article about 'intercultural problems' in the Pacific ('Peaceful Pacific?' 1931).

The *OED*'s 1955 quotation points to an early applied focus of interest in intercultural communication: 'In the interest of intercultural understanding various U.S. Government agencies have hired anthropologists.' The first documented use of 'cross-cultural' according to the *OED* is in the 1944 book *A Scientific Theory of Culture* by the famous anthropologist Bronislaw Malinowski: 'There is the comparative method, in which the student is primarily interested in gathering extensive cross-cultural documentations' and, also in the 1940s, another famous anthropologist, Margaret Mead, is cited by the *OED* as writing 'All people who have had the good fortune to learn several languages in childhood have a precious degree of cross-cultural understanding.' We can see that the partial overlapping of the two terms started early: while the Malinowski quote is in line with the comparative definition of 'cross-cultural' introduced in Chapter 1, the usage in the Mead quote aligns with the definition of 'intercultural' there.

Like multiculturalism, intercultural communication seems to have spread from academic publications into general discourse. A keyword search in the catalogue of the Library of Congress[5] for 'cross-cultural communication' and 'intercultural communication' documents that books that are relevant to these keywords first started to appear in the 1940s. A search in December 2016 yielded 4,141 entries. More than half of these (64.8 per cent; n = 2,684) had been published since 2000; 31.2 per cent (n = 1,292) were published in the 1980s and 1990s. That means that holdings filed under the keywords 'intercultural communication' or 'cross-cultural communication' have grown exponentially since they first started to appear in the 1940s.

Not considering undated entries, the first book on intercultural communication held by the Library of Congress is a 1944 Argentinean publication (Romero 1944), followed by 1947 conference proceedings in religious studies (Bryson, Finkelstein and MacIver 1947). The next holdings on intercultural communication date from 1959 (Bunker and Adair 1959; Hall 1959; World Confederation of Organizations of the Teaching Profession 1959), and after that date publications slowly start to take off. The early publications fall into three clearly identifiable strands: namely military (for example, Geldard and Bouman 1965; Gerver and Sinaiko 1978; Kraemer 1969); corporate business, particularly Japan–US (for example, Barnlund 1989; Carlisle 1967; Hall and Hall 1987); and missionary and religious studies (for example, G. Cooke 1962; Jurji 1969; Mayers 1974). These strands continue to be important in publications in intercultural communication today, but, as more and more publications have appeared, these have obviously become diversified.

What are the historical socio-economic contexts in which the exponentially growing interest in intercultural communication, particularly in the three key strands of activity, has been situated? As is the case with multiculturalism, the Cold War undoubtedly goes a long way to explain military interest in intercultural communication and many of the early developments in the field were associated with the US military. For instance, William B. Gudykunst (1947–2005), a key figure in intercultural communication studies and author and editor of numerous widely-read publications in the field started his career in the US Navy, where he once served as an intercultural relations specialist in Japan ('Communications Scholar William Gudykunst Dies' 2005).

A related source for intercultural communication studies is the Foreign Service Institute (FSI) of the US Department of State, which Wendy Leeds-Hurwitz (1990) identifies as the origin of intercultural communication studies, and which also appears in the 1955 *OED* quote cited above. Leeds-Hurwitz (1990) shows how the specific context of the FSI, which prepares US diplomats for their missions abroad, influenced the foundational assumptions of the fledgling discipline in the 1940s and 1950s. The FSI grew out of various language training programmes for military personnel during World War II. One of the anthropologists hired by the FSI, Edward T. Hall (1914–2009), whose books *The Silent Language* and *The Hidden Dimension* (1959, 1966) are widely considered to be classics in the field, became particularly influential. His approach to intercultural communication in turn was shaped by the practical concerns of his students:

> [T]he students in the FSI classes had no interest in generalizations
> or specific examples that applied to countries other than the ones to
> which they were assigned; they wanted concrete, immediately
> useful, details provided to them before they left the US. (Leeds-
> Hurwitz 1990: 263)

Consequently, Hall, an anthropologist by training, began to emphasise micro-cultural details over a more holistic view of culture. Specifically, he identified proxemics, time, paralanguage and kinesics as key aspects in need of attention in intercultural communication situations, and these continue to be cornerstones of many texts in the field. The basic idea is that people from different cultures – and cultures are usually equated with nations in this paradigm for obvious reasons – differ in their use of space, their conceptions of time, their ways of using paralinguistic phenomena such as intonation and pitch, and in the ways they move their bodies. In order to make these easily amenable to the needs of their students, Hall and his colleagues attempted to describe proxemics, time, paralanguage and kinesics in the same systematic way that descriptive structural linguists had developed for describing language, and particularly pronunciation:

> A microcultural investigation and analysis properly conducted can provide material which can be compared in the same way that phonetic and phonemic material from different languages can be compared. The results of such studies are quite specific and can therefore be taught in much the same way that language can be taught. (Hall 1960: 272)

Linguistics has long since moved away from structuralism with its emphasis on discrete units that contrast and combine to form the structure of a language, but the influence of structural linguistics continues to be felt in intercultural communication studies. This means that it is not only the field itself that developed in US military and diplomatic institutions of the mid-twentieth century, but also a very specific theoretical and methodological approach to intercultural communication. In this approach, 'culture' is equated with nation and is assumed to vary systematically on a set of universally meaningful variables.

Despite the fact that we can observe clear institutional links between early intercultural communication scholarship and the US military and diplomacy, the Cold War itself did not play out on the terrain of culture but on the terrain of ideology, with capitalism pitted against Communism. The key international conflict that has followed the Cold War – the War on Terror, as it is called from a Western perspective – is much more obviously based on a view of the enemy in terms of culture and is widely understood as a 'clash of civilizations' (Huntington 1993), particularly between 'the West' and 'Islam'.

The applied impetus behind intercultural communication studies is also apparent in other strands of intercultural communication: while the military and diplomatic strands alternatively seems to aspire to bringing world peace through intercultural communication on the one hand, and gaining a military advantage through intercultural communication on the other, literature in the business strand tends to be more unequivocal about the use of intercultural communication knowledge for the purposes of gaining a business edge. The period when intercultural communication studies started to take off in business studies in the early 1970s coincided with the rapid increase in Japanese exports and a perception, particularly in the USA, that Japanese imports in key sectors such as automobile manufacturing presented a threat to the national economy. Political economists usually identify the reasons for this surplus in the quota and tariff barriers Japan was subsequently pressured into dismantling (Reinert 2008). However, business studies and business commentators in the media widely held a view that the Japanese economic miracle, and particularly the Japanese export surplus, was a result of Japanese culture and character. Consequently, there emerged a strong desire to understand that culture in order to be able to meet 'the Japanese challenge' (Keegan 1984), and, incidentally, Edward T. Hall also made an important contribution in this context with his book *Hidden Differences: Doing Business with the Japanese* (Hall and Hall 1987).

In sum, interest in and concern for intercultural communication first became widespread at a time when there was an increasing awareness of international relationships in the USA but – unlike in the nineteenth century – that international world was no longer self-evidently inferior: there were the technological and scientific successes of the Soviet Union, the military and civil disobedience successes of former colonies that led to decolonisation, and the economic successes of Germany, Japan and other Asian nations. So the rise of the discourse of intercultural communication coincides with the rise of a US perception of the world in terms of international competition and threat. This is also the period when globalisation first became a widely used term (the interconnections between intercultural communication and globalisation will be explored in detail in Chapter 6).

KEY POINTS

This chapter made the following key points:

- If 'culture' does not self-evidently exist (as explained in Chapter 1), it is instructive to ask in which contexts 'culture' first came to be noticed and talked about. Or, to put it differently, in which contexts were culture and cultural differences talked into existence? In English, this was in the nineteenth century at a time of rapid colonial and imperial expansion of both the UK and the USA.
- In the nineteenth century, cultural differences were conceived in terms of an evolutionary hierarchy but when the idea of European superiority was called into question through various socio-economic and political developments in the second-half of the twentieth century, intercultural communication started to be seen as a means to overcome cultural

difference – be it cooperatively ('good intercultural communication leads to greater understanding') or competitively ('good intercultural communication helps to beat the other at their own tricks').

COUNTERPOINT

This chapter has told the story of 'culture', 'multiculturalism' and 'intercultural communication' exclusively from a Western perspective, where struggles over the definition and representation of cultural difference are embedded in colonial and capitalist expansion. However, discourses of culture are, of course, not unique to the West. China, for instance, has, since the founding of the People's Republic in 1949, pursued a multicultural project that is also embedded in a reification of cultural difference. China recognises fifty-six ethno-cultural groups known as *minzu*, which are assumed to be clearly demarcated by language, culture and, ultimately, blood lines and which are conceived as constituting a harmonious multicultural whole (Mullaney 2011). How would the story of the development of the terms 'culture', 'multiculturalism' and 'intercultural communication' in their social and historical contexts change if told from a Chinese or other non-Western perspective?

FURTHER READING

The compilation and explanation of English 'keywords' by Raymond Williams (1983) continues to be a profitable read and every student of intercultural communication should at least have read the entry for 'culture' (pp. 87–93). The same is true of the 'culture' entry by Tony Bennett (2005) in the *New Keywords* compilation. If you want to read some intercultural communication classics, *The Silent Language* and *The Hidden Dimension* by Edward T. Hall (1959, 1966) both make for enjoyable reading.

ACTIVITIES

The discipline-specific socio-historical contexts of intercultural communication

Consult a discipline-specific bibliographic database (for example, *Business Source Premier* for business studies, *LLBA* for linguistics, *PsycINFO* for psychology) and document when publications that had 'cross-cultural communication' or 'intercultural communication' as a keyword or as part of the title started to appear. Make sure also to consult the hard copies of the database before the records of the electronic version begin. Document the quantitative and qualitative development of intercultural communication for the discipline. In order to document the quantitative development, plot the number of publications against time in a diagram. In order to document the qualitative development, identify whether 'strands' or topical concerns stand out on the basis of the titles and abstracts.

The language-specific socio-historical contexts of intercultural communication

Alternatively, if you have access to bibliographic resources in a language other than English, consult a national equivalent of the catalogue of the Library of Congress, if such an equivalent exists, and document the quantitative and qualitative development of the translation equivalent of 'intercultural communication' for that language. If you want to write a more extensive research paper, you could also try to research the personal and institutional links, if any, between intercultural communication studies in the English-speaking world and its translation equivalent in your language.

NOTES

1. Background reading on Herder and the socio-political context of his ideas about culture is available at http://www.languageonthemove.com/herder-an-explainer-for-linguists/
2. Some of the images discussed here can also be viewed at http://www.languageonthemove.com/what-makes-foreigners-weird-a-quick-guide-to-orientalism/
3. Images of some of the cards can be viewed at http://www.languageonthemove.com/what-makes-foreigners-weird-a-quick-guide-to-orientalism/
4. The ad can be viewed at https://en.wikipedia.org/wiki/File:1890sc_Pears_Soap_Ad.jpg
5. See http://catalog.loc.gov

CHAPTER 3

Language and Culture

This chapter will enable you to:

- Familiarise yourself with the principles of linguistic and communicative relativity and to engage with them critically.
- Engage critically with discussions about the relationship between a specific language and a specific culture, and contribute to those discussions through critiques of existing writing in intercultural communication.

LINGUISTIC RELATIVITY

For years, I have started my classes on language and culture with two questions. First, I ask those in the audience who are afraid of spiders or who know someone who is afraid of spiders to raise their hands. Usually, more than half of the people in the audience raise their hands. Second, I ask those in the audience who are afraid that somewhere, somehow a duck is watching them or who know someone who is afraid that somewhere, somehow a duck is watching them to raise their hands. No one ever raises their hand and responses range from bewildered looks to giggles about the absurdity of the question – all followed by outright laughter once I show a *Far Side* cartoon[1] depicting a man sitting at his desk in front of a large window. The window is overlooked by high-rises with many windows, and in one of those windows there is a duck. The caption reads: 'Anatidaephobia: The fear that somewhere, somehow, a duck is watching you.'

Fear of spiders, or arachnophobia, is a concept that is readily available in many of the world's languages, grounded as it is in the actual fact that some spiders can be dangerous to humans. By contrast, fear of being watched by a duck, or anatidaephobia, is a word made up for a concept made up by a cartoonist and is known to only a very few people who are familiar with that particular cartoon. The observation that I would like my students to reflect on with this example is that a well-known concept is tied to actual experience: many people are afraid of spiders or know someone who is afraid of spiders. An obscure concept is not related to experience in the same way: no one I have ever met is afraid of being watched by a duck or knows someone who is.

Language thus offers us concepts for experiencing the world around us – and different languages sometimes offer different concepts for perceiving and experiencing the world around us, as I will illustrate with an example of kinship terms. Kinship relations and the terminology for those relations are characterised by rich variation among the world's languages and cultures (for an overview of anthropological research into kinship relationships and their representation in the world's languages, see Foley 1997: 131–149). In the example, let's concentrate on a small set of members of the preceding generation – the people referred to as 'mother', 'father', 'aunt' and 'uncle' in English. In Modern Standard English, the salient distinctions between these four terms and the relationships they refer to are relative to the directness of the biological relationship ('mother' and 'father' versus 'aunt' and 'uncle') and sex ('mother' and 'aunt' versus 'father' and 'uncle'). Contemporary German also has four terms with the exact same meanings (*Mutter, Vater, Tante, Onkel*). However, historically an additional contrast existed in German (W. J. Jones 1990). In addition to biological relationship and sex, different terms existed to denote side of the family. That means the English terms 'aunt' and 'uncle' had two translation equivalents each. 'Aunt' could be translated as either *Muhme* ('maternal aunt') or *Tante* ('paternal aunt') and 'uncle' could either be translated as *Oheim* ('maternal uncle') or *Onkel* ('paternal uncle'). This distinction was important as long as blood relationships were accorded a highly privileged position in law: one could be sure that maternal relatives were related by blood with a certainty that was impossible to achieve for paternal relatives before the emergence of paternity tests. Furthermore, the distinction between members of the paternal and maternal side of the family was important as long as women held a lower legal status than men and could not, for instance, assume guardianship of children born out of wedlock. In such a case, the mother's brother would have become the child's guardian. Therefore, the role of a maternal and paternal uncle was quite different and, obviously, required different words to identify it. However, when the legal and social status of blood relationships and of women changed – that is, culture changed – the language changed with it and first the meanings of *Muhme/Tante* and *Oheim/Onkel* started to overlap and eventually one term disappeared from each set of what were by then nothing more than duplicates.

While Modern Standard English and Early Modern German display an interesting difference in the way they use four or six terms, respectively, to refer to close relatives of the preceding generation, they are very similar in the way in which both sets of terms could be nicely slotted into a family tree. While one would need two additional slots for the Early Modern German model family tree, that really is a minor difference compared with kinship systems used by the indigenous people of the Western Desert in Central Australia. The kinship terms of the Western Desert languages differ from English not only in the way in which they classify relatives, but in two additional ways: they differ according to the way kinship terms are used in context and they differ in the fact that kinship terms refer to more than the relationship between members of the immediate biological family (Dousset 2003).

The kindship terms in the Western Desert languages are so different from what is common in European languages that it took European linguists quite some time to understand and describe them. The first formal description of the kinship systems of the Western Desert languages was provided by Adolphus P. Elkin (1891–1979), a key figure in Australian anthropology in the first-half of the twentieth century. During fieldwork in Central Australia in the 1930s, Elkin noticed that traditional Aboriginal people there apparently only had two terms for members of the preceding generation, *ngunytju* and *mama* (Elkin 1938–1940). He found *ngunytju* to refer to a person's mother, her sisters and, actually, to any female of their generation. *Mama* refers to a person's father, his brothers and can also be extended to any male of their generation. Elkin also recorded terms for paternal aunt (*kurutili*) and maternal uncle (*kamuru*) but that did not keep him and successive generations of anthropologists from focusing on the anomalies inherent in a system that apparently lacked ways of distinguishing between elementary kinship relationships such as immediate and extended relatives and where any member of the preceding generation could apparently be considered to be one's 'mother' or 'father'. Some anthropologists even went so far as to deduce a lack of a prohibition against sibling marriage from this system and even so famous an anthropologist as the French professor Claude Lévi-Strauss declared it 'aberrant' (Lévi-Strauss 1969). However, these anthropologists themselves were falling prey to linguistic relativity as they tried to understand the kinship terminology of the Western Desert languages through the lens provided by kinship terminology in European languages.

They overlooked two aspects, namely context of use and meanings

habits of speech as guides to an objective understanding of the nature of experience. This is the relativity of concepts or, as it might be called, the relativity of the form of thought. It is not so difficult to grasp as the physical relativity of Einstein nor is it as disturbing to our sense of security as the psychological relativity of Jung [. . .] but it is perhaps more readily evaded than these. For its understanding the comparative data of linguistics are a *sine qua non*. It is the appreciation of the relativity of the form of thought which results from linguistic study that is perhaps the most liberalizing thing about it. What fetters the mind and benumbs the spirit is ever the dogged acceptance of absolutes. (Sapir and Mandelbaum 1985: 159)

Even anthropologists as professional students of languages and cultures may be caught in the ways of seeing offered to them by the concepts of their own languages and (professional) cultures, as the history of research into kinship terminology in the Western Desert languages shows. Different views of the meanings of family – and the inability of Europeans to recognise other concepts of 'family' than their own – had tragic consequences in the forced removal of Aboriginal children from their families for much of the period since the European occupation of Australia (Haebich and Delroy 1999). Today it is hard to imagine anyone not being moved by the cruelty of the practice and the suffering inflicted on the Stolen Generations, their families and communities. At the same time, it is also apparent from the records that many of the white colonial officials behind the policy and implementation of forced removal actually thought they were 'doing the right thing' because they were incapable of conceiving of Aboriginal family relationships as valid, healthy and nurturing. The inability of the colonisers to recognise non-European family relationships is poignantly captured in the novel *Wanting* by Richard Flanagan (2008). The novel offers a fictional account of the British occupation of Tasmania and particularly the removal from her family of Mathinna, an Aboriginal girl, by Governor Franklin (1836–1843). Franklin and his wife were conducting a social experiment with the aim of establishing to what degree Aboriginal people could be 'civilised' through an English education. Remember that this was at a time when the races of the world were seen as inhabiting a cline topped by Northern Europeans and bottomed by the Aboriginal people of Australia (see Chapter 2).

In the scene I am quoting, the childless Lady Franklin is visiting Flinders Island in the Bass Strait, where the surviving Tasmanian Aborigines had been forcibly relocated. Lady Franklin is smitten by the beautiful seven-year-old Mathinna, who is made to perform a dance to greet the visitors.

Lady Franklin very much 'wants' the child. Therefore she tries to convince herself and her entourage that Mathinna is an orphan and it is thus in the best interests of the child to take her away from her family and bring her to the governor's residence in Hobart. The local Protector of Aborigines, who has just presented the boiled and flensed skull of Mathinna's father to the Franklins in response to their request for an Aboriginal skull for scientific purposes, is a bit more reluctant to hand a living person over to them. Therefore, he tries to explain that Mathinna may be an orphan in English terms but is not in Aboriginal terms:

> 'And that dear little girl then has neither mother nor father, nor family?' [asks Lady Franklin]
> 'She has family, Ma'am, but none immediate. They [= Aboriginal people] think of such things more loosely and more intricately than we. For us family is a string, for them it is lace.' [replies the Protector]
> 'She is an orphan, though.'
> 'By our reckoning,' said the Protector, 'she is an orphan.'
> (Flanagan 2008: 68f.)

Because 'our reckoning', the English reckoning of the Franklins, prevails, Mathinna is removed from her family, who had themselves already been forcibly removed from their ancestral lands, enters the Franklin household where she suffers all manner of injustice and indignity, only to be abandoned when Governor Franklin is recalled to Britain. Like the historical Mathinna, the fictional Mathinna in *Wanting* dies of alcoholism, loneliness and a broken heart at the age of twenty-one. The fact that the colonisers' insistence on a single valid world view wreaked havoc in Mathinna's life – as it has done and continues to do in the lives of so many 'Others' – is testament to the moral imperative to acknowledge the linguistic and cultural relativity of our views. The inability to see the world through lenses other than our own indeed 'fetters the mind and benumbs the spirit!'

LINGUISTIC RELATIVITY APPLIED

Linguistic relativity is probably one of the most popular and widely known linguistic concepts. Most people will have heard factoids such as the one that Eskimos have an amazingly large number of words for snow and will consider that as evidence that Eskimos think differently about snow than speakers of other languages. In reality, Eskimos have no more different words for snow than English speakers in the Northern Hemisphere, who may be able to distinguish between 'snow', 'slush', 'sleet' and 'blizzard,' as Pullum (1991) explains in an examination of how the supposed number of Eskimo words for snow ballooned from four in a 1911 publication by Franz Boas to many hundreds in some contemporary media texts. Furthermore, even if Eskimos had lots of different words for snow this would not in itself say anything more interesting about 'Eskimo culture' than the fact that specialists have a more sophisticated vocabulary about their specialisation than non-specialists.

The idea of linguistic relativity was further popularised in the 2016 Hollywood movie *Arrival* (Villeneuve 2016). The film features a linguist who is recruited by the US military to decode an alien language. The extraterrestrials have a 'circular' language that matches their non-linear conception of time. As the linguist learns to communicate in the alien language her world view changes and she is able to see into the future in the same way she remembers the past.

A multitude of Eskimo words for snow or a circular alien language that enables its speakers to see the future make linguistic relativity seem like an esoteric theory. However, as the example of the Stolen Generations has shown, it is much more than a quaint theoretical point about exotic languages. On the contrary, different ways of seeing the world may have significant consequences in intercultural interaction, particularly if these different ways of seeing are hierarchically ordered, as was true of the powerful 'English' ways of seeing family in colonial Australia which could afford to simply ignore Aboriginal ways of seeing family.

Another context where practical challenges resulting from linguistic relativity may be readily apparent is the provision of healthcare to transnational patients. For instance, in a study of understandings of mental health issues amongst East African refugees in Perth, Western Australia, Tilbury (2007) found that the term 'depression' did not have a direct translation equivalent in the languages of her interviewees. Instead, they described their emotions as frustration, uncertainty, hopelessness, shame, embarrassment, loneliness, disempowerment, shock, anger, loss of control and betrayal, as well as physical symptoms such as sleeplessness and stomach problems. In Australia, however, these emotions and symptoms were framed as 'depression'. Applying the hegemonic mental health language of the West to the participants' experiences had a number of consequences and created more 'depression' rather than less. It served to disempower migrants from the Horn of Africa in four ways: to begin with, '[i]t universalises an emotion state, rather than recognising its cultural situatedness' (Tilbury 2007: 454). Second, 'depression' is treated as an individual problem although the negative emotions described by the participants were clearly socially embedded. One participant explained the social rather than individual nature of his emotions with the following metaphor:

> Yes we do feel them [negative feelings] in Africa but it is different from the way I feel them here because their reasons are different. In Africa it was personal problems but here I feel I am a bird without wings – all my people who were supporting me in Africa are not here. (Tilbury 2007: 446f.)

Third, if the nature of the problem is misdiagnosed in this way, social and health services are bound to offer the wrong solution. Indeed, as the negative feelings of the participants resulted from financial stress, frustrations with being unable to find a job or the experience of underemployment, loss of control over their families or experiences of racism, the typical responses to 'depression' – counselling and medication – were rather useless. Fourth, as if adding insult to injury, universalised and individualistic diagnoses of 'depression' among new migrants and refugees sometimes served to justify arguments against immigration.

While Tilbury (2007) argues that different conceptualisations of mental health challenge us to question hegemonic ways of diagnosing and treating 'depression', other multicultural mental health practitioners aim to engage with different views of 'depression' while leaving the overall mental health framework unchallenged. An example comes from a mental health service project aimed at improving access to mental health services for asylum seekers from Afghanistan living in rural Australia (Griffiths, Qian and Procter 2005). Instead of purporting to treat 'depression' the project aims to treat *mualagh,* a Dari word for 'deep sad feeling like being suspended in the air'. The project is intended to enhance mental health outcomes by developing multilingual information on depression and the safe use of antidepressants. The intervention model adopted in the project was based on three assumptions: first, that healthcare workers needed to learn from Afghan patients about their perspectives on mental health; second, that Afghan patients needed to learn from each other about practical issues in coping with mental health issues; and, third, that Afghan patients also needed to learn from healthcare workers about the role of health providers in Australia, general and specific aspects of the healthcare system, and the availability and use of interpreters. On the basis of these reciprocal engagements, the project team eventually produced a set of resources in Dari to help educate Afghan patients about mental health issues and support services and another set of resources in English about the specific needs and expectations of Afghan patients aimed at healthcare providers.

COMMUNICATIVE RELATIVITY

The relativity of linguistic structure is obvious to anyone who knows more than one language. However, while the different ways in different languages to carve up, for instance, kinship relations usually make for good party talk and possibly even movie plots, the focus on formal relativity ('language A has no word for concept X') can easily obscure a much more fundamental relativity, namely that of function: humans do different things with language differently. We started to explore communicative relativity above with reference to the different contexts of use of Western Desert kinship terminology. The term 'communicative relativity' was, to the best of my knowledge, introduced by Foley (1997) but the concept itself originates in the work of the sociolinguist and anthropologist Dell Hymes (1927–2009), who explains it as follows:

> [I]t is essential to notice that Whorf's sort of linguistic relativity is secondary, and dependent upon a primary sociolinguistic relativity, that of differential engagement of languages in social life. For example, description of a language may show that it expresses a certain cognitive style, perhaps implicit metaphysical assumptions, but what chance the language has to make an impress upon individuals and behaviour will depend upon the degree and pattern of its admission into communicative events. [. . .] Peoples do not all everywhere use language to the same degree, in the same situations, or for the same things; some peoples focus upon language more than others. (Hymes 1974: 18)

Hymes contends that communicative relativity is most readily apparent in the case of multilingual persons, who use their different languages to do different things. I, for instance, am right now using English – in a fairly standardised international form – to write a book about intercultural communication for an international student audience. I could not use any of my other languages for this same purpose for various reasons: for one, the Bavarian dialect of my childhood is an oral language and does not have a written tradition. Standard German, the language in which I was schooled, does have an academic writing tradition and I am highly proficient in it, but I could not write this textbook because I have never taught intercultural communication in German and almost all of my reading in the field has been in English. Yet another language, Latin, a language I learnt to read and write to high levels, is out of the question because where would my audience come from? Finally, I can do many things with words in the other three languages in which I am relatively proficient – French, Persian and Spanish – but writing a book is not one of them.

Functional differentiation of languages is obvious in the case of multilinguals but the same differentiation can be found in monolinguals: the English used in writing a university textbook is very different from that used in typing a status update on *Facebook*, which in turn is very different from the English used in a quarrel among five-year-olds, and so on and so forth. The list could go on forever: English – just as any other language – is always an activity in context and these activities differ in what kind of a hold they have on the life of an individual and a community: writing textbooks is something relatively few speakers of English do, while playground quarrels may be much more influential in moulding our cultural identities.

The concept of communicative relativity can be further exemplified by returning to the example of the relationship between Aboriginal and non-Aboriginal Australians since the beginning of European settlement in 1788. In the example introduced above of Aboriginal children being removed from their families, the crux of the problem was the refusal of white Australians to recognise a kinship system other than their own. We can analyse that example by assuming a contrast between European languages on the one hand and Aboriginal languages on the other, with both languages playing the same role relative to 'European culture' and 'Aboriginal culture'. However, the story of the British occupation of Australia and the dispossession of Aboriginal people is characterised by a failure to recognise not only linguistic relativity but also communicative relativity, as is most obviously apparent from the idea that prior to European settlement Australia was *terra nullius*, a 'land belonging to no one'. The idea of *terra nullius* became one of the legal and moral justifications for the British occupation of Australia. While Aboriginal people obviously lived in Australia prior to the invasion in 1788, they were not seen as having a right to the land between Governor Bourke's 1835 Proclamation of *terra nullius* and the first successful native title claim in the Mabo case[2] of 1992 due to their supposed primitivism and barbarism. To Europeans, one of the indicators of Aboriginal people not having a right to their land lay in the fact that they did not have any written ownership records or title deeds. That means Europeans failed to recognise the communicative relativity of the ways in which land rights are communicated by different people. Of course, land rights and the idea of humans owning the land are themselves relative: maybe some of the ecological disasters of recent years could have been avoided if the dominant narrative of the human relationship to the earth was not one of ownership but one of custodianship?

The *Papunya School Book of Country and History* (Papunya School 2001: 8) explains how the strong connection to the land, including the spiritual relationship to the land, used to be communicated by Aboriginal people in the Western Desert:

> When the Tjulkura [= white people] came to Australia, they did not recognise that, between them, different groups of Aboriginal people owned all the continent. Because there were no pieces of paper saying which people belonged to which country, white people decided that the land was terra nullius. [. . .] The Tjulkura did not understand that Aboriginal people had been recording their ownership of their country in songs, stories, dances and paintings since the time when law began.

The observation that Australian history is only told from the invaders' point of view is not new. Egon Erwin Kisch, a refugee from Nazi Germany, observed as much in his 1937 travelogue *Australian Landfall*. One story he found particularly noteworthy was the way the word 'massacre' was used in Australia. As evidence he provides the example of the 'Hornet Bank Massacre'. The story of the 'Hornet Bank Massacre' as it is commonly told is as follows: on 27 October 1857, a group of Aboriginal warriors from the Yiman tribe attacked Hornet Bank Station, a newly-established large sheep run in Queensland. Three white men, two women and six children were killed in the attack. The women and an eleven-year-old girl were raped and one man was castrated before they were clubbed to death. Kisch observed that, by most counts, the events following 'the massacre' were more of a 'massacre' than the event that is called 'Hornet Bank Massacre'. For those 'events' following (and leading up to) the 'massacre' there is no name or single term. Those 'events' included that, in the lead-up to the 'massacre', the Yiman had been dispossessed of their lands on the Dawson Plains by white settlers establishing sheep runs. In the process, they had been subjected to violence and humiliation, including wanton killings and rape. After the 'massacre', an irregular paramilitary force, the so-called 'Native Police', as well as white vigilante groups, engaged in brutal revenge killings. The Yiman decorated themselves with crescent-shaped cicatrices on the chest and people with those characteristic markings were shot on sight. The numbers of those murdered in this revenge killing spree are debated but the most conservative estimate is that 150 Yiman and other Aboriginal people were killed in the eighteen months after the 'Hornet Bank Massacre'. Many others were maimed and displaced. Within a decade, the Yiman as a distinct group with their own culture and language ceased to exist.

Almost a century has passed since Kisch first observed that Australian history was only told from the invaders' point of view but surprisingly little has changed since then, in terms of the chances of an Aboriginal point of view 'to make an impress'. There still is no agreed-upon term for the colonial war of expansion fought in Queensland in the mid-nineteenth century. The 'Hornet Bank Massacre' continues to be remembered (for instance, it has a separate Wikipedia entry) but the 'events' that followed are not (they do not have a separate Wikipedia entry but do appear in Wikipedia's 'List of massacres of Indigenous Australians' for 1857 as 'Hundreds killed in retaliation for the Hornet Bank Massacre'). The 'Hornet Bank Massacre' also has a monument at the site where it took place, a 'cairn at Hornet Bank Station in memory of Europeans killed by the aborigines'.[3] There is no equivalent monument commemorating the Yiman who were killed, as far as I know.[4] There is an excellent book about the 'massacre' and its context (Reid 1982). However, it so happens that the book is out of print and not available digitally. My local public library does not hold a copy but Macquarie University Library does. There, it is located in the Automated Retrieval Collection, which means that it is not displayed on the shelves but has to be requested. Requesting an item from the Automated Retrieval Collection is easy enough but readers have to seek it out and will not have a chance to discover it surreptitiously by browsing the shelves. When I requested the book, the time stamps in the back of the book indicated that this particular copy has been taken out for loan on average every two years. This means that 'the chance to make an impress' of this detailed, fair and balanced account incorporating all available evidence and voices is evidently extremely limited.

One more piece of evidence that Australian history is told from the point of view of the colonisers and that the chance of other voices to be heard is small: William Fraser, the surviving son and brother of those killed in the 'Hornet Bank Massacre', 'never lost an opportunity of shooting a wild blackfellow as long as he lived' (contemporary, quoted in Reid 1982: 145). Despite the fact that there were witnesses to many of his murders, he killed with impunity. There never was even an inquiry into his murders despite the fact that simply shouting 'Watch out, Billy Fraser is about!' was a common tease of Aboriginal people at the time and sent them running away in terror. When he died in 1914, the local newspaper honoured him as 'one of the oldest pioneers of this part of Queensland [whose] death will be received with regret by a large number of old residents in Queensland' (quoted in Reid 1982: 153). This assessment of his character does not seem to have changed: the man who is reported to have killed more than a hundred Aboriginal people in his life has no entry in the Wikipedia 'List of mass murders in Australia'.

The *Papunya School Book of Country and History* which I mentioned above is one of an increasing number of books that tell the story of

Aboriginal dispossession from an Aboriginal perspective and are written and illustrated by Aboriginal authors and artists. Similarly, in 2009, the first Aboriginal account of the destruction wrought by British secret atomic weapons testing at Maralinga in South Australia between 1955 and 1963 (Yalanta and Oak Valley Communities and Mattingley 2009) was published to wide acclaim in Australia. In yet another instance of communicative relativity, these books are typically treated as children's books: they are located in the children's picture books section of bookshops rather than in the history section and they are considered for children's book prizes rather than history book prizes. I picked up my copy of *Maralinga: The Anangu Story* from the children's picture book section of a Melbourne bookshop in July 2009 and cannot but wonder whether I am the only customer to find it odd that a book about military invasion, forced deportation, the destruction of a people, the devastation of their land and its ongoing contamination should be placed on the same shelf as stories about fluffy animals, naughty little children having adventures with the tooth fairy and talking tank engines. Apparently, even in 2009, an Aboriginal telling of such horrors is still heard as less serious than a non-Aboriginal telling in mainstream Australia. In the same bookshop, I found the Maralinga memoirs of white Australian servicemen (Cross and Hudson 2006) duly located in the history section. And, in yet another layer of communicative relativity, both of these testimonies to the ravages caused even by the development – not to mention the actual use – of weapons of mass destruction are published as books – probably the mass medium with the smallest contemporary reach – by relatively small publishers in a country with a relatively small national market.

A LANGUAGE WITH A NAME

The exploration of linguistic relativity is undergirded by an implicit assumption that there is a direct relationship between language X and culture X, that is, that – for instance – the analysis of English kinship terminology tells us something about English culture. The above discussion of communicative relativity should already have thrown that relationship into question, with its focus on communicating in context and its explication of the relative impact potential of actual instances of communication. In this section, I will now explicitly address the question: 'What is the relationship between a particular language and a particular culture?' The short answer is that the relationship is relative. That means that there is not one single type of relationship that holds for all the languages of the world. English, for instance, is so diverse that many linguists today speak about English in the plural, Englishes. Not only are there many kinds of Englishes, but also many kinds of cultures in which English is used, such as Anglo culture, hip hop culture, international business culture, South Korean higher education culture, and so on. Obviously, the relationship between a particular variety of English and a particular culture where it is used is different in each case.

Furthermore, the relationship that pertains between Englishes and their cultures is different yet again from the relationship that pertains between other languages and cultures. An obvious example would be a comparison between a widely spoken language such as English, which is used by many people, with many different proficiency levels in many different contexts, and a small language spoken by only a few people in only one or two domains. Clearly, the language-culture relationship for English is very different than it is for, say, Adnyamathanha, a language spoken in South Australia's Flinders Ranges by a few dozen people (Sehlin MacNeil 2016).

Despite the fact that the relationship between a particular language and a particular culture is obviously relative, a universal relationship is often assumed and asserted in the literature on intercultural communication, particularly when it comes to official national languages and the national cultures they are supposedly matched to. I will now explore the fallacy of the language X–culture X relationship in more detail on the basis of examples from the intercultural communication literature.

As I have pointed out earlier, intercultural communication studies are carried out in a range of disciplines and most of those pay little attention to real language. However, in the limited treatment of the role of language in intercultural communication, linguistic relativity usually figures prominently and is undergirded by an assumption that a national language is mapped onto a national culture in a straightforward way, as in the following two examples from the widely used textbook *Intercultural Business Communication* (Chaney and Martin 2014). In its 'Language' chapter, this book includes a table that matches 'verbal style' with 'ethnic group'. The layout suggests that whatever information is provided under the heading 'verbal style' has the same relationship to the 'ethnic group' to which it is related. I am going to discuss the entries for 'German' and 'Japanese' in some more detail here. Under the heading 'Germans' the authors offer the following entry: 'In the German language, the verb often comes at the end of the sentence. In oral communication, Germans do not immediately get to the point' (Chaney and Martin 2014: 119). Linguistically speaking, this entry is based on the false assumption that having the verb at the end of the sentence says something about when 'the point' is being made. As a matter of fact, the statement that the verb 'often' comes at the end of the sentence is imprecise as the position of the verb in German is purely a matter of syntax (that is, sentence grammar) and strictly rule-governed. The rule is that, in a main clause, the verb is always the second constituent. In a subordinate clause, the place of the verb shifts to the end of the clause. By contrast, the position of 'the point' – or the theme in linguistic terminology – is a matter of pragmatic choice. The theme of a sentence – or more often a whole text – can be expressed in many different ways and is in no way tied to the verb or its position. As a matter of fact, the theme does not even need to be expressed grammatically although it frequently is. In German, the word order of those constituents which – unlike the verb – can be moved around freely is a frequently used means to make a point. So, grammatically speaking, the position of any part of a sentence or clause other than the verb is a more useful means to make a point in German. Non-grammatical means to make a point include intonation (placing stress on the important bit) in spoken language or emphatic capitals or other typographic means of emphasis in written language. Not only can 'the point' be expressed in many different ways, it may also be located anywhere in a sentence and across syntactic boundaries (or even outside of the strictly linguistic message altogether).

Another example from the same table comes from the entry for 'Japanese'. Under that heading, the authors state rather cryptically: 'The word "yes" has many different meanings' (Chaney and Martin 2014: 118). The implication of such an entry is that such polysemy and multi-functionality are special to the Japanese and presumably an aspect of their stereotypically inscrutable character. However, in fact, there is absolutely nothing special about a word having many different meanings in any language. Polysemy – a word having more than one meaning – is a characteristic of all natural languages. Just like in Japanese and any other language, English words, too, can be used to mean the exact opposite of their 'real' meaning, that is their core or dictionary meaning: just think of the 'start' button many of us need to press to shut down – that is, 'end' – our Microsoft Windows computers. The English word 'no' is another good example: just like the Japanese word for 'yes', it can have many different meanings as Kulick (2003) demonstrates for its uses in sexual contexts. Both the intended meaning and the understood meaning of 'no' can vary widely in sexual contexts alone. 'No' may mean 'yes' in sadomasochistic scenes, for instance. Even if the speaker actually intends 'no' to mean 'no', the recipient may claim they thought it meant 'yes', and they may even have that understanding considered as a legitimate defence in sexual harassment and rape cases (see also Ehrlich 2001).

In the context of the 'Language' chapter in *Intercultural Business Communication* both these examples are intended to convey a message about the relationship between an aspect of the German and the Japanese language and German and Japanese culture, respectively. As I have just shown, they do so in a way that cannot be called anything but linguistically misinformed. Even if the actual linguistic facts were to hold up to scrutiny, the tidbit character of the information provided would make it impossible to use those facts in any meaningful way. So, what do examples such as these achieve in the guise of providing intercultural communication advice? While the examples purport to say something about the German and Japanese languages and their relationship to German and Japanese culture, they actually naturalise a national view of culture that sets up an equation in which the German and Japanese languages match German and Japanese culture, which in turn match the German and Japanese nation states. Rather than teaching readers something about intercultural communication, these examples are complicit in naturalising a particular version of a language, the so-called standard, as the language. The sociologist Pierre Bourdieu (1930–2002) has criticised such simplistic views of language: 'To speak of the language, without further specification, as linguists [and writers on intercultural communication] do, is tacitly to accept the official definition of the official language of a political unit' (Bourdieu 1991: 45).

Examples such as these which map 'the German language' onto 'German culture' and 'the Japanese language' onto 'Japanese culture' are ultimately nothing more than exercises in banal nationalism, a concept to which I will return in more detail in Chapter 4. They do not explain the relationship between language and culture; rather, they are themselves in need of an explanation. Before I return to the culture-equals-nation part of this equation in Chapter 4, I will now illustrate how languages came to be 'naturally' associated with nations with three examples from the history of the invention of the German language, the Tolai language and the Thonga language.

'Culture with a (national) name' is often an a priori assumption in the literature on intercultural communication and the same is true for language. 'Languages with a (national) name' such as 'English', 'German' or 'Japanese' are all a priori assumptions that have their origin in the same source that the frequent identification of 'culture' with nation and/or ethnicity has, namely the strong hold that nationalism has had on European, and later global, human identity making since the eighteenth century. Historically, language names mostly derive from a generic term for '(our) language'. The German term for the German language (and 'culture' and nation), for instance, is *Deutsch*. This term derives from a Latin term, *theodisce*, which simply meant 'vernacular' or 'non-Latin'. From around the eighth century, the formula *tam latine quam theodisce*, 'both in Latin and the vernacular', was used to indicate that a religious text was available in Latin and any of the – not-yet-standardised – vernacular languages of Central and Western Europe (Schmitt 1970). These languages or language varieties formed a so-called dialect chain, that is, a continuum of mutually intelligible ways of speaking where people from one place understood the people from neighbouring villages or cities, and where it was impossible to ever find a point of non-intelligibility even if the people who lived on points of the chain that were removed from each other to various degrees could not understand each other. Such was the linguistic situation in medieval Europe, and such it was in much of the rest of the world in pre-colonial times. It was only the imposition of nation states that started to break up those chains, and people living in neighbouring villages on different sides of a national border often lost the ability to communicate. As far as *theodisce* is concerned, it was only much later that the term *Deutsch* came to be used for the national language of Germany (a country not in existence until the nineteenth century!). The fact that the term started out meaning the vernacular of various Germanic tribes also explains the similarity between the German term for 'German', *Deutsch*, and the English term for the language of the Netherlands, *Dutch*. They are so similar that it is easy to confuse them, as is the case, for instance, in the Pennsylvania 'Dutch' Country, an area of Pennsylvania characterised by *German* settlement in the seventeenth and eighteenth centuries.

Not to have a specific name for a particular language variety and to simply refer to it as '(our) language', and to not be aware of where it begins and where it ends, was the normal pre-national state of affairs. However, that fact of European history had been forgotten by the time European missionaries and linguists started cataloguing and describing the languages of the non-European world: to them, the fact that the natives often did not seem to have a name for their language or could not neatly identify who spoke their language and who did not became another indicator of their primitivism and lack of civilisation (see Chapter 2).

In their survey of the Oceanic languages – a group of languages spoken in Polynesia, Melanesia and Micronesia – Lynch, Ross and Crowley (2002: 21f.) provide an overview of how those languages were named by missionaries and linguists: frequently, competing missionaries and explorers would assign a different name to a language – most often on the basis of the indigenous word for 'language' or on the basis of a place name, often that of the mission station. As a striking example, the authors list the ten different names under which the language of the Tolai people of the Gazelle Peninsula of New Britain, Papua New Guinea, is known in English. One of these, rather amusingly, is *Kuanua*, which is an indigenous word of the neighbouring Duke of York Islands for 'over there' but was apparently understood to be a proper noun by Methodist missionaries.

For a detailed account of the invention of a language with a name, I will now describe the history of the Thonga language of the Transvaal. Thonga, which is also known as Changana, Gwamba, Shangaan, Shangana, Shitsonga, Thonga, Tonga, Tsonga, Xichangana and Xitsonga, is spoken by more than eight million people in an area divided between four nations, namely South Africa, Mozambique, Swaziland and Zimbabwe ('Tsonga' 2016). Although spoken in one form or another since time immemorial, Thonga as a language-with-a-name emerged only in the nineteenth century, as Errington (2008: 113–116), on whose account I draw here, explains. In 1872 Paul Berthoud and Ernest Creux, two Swiss missionaries sponsored by the Paris Missionary Society, arrived in the Transvaal to proselytise in Sotho, a language they had learnt during their previous work in neighbouring areas. As it turned out, no one in the Transvaal spoke Sotho and so Berthoud and Creux took it upon themselves to learn the local language in order to spread their faith in that language. It did not take them long to realise that in fact a number of different – even mutually unintelligible – varieties were spoken in the area they took to be their own. However, they had practical reasons not to admit the multilingualism of the Transvaal. To begin with, they could not attempt to learn and describe more than one language and they did not have the funds to print religious-instructional materials in more than one language. Second, they needed the Transvaal to be seen as one unit in order to strengthen their claim to the region and to defend if from the incursions of rival missionaries who were operating in surrounding areas. So, they set about their work partly describing and partly inventing Thonga:

> With hindsight, the Berthoud brothers can be seen to have worked against the grain of historical and linguistic reality to create written Thonga and its history. But they succeeded in making them social facts among their literate converts. Once they had some intellectual purchase on local conditions and linguistic cultural difference, they could teach Thonga literacy and so also the Thonga language itself. (Errington 2008: 116)

Not only did missionaries create the Thonga language, they also monopolised its literate forms and uses, thus establishing their version of what it means to be Thonga. They were so successful that the fact that they had invented Thonga was soon obscured and a later missionary quoted by Errington (2008: 116) saw nothing wrong with describing the language as 'one of the most trustworthy and complete manifestations of [the Thonga nation's] mind' and 'the oldest element in the life of the tribe [. . .] the great bond which bound the Thonga clans together in past centuries'.

The association between the Thonga language and Thonga culture is obviously a discursive artefact. However, the process itself is not uncommon. A language with a name is an invention and once it has been invented, an eo ipso claim about how that language is a direct expression of the culture associated with that language is never far away. Once a language has become accepted as a fact – once it has been named, described and codified in grammars and dictionaries – the relationship between language X and culture X may seem self-evident.

The strong association of a particular language with a particular nation as expressed in the slogan 'one language, one nation' has its origins in the French Revolution and has influenced the language policy of the French state and many others ever since (Spolsky 2004). However, it is important to recognise that the French language – just as the Thonga language – did not somehow precede the French state nor exist independently of it. The French language – as all national languages – was invented by the French state, as the historian Eric Hobsbawm (1990: 54) explains:

> National languages are therefore almost always semi-artificial constructs and occasionally, like modern Hebrew [or Thonga], virtually invented. They are the opposite of what nationalist mythology supposes them to be, namely the primordial foundations of national culture and the matrices of the national mind. They are usually attempts to devise a standardised idiom out of a multiplicity of actually spoken idioms, which are downgraded to dialects.

Max Weinreich (1894–1969), a famous scholar of Yiddish, is widely quoted as quipping that 'A language is a dialect with an army and a navy.' Or, to put it differently, 'a dialect is a language that gets no respect', as Lippi-Green (2012) adds. The constructed nature of 'a language with a name' is an old hat in sociolinguistics. 'No one who has studied the history of any national or standard language (unless for partisan purposes) has come up with a different conclusion' (Joseph 2004: 120). However, intercultural communication scholarship has to date by and large chosen to ignore this central sociolinguistic insight. It has done so at the cost of intellectual integrity. If intercultural communication scholarship is to be more than the reproduction of nation-language stereotypes, it will need to stop treating a specific language as a given. Language with a name does not predate intercultural communication as some sort of independent variable; instead, language with a name is discursively constructed in intercultural communication. These discursive constructions of language X are necessarily interested and hegemonic, that is, they serve the interests of some speakers while excluding and marginalising other speakers. Generally speaking, this is the nature of politics and hegemonic power: the power of the state and influential groups tends to lie in their success in creating apparently natural hegemonic constructions of a particular group, and to thus make those disadvantaged by such arrangements complicit in their own disadvantage and marginalisation. Language with a name is a powerful ingredient in cultural politics where it 'serves as a cause, a solution, a muse for the national self, and a technology of the state' (Ayres 2009: 3). However, it is not the role of intercultural communication scholarship to be complicit in hegemonic cultural politics, but to help us understand how these work.

KEY POINTS

This chapter made the following key points:

- Language forms are relative and different languages encode different world views. The inability to engage with, and the unwillingness to acknowledge, different ways of seeing was a central facet of colonialism. Conversely, intercultural competence is characterised by the ability and desire to engage with realities other than our own.
- Formal linguistic relativity is undergirded by a more fundamental difference of communicative relativity, which means that communication itself is relative. There are differences in what is communicated when and by whom in which way. Communicative inequality is a key aspect of communicative relativity: ways of communicating are not only relative but also have unequal chances of making an impact.
- Languages with a name are not just a natural fact but are inventions and tools of the state. Intercultural communication advice that assumes a one-on-one match between a particular language and a particular culture is just another discursive practice that creates and maintains a particular language variety as the dominant language and associates it closely with a particular national culture. Critical intercultural communication studies engage with sociolinguistics to gain an understanding of the ways in which the discursive construction of a particular language is used in intercultural communication.

COUNTERPOINT

We are all used to speaking of a particular language with a name as if it were 'a real thing'. Whenever we use language names and treat entities such as 'English', 'German' or 'Thonga' as 'real' we are complicit in reproducing official hegemonic views of the political unit with which the language is associated. In fact, despite the argument I have put forward here, I will continue to refer to specific languages throughout this book, sometimes with the addition of scare quotes but often without. Mostly I do so for reasons of convenience and for the sake of readability. Is it possible to continue to use established terms without 'tacitly accepting the official definition of the official language of a political unit'? How can we escape complicity while maintaining readability and accessibility?

FURTHER READING

Hymes (1996) is a must-read introduction to communicative relativity and communicative inequality. The invention of languages with a name as colonial practice is well-illustrated in Errington (2008), and Ayres (2009) is an engaging case study of the invention of Urdu and its use in Pakistani nationalism.

ACTIVITIES

Feeling disgusted

Work in teams of two or more, with at least one team member having English as their strongest (or only) language and at least one team member having another language as their strongest language. Divide a piece of paper (or a word-processing document) into two columns, one headed 'disgust' and the other with the translation equivalent of 'disgust' in the other language. Discuss and compare how the feeling of 'disgust' and its translation equivalent is created, and how the feeling is expressed and what determines how it is expressed (or whether it is expressed at all). In a next step (if you are working on your own you can only do the second part of this exercise) carry out an online search for 'I felt disgusted' and its translation equivalent (make sure to add the quotation marks so that you only get hits for the exact phrase). Are there any differences in what the causes of feelings of disgust recorded on the Internet are in the top twenty hits for each language?

Explaining a linguistic-cultural rich point

Read the chapter entitled 'Situations' in Agar (1994) (if you have more time, read the whole book!) and take note of the way in which he goes about understanding the Viennese concept *Schmäh*, which he identifies as a 'rich point' in Viennese culture. Identify a 'rich point' in a languaculture

(Agar's term for the intersection of language and culture) that you are very familiar with, follow the author's way of understanding and explaining *Schmäh*, and explain your rich point in a blog post to outsiders to your language and culture. Use the blog post about Danish *hygge* by Knudsen (2016) as a model.

What can you do with your languages?

What are the things you can and cannot do with the languages and language varieties you know? What are the factors which make it possible for you to do some things but not others? Bear in mind that some of these factors will be related to your own proficiency and some to the place of a language or variety in society. What can you do to extend the range of things you can do in one or other of these languages?

Sharing knowledge on Wikipedia

Examine in which languages knowledge is created and made available on Wikipedia. Visit the 'List of Wikipedias' page and see in which languages entries are available. What differences between the availability of encyclopaedic knowledge in different languages can you observe? Do some languages dominate encyclopaedic knowledge production? Are others absent? What are the consequences of the differential use of languages in global knowledge production? How do your findings relate to those in Piller (2016c)?

NOTES

1. The cartoon can be viewed at http://dailyapple.blogspot.com.au/2011/01/apple-504-fear-of-being-watched-by-duck.html
2. For further information on the Mabo case and a wide range of related resources, visit http://www.mabonativetitle.com/
3. See http://monumentaustralia.org.au/themes/conflict/indigenous
4. My efforts to find a memorial are documented at http://www.languageonthemove.com/yiman-does-not-have-a-word-for-massacre/

Nation and Culture

CHAPTER OBJECTIVES

This chapter will enable you to:

- Understand the central role played by nationalism in intercultural communication as well as in the literature about intercultural communication, and to engage critically with methodological nationalism in intercultural communication.
- Familiarise yourself with the concept of 'banal nationalism' and use it to engage critically with the concepts of 'cultural values' and 'cultural scripts' and the intercultural communication advice literature.

STEREOTYPES

As most readers will be aware, intercultural communication advice is a well-established genre that fills shelves and sections in bookshops and your local library, and has, of course, an established presence on the Internet and in training workshops. On my bookshelf, for instance, I have titles such as *Beyond Chocolate: Understanding Swiss Culture* (Oertig-Davidson 2002), *Don't They Know it's Friday? Cross-cultural Considerations for Business and Life in the Gulf* (J. Williams 1998) and a few *Xenophobe's Guides* (Bilton 1999; Hunt and Taylor 2004; Yang 1999). These last are part of a 'series that highlights the unique character and behaviour of nations'.[1] The website lists the available *Xenophobe's Guides* by nationalities from 'the Albanians' to 'the Welsh' and in this way is typical of many websites that provide intercultural communication advice and that usually provide intercultural communication advice sorted into national categories. Reading such literature reminds me of those silly national stereotype jokes most of you will also be familiar with. To give you an idea of what I am talking about, I shall start with an example of such a joke; I imagine that most of you will easily be able to add your own favourite (best-loved or best-hated) examples from the genre. I will follow this with two examples which I am quoting from intercultural communication advice.

> An Englishman, a Frenchman, an American and a Mexican are on a plane that is crashing because it is too heavy. They all throw their baggage from the plane but it is still too heavy. Realising that this calls for extreme heroism, the Englishman shouts, 'God save the Queen!' and jumps out. The Frenchman shouts, '*Vive la France!*' and jumps out, too. Then the American shouts, 'Remember the Alamo!' and chucks out the Mexican.

This joke is based on national stereotypes and you need to be familiar with the national stereotypes invoked to get the joke. National stereotypes are used to achieve a humorous effect and it is the very reduction to a stereotypical type of an Englishman, a Frenchman and an American that makes us laugh. Now consider the following example from a Swiss newspaper article that offers advice to readers on how to communicate with Chinese tourists and business people:

> Chinese communication style. A 'no' can mean 'yes' and a 'yes' doesn't mean anything, as in the following example:
>
> *S (Swiss person): Can I offer you a cup of tea? // C (Chinese person): No, thank you. // S: Are you sure you don't want a cup of tea? // C: No, thank you very much. // S: But a cup of tea would make you feel better in this cold weather. // C: I don't want to cause you any troubles.*
>
> The Chinese person had wanted a cup of tea from the beginning but it would have been impolite to say so directly. Whether you offer a drink, support or a present: the Chinese will always say no. All other questions will be responded to with yes. (Müller 2006; my translation)

The next example comes from an advice booklet produced by the Japanese External Trade Organization (JETRO), which is aimed at 'Western' business people operating in Japan or working with Japanese colleagues internationally.

> When the French want to say 100 things, they will verbalise 150
> things. When Japanese say 70 things, they are trying to get the
> other person to understand 100. (JETRO 1999: 9)

Just as with the joke in the first example, the advice in the two subsequent
examples 'works' because it reduces characters to national stereotypes.
Disparate as the joke and the pieces of intercultural communication advice
may seem, the three examples have one thing in common: each text relies
on stereotypes to make its point. Those stereotypes are of a typical national
in each case: it is the stick-figures of an Englishman, a Frenchman, an
American and a Mexican who are meant to make us laugh in the joke,
and it is the stick-figures of a Swiss person and a Chinese person, and a
Japanese person and a French person who are meant to teach us about
intercultural communication in the advice samples. The national character
stereotypes which populate jokes and intercultural communication advice
alike are completely mono-dimensional and are not inflected by any other
aspects of their identities. The national characters in these examples are
presented as free of class, gender, ethnicity, regional background, personal
traits or any other individuating aspects of their being – all that matters
for the purposes of the joke and the intercultural communication advice is
their national identity.

Due to their common reliance on national stereotyping the three texts
share textual effects as well: they all create, re-create and sustain national
belonging as a key aspect of contemporary identity. Ostensibly, the joke
and the examples of intercultural communication advice seem to have
completely different aims: it is the central function of a joke to produce
humour and to make us laugh, while it is the central function of intercultural communication advice to teach us better communication skills, to
make us more aware of difference and diversity. However, despite these
seemingly very different aims, both text types actually do the same kind of
additional discursive work: they sustain the nation as a key category, they
present national belonging as overriding any other aspects of identity, and,
consequently, they render other aspects of identity invisible – in short,
they are examples of banal nationalism.

BANAL NATIONALISM

The term 'banal nationalism' was introduced by the social psychologist
Michael Billig 'to cover the ideological habits which enable the established
nations of the West to be reproduced' (Billig 1995: 6). Many people think
of nationalism as extremism and as extreme forms of national ardour such

as those of Nazi Germany or the disintegrating Yugoslavia. However, Billig points out that nationalism is the endemic condition of established nation states, that it is enacted and re-enacted daily in many mundane, almost unnoticeable, hence 'banal', ways. It is these banal forms of nationalism that lead people to identify with a nation. Examples of banal nationalism are everywhere although they often go unnoticed. Typically, the discourses of banal nationalism emanate directly from state institutions. However, they are then taken up by non-state actors and become enmeshed with a range of discourses that at first glance have nothing to do with nationalism at all, such as the jokes and intercultural communication advice I quoted above. In order to exemplify the concept, I will now discuss two examples of banal nationalism in detail: one comes from the context of schooling and the other comes from the world of food packaging and consumer advertising.

The discourses of banal nationalism are often embedded in the practices of state institutions. Schooling is a prime example of the way in which children are socialised into a national identity. It is school where we become members of the nation and where we are taught to think about ourselves as nationals. The Pledge of Allegiance in many public schools in the USA is an oft-quoted example. The Pledge of Allegiance is often part of the morning ritual, with a class standing to attention, facing the flag and, with the right hand over their heart, jointly reciting the Pledge:

> I pledge allegiance to the Flag of the United States of America, and
> to the Republic for which it stands, one Nation under God,
> indivisible, with liberty and justice for all.

On the other side of the world, in Australia, many public schools hold a weekly assembly, where the school community comes together to listen to a speech, watch a performance or be part of an award ceremony. The joint singing of the national anthem plays a central part in the school assembly. In yet another example, Indonesian public schools conduct a flag-raising event every Monday morning and also on every 17th of the month (in commemoration of the national Independence Day, which is celebrated on 17 August). Pasassung (2004: 182–183) describes such a flag-raising ceremony as follows:

> It is imperative for every school member to attend this 'flag-raising' ceremony. [. . .] It is part of school formal and regular activities throughout Indonesia. In this ceremony, the *Pancasila* – the philosophical foundation of the nation that contains the five

philosophical and ideological principles of the nation: believing in one God, civilised and just humanity, the unity of Indonesia, democracy, and social justice – and the Preamble of the State Constitution are read. The remembrance of and praying for the national heroes are also essential parts of the ceremony. The ceremony participants are required to repeat the five points of the *Pancasila* after the inspector of the ceremony, who is usually the principal. In every ceremony there is time provided for the ceremony inspector to deliver a speech.

The induction into a national identity is part of the hidden curriculum in many schools around the world. The term 'hidden curriculum' is used in the sociology of education to refer to the values, dispositions, and social and behavioural expectations inculcated through schooling without being explicitly taught. In addition to ceremonial activities such as those just described, the socialisation into the nation is also part of teaching content in many schools around the world: consider, for instance, the lyrics of national poems that are used to teach students how to read and write, the national anthem that is taught in music and recital lessons, the focus of much teaching on national history, or the valorisation of the national language as the only legitimate medium of educational activities. Let's look at an example to examine the ways in which socialisation into the nation is enmeshed with the teaching of reading and writing. The example comes from the Persian-language primer that has been used in elementary schools across multilingual and multicultural Iran for generations – both during the Shah regime and the Islamic Republic – and that is also used in many Persian-language heritage schools outside the country (*Farsi: Aval Dabestan* n.d.: 74f.).[2] The exercise begins with a reading passage titled 'Motherland' and set against an outline of the map of Iran:

> Our country is Iran. // We live in Iran. // We are Iranian. // The land of Iran has many cities and villages. // Some Iranians live in cities. // Some Iranians live in villages. // Wherever Iranians live, they are Iranian. // Our motherland is Iran. // We love our very own motherland. (My translation)

The passage is followed by a poem called *Farzandan-e Iran-im*, 'We are the Children of Iran' by the progressive educator and children's author Abbas Yamini Sharif (1919–1989). The poem is followed by a drawing of children dressed in the costumes of various ethnic groups of Iran and dancing together in a circle so as to represent national unity in diversity:

We are smiling flowers. // We are the children of Iran. // Our country is to us like our body. // We have to be wise, // Watchful and alert. // For the protection of Iran // We've got to be strong. // Oh Iran, develop well! // Oh Iran, be free! // Oh Iran, may your heart // Take pleasure in us, // Your children!

The power of the poem 'We are the Children of Iran' to produce national identity is beautifully illustrated in the Iranian film *Bashu* (English title: *The Little Stranger*), directed by Bahram Beizai (1989). *Bashu* tells the story of a ten-year-old boy from Southern Iran, who becomes orphaned during the Iran–Iraq War (1980–1988). The boy flees his home on the shores of the Persian Gulf and, as a stowaway on a truck, travels north across the country, for almost 2,000 kilometres, and winds up in a little village in Northern Iran. There he hides in a little granary, where he is found by a village woman: the two look at each other across a social, cultural and linguistic chasm: a traumatised, Arabic-speaking, dark-skinned child and a no-nonsense, Gilaki-speaking, light-skinned farmer and mother, who has never been outside her village. The woman tries to catch the little boy as one would try to catch an animal, all the while asking, in her language, who he is, whether he is an animal or an evil spirit, and the boy shrieking as he tries to escape. Finally, as the woman corners him, the boy starts to chant *Farzandan-e Iran-im*, 'We Are the Children of Iran'. It is only at that moment that the woman recognises the boy as human – the national poem from the primer becomes their common bond. Although both have only a very limited grasp of Persian, the official language of Iran and the language of the poem, they form a strong relationship, and the woman takes Bashu into her family.

Schooling is widely controlled by the state and the fact that it is used as a vehicle to socialise students into the nation is maybe not particularly surprising. However, the discourses of banal nationalism also emanate from less likely sources. Billig's (1995) example of the daily weather forecast on TV is a particularly convincing one: the daily weather forecast is usually presented against an image of the national map – as if national borders were meaningful to weather patterns. Banal nationalism in sports has also been widely studied (for example, Bishop and Jaworski 2003; Darnell 2014; Koch 2013): sporting competitions are typically framed as national competitions and most spectators are more likely to support co-national competitors on the basis of their nationality rather than using more pertinent criteria such as sportsmanship or elegance of the game.

Yet another domain of banal nationalism can be found in consumer advertising, where national imagery is used to create positive associations with a product or service or consumption in general. At the same time, the use of national imagery in consumer advertising increases the presence of national imagery in the mundane spaces of everyday life and thereby continually reinforces the message of national belonging. The discourses of banal nationalism that come associated with consumer advertising have come to pervade our private lives. For instance, a cornflakes box[3] that has graced my very own breakfast table countless times sports the following 'poem':

> Sanitarium corn flakes are as Australian as . . . // A Didgeridoo // and a Kangaroo // As a Rubber Thong // and a Billabong // As Uluru // and a Cockatoo // The Barrier Reef // and a Eucalyptus Leaf // The Harbour Bridge // and Lightning Ridge // A Melbourne Tram // and a Merino Ram // A sun that Blisters // and those Three Sisters.

The poem lists a number of Australian icons against a blue background. Blue is widely considered to be the Australian national colour, an association reinforced in collocations such as 'a true blue Aussie' meaning a 'real' Australian. The words of the poem are set against the background of the Australian flag and surrounded by pictures of all the national icons referred to in the poem. Associating products with national imagery is a widely used marketing strategy in Australia, just as it is in many other countries.[4] Through everyday items such as a cornflakes box – and many other similar items of product packaging – national symbols enter mundane everyday spaces such as supermarket shelves and the breakfast table in our homes. They keep circulating in those spaces as constant small reminders of national identity.

In sum, the discourses of banal nationalism socialise people into seeing themselves as members of a particular nation who live in a wider world of nation states. These discourses of banal nationalism train us to see ourselves in national ways and they become part of who we are to such a degree that they enter our emotional make-up. Internet comments in response to national songs, videos or images often provide evidence of national belonging as a deeply felt emotion. For instance, 'top' comments on a rendition of the song *I Am Australian* include the following:

> I love this song it should be national anthem im born here and mixed blood. Dutch, indonesian, english, irish, aboriginal, south american. // *puts my hand on my heart and sings along with a tear ^^ * // I'm an Aussie and bloody proud of it!! I love this country!! // Another fiercely proud Australian. I always get that same shiver down the spine and a tear in my eye.[5]

References to 'love', 'pride', 'tears' and a 'shiver down the spine' all testify to national identity as a deeply-felt emotion of the posters. While these commentators' feelings of community may be heartfelt, the community they belong to is an 'imagined' one (Anderson 1991). That means that members of a nation imagine themselves and are imagined by others as group members. However, the groups themselves are too large to be considered 'real' communities, that is, no group member will ever know all the other group members. Critical theorists have written extensively about the ways in which identity is socially constructed and intimately linked to power relationships in society, as the socialisation into particular subject positions – those of national subjects in this case – predisposes us to certain kinds of activity that fit with the demands of a particular national society and of a global society of nation states in general. As we become nationals and live out the requirements of the ideologies of a particular national identity and that of the importance of being national in general, 'we are under the illusion that we have freely chosen our way of life' (Widdicombe 1998: 200).

In this section, I have shown that national identity is a discursive construction – a highly pervasive one but a construction nonetheless. However, while this point is basic to most of the contemporary social sciences, it is rarely acknowledged in the literature on intercultural communication, where national identity tends to be treated as a given. In the following section, therefore, I will consider intercultural communication advice as another instance of banal nationalism, a discourse that reinforces readers' sense of national belonging rather than one that leads them to genuinely engage with difference and diversity.

INTERCULTURAL COMMUNICATION ADVICE

In Chapter 2, I introduced the work of Leeds-Hurwitz (1990), who shows how a major strand of intercultural communication research grew out of the need to train US army and diplomatic personnel for their missions abroad. As a consequence of that applied focus, much work in intercultural communication is predicated upon a conflation of culture, nation and language. It is a simple equation: Australian culture can be found in Australia, where people speak Australian, which is an expression of Australian culture; Chinese culture can be found in China, where people speak Chinese, which is an expression of Chinese culture; Zambian culture can be found in Zambia, where people speak Zambian, which is an expression of Zambian culture; and so on. Those readers who are familiar with any of these countries will probably find what I have just written absurd. Regarding Australia, they could point to the fact that Australia is a country with high levels of immigration and that in the 2011 census more than twenty-three per cent of the population spoke a language other than English at home ('2011 Census Quickstats' 2016). Regarding China, they could point to the fact that two countries claim to be 'China' – the People's Republic of China or 'Mainland China' and the Republic of China or Taiwan – and that consecutive waves of Chinese emigration have established a Chinese diaspora across Southeast Asia, and, more recently, internationally (S. Lee and Li 2013). Regarding Zambia, they could point to the fact that a language called 'Zambian' does not actually exist, and that the state of Zambia is home to more than forty different indigenous ethnic groups with their own languages. The official language of Zambia, incidentally, is English, although only a minority of Zambians can speak it and even fewer are literate in it (E. Williams 2014).

It is obvious from these examples that the one-on-one mapping of culture onto nation onto language is factually wrong. However, it is a staple of the intercultural communication advice literature nonetheless. The one-on-one mapping of culture onto nation onto language is discursively constructed in a number of ways. The most obvious one is through titles in the intercultural communication advice literature that conflate 'culture' with nation. Examples include the Halls' classic *Hidden Differences: Doing Business with the Japanese* (Hall and Hall 1987), or more recent titles such as 'Communication with Egyptians' (Begley 2015), 'Russian Cultural Values and Workplace Communication Patterns' (Bergelson 2015) or 'Some Basic Cultural Patterns of India' (Jain 2015). Another way to make the nation the scope of culture (see Chapter 1) can be found on websites and smartphone apps devoted to intercultural communication advice. There, intercultural communication advice is most frequently organised in lists of national names or national flags. A smartphone app called 'CultureGPS',[6] for example, has a world map on its entry page and allows users to look up country profiles. The app is described as 'a global positioning system to navigate through intercultural differences' and is supposed to help a user 'predict to a certain degree, which interactions evolve when people from different nationalities meet'. Despite a somewhat cryptic disclaimer that '[not] everyone in a given society is programmed in the same way', the iconic association of country names with communication advice creates the impression that communication style is nation based. The app creates a strong image of banal nationalism and essentialises the nation as the locus of culture and communication.

The 'CultureGPS' app is typical of a substantial segment of intercultural communication scholarship, where the nation is the basic unit of intercultural communication. The nation is salient to intercultural communication researchers for the same reason it is salient to most people: because of the pervasiveness of the discourses of banal nationalism. However, intercultural communication scholarship that simply takes the nation as given does little more than reproduce the discourses available, that is, those circulating in society at large, rather than analysing those discourses critically. Much of the academic justification for treating the nation as the basis for culture in the intercultural communication literature rests on the work of the Dutch psychologist Geert Hofstede. I will introduce Hofstede's work in Chapter 7. Here, my key concern and argument has been that intercultural communication advice premised on monolithic and essentialist views of the nation as the foundation of culture are not useful to understanding and appreciating difference and diversity, but are little more than instances of banal nationalism, much in the same way that a flag-raising ceremony in Indonesian schools or an Australian cornflakes box adorned with national imagery are examples of banal nationalism. Such understandings are theoretically and practically inadequate. Theoretically, they are inadequate because there is no acknowledgement of the multiplicity of our identities. We are never just members of a nation but perform many other identities, too, simultaneously and at different points in our lives. Practically, they are inadequate because national identity has lost some of the sway it once held in an age characterised by globalisation and transnationalism.

GLOBALISATION AND TRANSNATIONALISM

As I have shown in this chapter, nations are discursive constructions. However, that does not mean that they are not important. When I lived in Basel, a Swiss city that borders France and Germany, even mundane activities such as grocery shopping (cheaper in Germany) or attending a children's birthday party (school friends of my child living in France) reminded me of national borders on an almost daily basis. They also reminded me of, and inscribed, my identity as a German citizen because this is the passport I carry, and this is the passport I must not forget to put in my car in case I was checked as I crossed one of those borders. Furthermore, in comparison with an Indian friend of mine, those reminders and ascriptions of my national identity were relatively benign: Indian citizens cannot just cross those borders by only showing their passport. Rather, whenever my friend wanted to cross into Germany or France, she would first need to travel to Berne, the Swiss capital, and apply for a visa to the Schengen Area – the union of European countries that form one 'visa area' and of which Switzerland was not yet a member at the time – at one of the embassies there. This involved paying fees, completing paperwork and providing various types of evidence, queuing for a significant amount of time outside the embassy, and so on. Predictably, she did not take advantage of cheaper grocery shopping in Germany or let her child attend birthday parties in France. State practices such as these obviously powerfully construct my friend and me as Indian and German, respectively, and both of us as non-Swiss, and they make national identity a salient aspect of our identity to us. So, national identity is obviously real and powerful. However, it works in ways that are quite different from those imagined in the intercultural communication advice literature, where national identity is made to rest not in institutional practices but in an individual's speech styles, behaviours, values and communicative preferences. As a matter of fact, those speech styles, behaviours, values and communicative preferences which are the locus of intercultural communication advice are increasingly decoupled from the nation in the context of globalisation and transnationalism. In today's world, the coercions of bureaucratic practices, 'the passport identity', have become increasingly more powerful due to the ascendancy of security concerns. However, cultural and communicative styles and values have become diluted and have acquired a mix-and-match flavour as more and more people travel and migrate and as mediated cultural flows criss-cross the globe.

The obvious point is that, given the state of connectedness of our world, no (national) culture exists in isolation. In a magazine article in *CNN Traveller*, for instance, a Thai informant explains Thai culture to an American journalist as follows:

> The Thai people like cowboy films. We identify with them. We grew up with *Stagecoach* and *Wyatt Earp*. The first film I ever saw was a Wayne – *Rio Grande*. 'You must learn that a man's word to anything, even his own destruction, is his honour,' he quotes.
> (Taylor 2006: 54)

The example is mundane: I could have chosen any number of examples making the same point, and each reader will be able to add their own examples to show that culture is in a constant state of flux and cross-fertilisation. Given that each of us belongs to many cultures in this sense, and that all these combinations are slightly different, it is possible to argue that, seen this way, all communication is intercultural, as Holliday, Kullman and Hyde (2017) have done.

Identities are always complex, multiple, hybrid and diverse and cannot simply be reduced to the national. We live in a world where people cross in and out of cultural styles (Rampton 2011), engage in cultural fusions (Pennycook 2007), are part of third cultures (Moore and Barker 2012), and where hybridity carries enormous identificatory and analytic purchase (Maher 2010). There is a strong sense today that identities are becoming ever more complex – a phenomenon sociolinguistics has attempted to capture with terms such as 'super-diversity' (Blommaert 2015), 'metrolingualism' (Pennycook and Otsuji 2015) or 'translanguaging' (Garcia and Li 2013). The sense that contemporary diversities are more complex than ever before may be a fallacy as diversity has always been central to the human experience (Piller 2016b). However, the perception of complex, multiple, hybrid and diverse identities demonstrates that homogeneous, nation-focused intercultural communication advice is not only stereotypical, it is also out of touch.

Explorations of crossing, cultural fusions, third cultures and hybridity are often conceived as challenges to dominant accounts of a uniform national culture. Even so, these accounts still take the nation and/or ethnicity as their point of departure. This approach has been called a 'big culture' approach by Holliday (1999), who argues for a shift of focus to 'small culture'. We sometimes speak about a 'company culture' or a 'family culture', and it is groups such as these that a 'small culture' orientation focuses on. 'Small cultures' are characterised by 'relating to cohesive behaviour in activities within any social grouping' (Holliday 1999: 241). As I have done above, Holliday takes issue with the essentialism and reification of culture that mars a lot of what is being written and said about intercultural communication, both inside and outside academia.

While researchers such as Holliday (1999) conclude that in a globalised and transnational world all communication is intercultural, others have concluded that the concept of intercultural communication has become completely meaningless as decontextualised discourses float around the globe in a time- and space-free manner (Kramsch and Boner 2010). Just as the global flows of images, discourses, ideas and lifestyles call static views of intercultural communication as communication between people from different cultural backgrounds into question, so do actual people flows. The former are often discussed under the heading of globalisation whereas the latter are more typically discussed under the heading of transnationalism (and also migration studies). In the following, I will present a detailed case study of transnational migration between Mexico and the USA and explore its implications for the national basis of intercultural communication studies.

Mexican migrants are often seen as one homogenous group in the USA. However, in the title of the study I am drawing on here neither 'Mexican immigrants' nor 'the USA' appears. Instead Marcia Farr's (2006) fifteen-year-long ethnographic engagement was with *Rancheros in Chicagoacán* – that is how the transnational people she studied described themselves ('rancheros') and the place they inhabited ('Chicagoacán'). The literal translation of ranchero is 'rancher' and the emergence of rancheros in the Americas is related to European settlement and particularly to the development of cattle ranching, with North American cowboys as the 'cultural cousins' of the rancheros. Rancheros are a recognisable group within the rural population of Western Mexico, where they are different from wealthy *hacienda* ('large estate') owners as well as indigenous *campesinos* ('peasants'). Rancheros have their own cultural norms and practices, and it was one of the aims of Farr's research to raise awareness of rancheros as a distinct subgroup of Mexico's rural population. Reading her account of the identities performed in this group and their language practices, it becomes quite apparent that reference to Mexicans as a cultural group is quite meaningless. What is more, rancheros are not a uniform group, either: 'If Hispanics are diverse, and Mexicans are diverse, rancheros are diverse as well', as the author points out (Farr 2006: 270). Gender in particular is a key aspect of internal variation, and gender identities themselves are shifting in the migration context where migrating husbands often leave their wives behind as heads of the household. This, together with the fact that migrating ranchero women are likely to be in paid employment in Chicago factories, has resulted in women taking on responsibilities and roles of authority that were traditionally considered male in this community. The lives of rancheros are far removed from the pseudo-scientific description on an intercultural communication website, which has this to say about Mexicans and their 'culture':

> Mexico is a hierarchical society. [. . .] subordinates expect to be told
> what to do [. . .] people 'live in order to work' [. . .] there is an
> emotional need for rules (even if the rules never seem to work)
> [. . .] Mexican culture is normative. People [. . .] exhibit great
> respect for traditions, a relatively small propensity to save for the
> future, and a focus on achieving quick results. [. . .] Mexican
> culture has a definite tendency toward Indulgence. People [. . .]
> place a higher degree of importance on leisure time, act as they
> please and spend money as they wish.[7]

In her fifteen-year-long engagement with a group of migrant ranchero families, where the researcher was a participant observer both in their homes in Mexico and in the USA and where she also recorded and analysed almost 200 hours of naturally occurring conversations, Farr came up with a much more complex picture of the values of her participants. In direct contrast to the statement about people expecting to be told what to do quoted above, *franqueza* (frankness) emerged as a highly prized way of speaking in this community. *Franqueza* was considered an expression of individualism, serving the dual purpose of establishing a person as a unique individual able to defend themselves and, simultaneously, to defend their place in the family.

> [T]he importance of both individualism and familism among rancheros disrupts another stereotype based on the commonly perceived dichotomy between (U.S.) individualism and (Mexican) familism. [. . .] The unexamined stereotype of Mexicans as communal (and even worse as submissive) likely derives from generalizing all campesinos as Indian and, in turn, from generalizing (and romanticizing) Indians as communally oriented or, more importantly, as different from 'us.' (Farr 2006: 269–270)

The USA to which rancheros migrate is of course not a mythical homogenous country, either. Most of them spend most of their lives in *el Norte* (the North) – as the USA is commonly referred to in Mexican Spanish – living in a close-knit network with other ranchero migrants who inhabit a few closely circumscribed quarters of Chicago. The name they have given to this area, *Chicagoacán*, is a blend between the name of their destination city, Chicago, and the name of their province of origin, Michoacán. To make the story even more complex, Farr's participants do not simply migrate from Michoacán to Chicago: not only do they create a new space and a new community in Chicagoacán, they also travel back and forth and 're-migrate' with some regularity, leading transnational lives.

In sum, in order to remain relevant, intercultural communication studies need to engage with globalisation and transnationalism and place them at the very centre of their enquiry. Not only have these processes increased the potential for intercultural encounters to take place exponentially, they have also changed the ways in which we need to approach intercultural communication as an object of enquiry. They demonstrate quite clearly that nation-based ways of approaching intercultural communication have become obsolete. In order to overcome the banal nationalism that can be found in a large segment of the intercultural communication advice literature, ethnographic studies of communication and identity making in context, such as the one by Farr (2006) I have just described, are of paramount importance. The fallacies of banal nationalism in intercultural communication research can only be avoided by a commitment to studying language, culture and communication in context. Rather than taking the 'nation equals culture equals language' formula for granted, the key question of intercultural communication research needs to be: Who makes culture relevant to whom in which context for which purposes?

KEY POINTS

This chapter made the following key points:

- Stereotypes underlie much intercultural communication and as participants in intercultural encounters we often approach each other through stereotypes. We need to understand stereotypes for what they are – interested generalisations – in order to engage with people from different backgrounds in a meaningful way. Elevating stereotypes to heuristic devices is not only useless but also damages our capacity to engage with others.
- Banal nationalism is a ubiquitous way of stereotyping which socialises us into national belonging in mundane, often overlooked, but pervasive ways. National socialisation is part of the baggage most if not all of us bring to intercultural encounters.
- A large segment of the intercultural communication advice literature is nothing more than an instantiation of banal nationalism. Such advice often purports to teach about intercultural communication but peddles nothing more than national ways of seeing the world and stereotypes about essentialist and homogeneous national identity.
- Globalisation and transnational migration further throw nation-based approaches to intercultural communication into question. As the media broadcast cultural styles and values around the globe and as more and more people travel (or are travelled to), intercultural communication itself is best seen as a mobile resource and the question of who makes culture relevant to whom in what context for what purposes is ever more important to gain an understanding of the interested nature of communication.

COUNTERPOINT

I have argued here that intercultural communication research needs to escape from the trap of methodological nationalism through ethnographic and discourse-analytic work that examines who makes culture relevant to whom in what context for what purposes. However, does it actually make sense to retain such a tainted and overburdened concept such as 'intercultural communication'? Or have globalisation and transnational migration resulted in all communication being intercultural? Have they resulted in making the intercultural meaningless as dominant cultures impose their discourses on others as supposedly culturally-neutral texts?

FURTHER READING

It is well worth reading Billig (1995) in the original. The contributions to *The Handbook of Language and Globalization* (Coupland 2010) provide a wide range of perspectives on globalisation and communication. An in-depth study of 'super-diversity' in the linguistic landscape of Antwerp provides an intriguing 'chronicle of complexity' (Blommaert 2013). Holliday et al. (2017) is a collection of resources of intercultural communication that engage with and go beyond nation-based approaches to intercultural communication.

ACTIVITIES

Banal nationalism around you
Document instances of banal nationalism in the spaces you frequent and the activities you engage in during the course of a day. If possible, use a digital camera or mobile phone to record all displays of your country's name, the flag and any other national imagery you encounter on campus, in the street, on public transport, in the mall, and so on. Also, create a record of any other reminders of national belonging you are exposed to as part of your normal activities (for example, during work, while eating, in your study materials, in the media, and so on). Once you have completed your data collection and compiled your documentation, consider whether the number of instances of banal nationalism differs from your expectations. Are there instances of banal nationalism that you must have encountered already but that you had never noticed before? Who is included and who is excluded by the instances of banal nationalism that you have encountered?

Banal nationalism in intercultural communication websites
Choose an intercultural communication advice website or a smartphone application and analyse which scope of culture is encoded in the design. How is that encoding achieved (for example, through maps, lists of country names or flags as organising devices)? If the scope of culture is not the nation, what is it? If you want to turn this activity into a more substantial exploration, you might want to read up on multimodal analysis, to which Kress and van Leeuwen (1996) provide an excellent introduction.

Global and local intersections in your life
Keep a close record of the local or global origins of what you do for one day. Where do the things you use come from (for example, clothes, food,

furniture, books, computer)? Most of these will have multiple sources (for example, clothes designed in one place, material grown in another, assembled in yet another); can you determine all the sources for the things in your life? What about the practices and ideas that you engage in? Where do they come from? On the basis of this record write a short essay about global and local intersections in your life.

NOTES

1. See http://www.xenophobes.com/
2. An image of the page can be viewed at http://www.languageonthemove.com/the-banal-nationalism-of-intercultural-communication-advice/
3. An image of the cornflakes box and can be viewed at http://www.languageonthemove.com/the-banal-nationalism-of-intercultural-communication-advice/
4. For a collection of images of products and streetscapes infused with national imagery of the United Arab Emirates, visit http://www.languageonthemove.com/happy-birthday-uae-2/
5. See https://www.youtube.com/watch?v=jD3SkTyXzcE; spellings as in the original.
6. Published by Itim International; last downloaded from the Apple App Store on 2 January 2017.
7. See https://geert-hofstede.com/mexico.html

CHAPTER 5

Intercultural Communication in a Multilingual World

CHAPTER OBJECTIVES

This chapter will enable you to:

- Familiarise yourself with sociolinguistic approaches to intercultural communication and to understand intercultural communication as shaped by language proficiency and language choice.
- Gain an understanding of multilingualism, language learning and language choice that does not see languages as clearly bounded autonomous systems but as truncated repertoires that can best be understood by exploring beliefs about language, language practices and the political economy of languages.
- View misunderstandings as linguistic rather than cultural problems and apply a real-language perspective to intercultural communication.
- Engage critically with state and commercial language regimes, particularly in the context of language and the law, and the commercialisation of language teaching.

LANGUAGE PROFICIENCY

There is yet another perspective from which the 'nation equals culture equals language' formula is problematic. In Chapter 3, we examined how a language with a name is a discursive construction but we largely took a monolingual view. However, the complex identities resulting from globalisation and transnationalism which we observed in Chapter 4 are also related to significant linguistic complexity: the majority of the world's population uses more than one language on a regular basis and monolingualism is by and large a historical and Anglophone anomaly. That means that attention to linguistic diversity needs to be placed at the centre of all intercultural communication enquiry because diverse communicators bring to the table their diverse linguistic repertoires, trajectories and proficiencies. Intercultural communication is characterised by multilingual practices, is embedded in beliefs about language, and plays out in the political economy of language. To put it differently, all human communication, whether we consider it as intercultural or not, takes place in and through language. Natural language can be characterised as a system of choices to which speakers enjoy differential levels of access. Within the choices available to them, speakers choose on the basis of practices ('what is normally done') and on the basis of beliefs ('what is the best/appropriate/right thing to do'). Language choice – as practice and ideology – is a crucial aspect of intercultural communication and it is the aim of this chapter to focus attention on real language in intercultural communication.

Let's consider two examples that demonstrate the vital role of language proficiency in intercultural communication. The first example comes from my research with bilingual couples, where one partner came from a German- and the other from an English-speaking background (Piller 2002a). As part of the research, I interviewed a woman I will call Tracy. Tracy was an educational counsellor from New York City with a graduate degree in educational psychology and many years of professional experience. In her late thirties, she followed her German husband to live with him in his native town, a small city in Southern Germany, where she became a stay-at-home mum. When I first met her, Tracy had lived in Germany for almost five years but her German was still very basic. Her failure to learn German resulted from a combination of factors: her husband and all their circle of family and friends spoke English well and were all too happy to accommodate to her to practise their English; the local dialect is very different from the standard German that can be found in textbooks and is taught in formal language classes; she wanted to raise her children bilingually and give them as much 'native-speaker' input in English as possible; she felt she did not have a talent for languages, and overall she felt ambivalent about life in Germany and would have much preferred to return to the USA if her husband's job and the family's circumstances had allowed it. Unsurprisingly, given her professional background, Tracy took a strong interest in her children's schooling and volunteered her services for all kinds of roles on the parents' council. However, all such attempts came to naught and while she was tolerated in general assemblies, she was never elected to one of the offices she aspired to and to which she felt she had so much to contribute. It pained her that her professional expertise counted for nothing in the face of her language difficulties and she was angered by this lack of recognition. She said that other parents made her feel stupid because she could only make her contributions in basic, faltering German.

Now consider another example from a published intercultural memoir by Corey Heller, who, like Tracy, is a white English-speaking woman from the USA residing in Germany. In the account, Heller recalls the frustrations of her early days living in a new country:

> One day I was purchasing goods in a store and after giving the cashier fifty marks, she only returned a ten mark bill plus some change. I went into a sudden internal panic. She should have returned a twenty mark bill plus change! I tried to tell her as much but I had not yet learned the past-tense in class. So, I stated, 'You give me ten marks.' But the tired, annoyed cashier just looked at me blankly and called the next person. I didn't budge. I kept trying to make myself understood, becoming breathless and turning bright red in the process. 'You give me twenty marks, but you give me ten marks.' It was hopeless. Finally, a kind gentleman behind me asked if I spoke English. Relieved, I explained the situation to him, he translated it for the cashier and I did get my correct change back (along with a very dirty look from the cashier). I felt small and insignificant. I felt like telling everyone, 'I come from America. I am educated. I am not as tiny and stupid as it seems. I am like you!' But instead I said '*Danke*,' [= thank you] walked home and cried. (C. Heller 2009: 126f.)

In both these examples, intercultural communication is mediated by language proficiencies and language ideologies: Tracy's limited proficiency dovetailed with the beliefs held by the members of the parents' council that voices other than those of proficient German speakers are not worth listening to and that language proficiency is an indicator of expertise. Heller similarly finds her identity reduced to that of a 'small and insignificant' and 'tiny and stupid' language learner. The examples demonstrate that an analysis of intercultural communication in terms of cultural values and intercultural communication advice based on cultural values is not only stereotypical banal nationalism, it is also utterly useless as the expression of a person's values – cultural and other – and their identity is mediated by their linguistic proficiency. Who we are in intercultural communication is to a large extent a function of our linguistic proficiency: you cannot 'be' an educational expert or a competent shopper if you do not sound like one. 'Being' an educational expert or competent shopper involves performing these identities: you have 'to do being'.

As these two examples demonstrate, the identities you would like to claim and your linguistic ability to do so may sometimes come into conflict. Most readers will readily accept that in these examples the failure to hold an audience of fellow parents or the experience of being pushed around in a service interaction is related to linguistic proficiency rather than the cultural traits and values of Americans. However, that point seems to get lost as soon as it comes to English-language learners, particularly if their proficiency is more than just basic. For example, I have often read in the intercultural communication literature and have also been told by colleagues that English speakers form a negative impression on first meeting a Japanese person if that Japanese speaker says 'Please take care of me' as part of the introduction. Some English speakers view such a request as a sign of a weak and dependent character, others take it as an expression of Japanese cultural values, such as being hierarchically oriented and attempting to curry favour and engender sympathy (e.g., Melville 1999). However, unless they are familiar with Japanese or Japanese-influenced English, few English speakers take this expression for what it is: lack of familiarity with more conventional greeting and introductory routines in English. 'Please take care of me' is a literal translation of *yoroshiku onegai shimasu*, a formula used in Japanese on first introduction. The conventional (rather than the literal) equivalent in English is 'Pleased to meet you'! Far from seeing it as an expression of their cultural values, many Japanese speakers who say 'Please take care of me' in English feel just as constrained and reduced in the identity they want to perform as the English speakers above.

'I'M NOT LISTENING TO YOU!'

As these examples demonstrate, what you can do with your language proficiency is not only a matter of performance but also of perception. The cashier in Heller's shopping misadventure clearly would have preferred not to hear her explanation. That is not an unusual reaction and we humans overall tend to hold rather dim views of people whose language we do not speak or understand. The ancient Greeks, for instance, referred to non-speakers of Greek as *barbaros*, 'blablas' – a word that has been borrowed into many European languages, including English, as 'barbarian'. However, 'barbarian' has long since lost its original meaning of 'non-speaker of Greek' or 'foreigner' more generally, and the only aspect that remains is the decidedly negative value judgement of the original. A similar example can be found in Arabic, where *ajam* means 'mute, non-speaker of Arabic, foreigner, non-Arab'. Just like 'barbarian', it is not a neutral term for a non-speaker of Arabic but carries derogatory connotations to the degree that *ajam* has become an insulting term for those tongue-tied foreigners, particularly the Persians, whose empire the Arabs took over in the seventh century to become the foundation of their own (Hourani 2005). The Persians in turn converted the term *ajam* into a proud self-identification, which served to mock the naïve assumption of their speechlessness.

Like the Ancient Greeks and Arabs who felt superior to non-speakers of their languages, speakers of powerful languages often may not feel the need to try and understand what is being said in other languages. The Roman politician Marcus Tullius Cicero (106–43 BCE) summed up this attitude when he quipped 'we are completely deaf to the innumerable languages which we don't understand' (Cicero 45 BCE: 5, 116). In fact, turning a deaf ear to speakers of other languages may be a frequent feature of intercultural communication, as the following examples from twenty-first-century healthcare show.

In 2016, two cases were reported in the Australian media relating to the fatal consequences of patients with limited English proficiency not being listened to: in one case, a seventy-five-year-old woman 'who did not speak fluent English' (Menagh 2016a) died under the care of a homecare team. During the inquest into her death it emerged that she had received substandard care to the degree that her infected pressure wounds were contaminated with dried faeces and her dentures had turned mouldy in her mouth. In their defence, the carers described the woman as 'stubborn', 'very quiet' and 'not cooperating with the nurses and carers' (Menagh 2016a, 2016b). Her family, by contrast, argued that her English was basic and she simply would not have understood instructions. In a similarly chilling story, Faysal Ishak Ahmed, a twenty-seven-year-old man from South Sudan died in immigration detention after he collapsed with a seizure. After his death, it emerged that the young man had presented at the detention healthcare service repeatedly over a period of several months for a range of health issues such as stomach upsets, high blood pressure, fevers and heart problems. However, he never got to see a doctor and each time was dismissed by the nurse on duty. He described one such incident to his friends shortly before his death:

> I went to the [health care provider] and then [they] told me that, hey you don't have anything, you are not sick and you're pretending to be sick, and from now on, we don't want you to come down here, so please stop coming here. (Quoted in S. Kim 2016)

Cases such as these where patients with limited proficiency in the dominant language are not taken seriously and oftentimes simply ignored are not unique to Australia, as a US study of doctors and nurses working with patients with limited English proficiency (LEP) demonstrates (Kenison et al. 2016). The researchers review a body of earlier research that has found that LEP patients have a higher likelihood than non-LEP patients of: misunderstanding their diagnosis, treatment and follow-up plans; using medications incorrectly; lacking informed consent for surgical procedures; suffering serious adverse events; and, overall, reporting a lower-quality healthcare experience. Based on these findings, the researchers examine how these negative outcomes for LEP patients come about from the perspective of doctors and nurses. They identify negative role modelling, systems factors and organisational culture as key problems. Negative role modelling refers to the dismissive attitude that junior doctors and nurses observe in the interactions of more senior colleagues with LEP patients. For instance, in a quote that has almost uncanny echoes of Faysal Ishak Ahmed's experience on the other side of the world, one junior doctor reported this conversation with a senior clinician to the researchers:

> And he said, 'Oh, you know we see this, a lot of this Haitian chest pain.' And I said, 'What do you mean by that?' And he said, 'Well, they come in and the tests are negative, and they have a different perception of pain than other people.' He kind of wrote it off that way. I felt a little weird that it was written off that quickly. To write off the chest pain on a patient who is having trouble communicating because she's using a phone interpreter. (Kenison et al. 2016: 3)

In addition to explicit negative role modelling as in this example, another major reason why LEP patients were ignored was related to system factors such as time pressures, inadequate interpreting services or lack of training on how to identify language needs or how to use the telephone interpreting equipment. Finally, the organisational culture in hospitals was such that 'efficiency' was valued more highly than good communication, and LEP patients were simply assigned a low value. One doctor summed up how all these factors conspired to result in the substandard care of LEP patients by comparing them to patients with infectious diseases:

> [. . .] there are all sorts of reasons why patients receive different treatment. Even wearing the yellow gowns and entering a room of a patient who has MRSA [= methicillin-resistant staphylococcus aureus; a highly contagious penicillin-resistant bacterium also known as 'superbug'] we are less willing to go into those rooms or hop in and say something because there's a barrier. I feel like

language is a similar barrier that's even more extreme because it requires extra resources and extra brain power as well. [. . .] the level of empathy lost for a patient who is LEP might be kind of similar to the empathy you lose towards the patient who complains a lot or something, and it's through no fault of that patient themselves. (Kenison et al. 2016: 6)

The junior doctors and nurses interviewed by Kenison et al. (2016) were for the most part idealistic and themselves disturbed by the differential treatment they observed LEP patients receiving. However, they also observed that the hospitals in which they worked were set up in a way that made it very difficult for individual doctors and nurses to address any language barriers. When a problem is out of the control of an individual doctor or nurse, ignoring it is an entirely rational response. In some other contexts, refusing to listen to speakers of other languages may draw even harsher responses that include victim blaming and exploitation of language barriers. With language being the main criterion that distinguishes humans from the rest of the animal world, the seeming speechlessness of the linguistic other has at times invited extreme cruelty – a facet of intercultural communication that is difficult to face. Like everything we repress, cruelty as intercultural communication also needs to be recognised to overcome it. Cruelty towards non-speakers of a particular language is closely linked to the human rights' abuses involved in slavery and human trafficking. Human trafficking itself has emerged as an increasing human rights' concern linked to transnational migration (Piller and Takahashi 2011). Placing people in contexts in which they do not speak the language and thereby become speechless, 'small and insignificant', 'stupid and tiny', 'stubborn and non-compliant' or 'requiring extra resources and extra brain power' may in itself be a tool of abuse as bell hooks (1994: 169) explains with reference to the transatlantic slave trade from the sixteenth to the nineteenth centuries:

When I imagine the terror of Africans on board slave ships, on auction blocks, inhabiting the unfamiliar architecture of plantations, I consider that this terror extended beyond fear of punishment, that it resided also in the anguish of hearing a language they could not comprehend. The very sound of English had to terrify. [. . .] How to remember, to invoke this terror? How to describe what it must have been like for Africans whose deepest bonds were historically forged in the place of shared speech to be transported abruptly to a world where the very sound of one's mother tongue had no meaning?

Terrors such as those imagined by bell hooks for the victims of the transatlantic slave trade are as real in the twenty-first century as they were then, as is evident from examples from contemporary refugee crises such as the one faced by the Rohingya. The Rohingya are an indigenous Muslim minority in Myanmar, who are not recognised as Burmese citizens and who are subjected to grave human rights' abuses ('Who are the Rohingya Refugees?' 2016). Rather than putting them out of harm's way, fleeing Myanmar may court further tragedy as happened in December 2008 when a couple of boatloads of Rohingya refugees arrived in Thailand. Instead of finding refuge and receiving help, these refugees were detained, beaten and then put back on boats and towed out to sea, where they were finally cast adrift. Interviews with some of the survivors who were later rescued off Aceh, Indonesia, more dead than alive, show that their utter incomprehension of what was being done to them was aggravating their situation ('Rohingya Migrants Claim Thai Abuses' 2009). One of the survivors, interviewed on Al Jazeera TV, stated that it was only his belief that God 'comprehends' that had kept him alive. For the Rohingya, as for many other victims of human rights' abuses around the world, the inability to communicate, to understand the threats of the soldiers, is not only a human rights' concern in the immediate context of being subject to military brutality. The fact that their oppression is rarely communicated in English or any other language of wider communication also results in the invisibility of their plight on the global stage. The human rights' situation of the Rohingya – both inside and outside Burma – is catastrophic. Yet, in a world where the plight of so many is competing for attention, their oppression remains largely invisible. This gives their abusers a free reign and stands in the way of international condemnation, solidarity and support.

Humans are social creatures and being able to communicate with one's fellow humans is clearly a basic human right. The abuse involved in rendering another human being 'speechless' by placing them in a situation where they cannot communicate or cannot communicate effectively has largely gone unnoticed by communication scholars and human rights' activists alike. This may be due to the fact that for slaves, the victims of trafficking and boat people, their inability to comprehend what is being done to them and to communicate is only one facet of a much larger atrocity. In such cases, it is probably strategically ineffective to point to their inability to communicate as a human rights' abuse because 'speechlessness' is likely to be perceived as a minor infringement compared with the overall brutality of their situation.

However, being placed in a situation where one is unable to communicate is a human rights' violation that does not only occur as part of the outrages of slavery and human trafficking. In some cases it can also be brought about by the asylum-seeker policies of countries that are signatories to the United Nations Universal Declaration of Human Rights (1948), as the following examples from the UK and Australia demonstrate.

The first example is situated in the context of the UK's policy of regionalisation, which is an attempt to disperse asylum seekers away from London. Suleiman Dialo, an asylum seeker from Guinea in West Africa, was sent to Newcastle upon Tyne, a city in the North East of England, in 2000, while his claim for asylum was being assessed. One-and-a-half years later his application was refused and he was awaiting deportation back to Guinea when he committed suicide. During all that time he had been the only Fula speaker in the region.

> This is not a plaintive tale about a cruel bureaucracy condemning a vulnerable young man to death; rather, it is a story about the loneliness and fear which are common to asylum-seekers everywhere, made worse perhaps in Dialo's case by the fact that his native language was Fula, which is spoken across parts of West Africa, and that there were no other known Fula speakers in the whole of north-east England; that his French was very poor and that he spoke scarcely a sentence of English; and that, in all his childhood in Guinea, he had never learnt to read or write. Signposts, letters, instructions, telephone calls, the television and radio, ordinary, daily conversation – none of this meant much to him in England; and his sense of aloneness was both overwhelming and shocking to him. [. . .] 'He didn't ever really understand what was happening to him. [. . .] The world about him had shrunk to almost nothing.' (Moorehead 2006: 129)

In the UK, asylum seekers such as Dialo are allowed to live in the community while their asylum claim is being processed. While their mobility is restricted within the region to which they have been assigned, Australia has since the early 1990s restricted the mobility of asylum seekers in a much more drastic fashion. There, the policy of mandatory immigration detention means that asylum seekers are held in detention centres while their claim for asylum is being assessed. Detention centres are located in remote locations in Australia or outsourced to neighbouring countries such as Papua New Guinea and the tiny Pacific Island nation of Nauru. Now let us meet Aladdin Sisalem. Sisalem is a Kuwait-born Palestinian, a group that had been subjected to a violent campaign of ethnic cleansing in the early 1990s (El-Najjar 2008). Sisalem tried to reach Australia by boat from Indonesia in order to seek asylum there and was detained in an off-shore processing centre on Manus Island, which is part of Papua

New Guinean territory. In July 2003, when he had been in the detention centre for about a year, the Australian authorities were preparing to close down the centre (it was finally formally closed in 2008 but reopened in 2012). All other inmates were resettled, either in Australia or New Zealand. However, Sisalem's case had not yet been resolved at the time and he was left behind as the only inmate for another ten months before he was finally granted an Australian visa (Loewenstein 2016). When he was finally released, he had this to say about the company he had kept for ten months: 'Honey, a stray cat [. . .] was the only company I had since I was left alone in detention 10 months ago' (A. Jackson 2004).

Even in cases where other detainees are present in detention centres in Australia, detainees from different language and national backgrounds may not necessarily be able to communicate with each other or with English-speaking guards. The violation entailed in detention without communication is most powerfully symbolised by detainees sewing up their own lips in a desperate bid to draw attention to their plight (Cox and Minahan 2004). Many media commentators have condemned the practice as evidence of the detainee's barbarism. However, remember the etymology of 'barbarism'. In order to be competent, in control and balanced, you need to be able to do being competent, in control and balanced. Above, we saw competent, educated, privileged American middle-class women lose control because they could not communicate in much less serious circumstances that were far removed from being stuck in a desert detention camp in the Australian outback for months, and in some cases even years, on end.

In sum, being placed in a situation where one cannot communicate can be terrifying and abusive. However, instead of making extra efforts to bridge language barriers, those who are linguistically privileged often prefer to close their ears – and hearts – to those they find difficult to understand. The perceived speechlessness of the linguistic other more often seems to invite dismissal, even cruelty, abuse and hatred than solidarity, compassion and kindness.

THE MONOLINGUAL MINDSET

So far, I have argued that language matters. However, much of the literature in intercultural communication studies gives the impression that intercultural communication takes place in some kind of linguistic never-never land: we are never told which language is the language in which a particular interaction takes place or how proficient the interlocutors are in that language. This does not mean that language is not important in intercultural communication; it just means that language choice is rendered invisible. In effect this results in naturalising a particular language choice, namely that of the dominant language, which in intercultural communication studies is usually English. The sociolinguist Michael Clyne (2005) has termed this myopia the 'monolingual mindset'. For the monolingual mindset the use of one single language, that is the absence of linguistic choice, seems normal and natural. As a consequence, language choice, language proficiency and language diversity are either ignored altogether or trivialised. Where the fact that intercultural communication occurs in a multilingual world is ignored, cultural stereotypes often flourish instead, as we saw with the example of 'Please take care of me' above.

A research tradition that has consistently challenged the monolingual mindset over many years can be found in interactional sociolinguistics as pioneered by John Gumperz (1982a, 1982b). Interactional sociolinguistics has an empirical focus on naturally occurring face-to-face interactions between people from different kinds of backgrounds. As an example, I will now describe a study in this tradition in more detail to give you an understanding of the approach as well as to further exemplify that language matters in intercultural communication (Roberts et al. 2005). This is a study of general practice consultations in four inner-London medical practices in a local government area characterised by high ethnic diversity. The researchers obtained permission to video-record 232 such consultations and then identified all misunderstandings that occurred. They found that twenty per cent of all the consultations they filmed contained misunderstandings. Crucially, they found that these misunderstandings resulted from linguistic problems. Linguistic proficiency was the main problem in medical encounters in this multilingual community and not culturally-specific health beliefs, as some might have expected.

The following is an example of a consultation where a misunderstanding occurred. The purpose of the consultation was not actually health related but for the general practitioner (GP) to confirm the patient's identity for a passport application. The GP is of Anglo-Saxon background and the patient is originally from Bangladesh.

1	Doctor	this is for you M, isn't it?
2	Patient	yeah, M B's my name.
3	Doctor	how long have I known you, B?
4	Patient	[pause] my name?
5	Doctor	[pause] how long [pause] how long do I know you for, how many years?
6	Patient	oh um [pause] eh nine years [pause] I come to this country in er [pause] 1990 [pause] but [. . .] (Roberts et al. 2005: 468)[1]

The misunderstanding, which occurs between turns 3 and 4, is evidenced by the fact that the patient fails to provide a relevant answer to the doctor's question. The researchers identify five different causes of the misunderstanding. First, there is a pronunciation problem: '*known*' and '*name*' may sound the same to the patient. Second, there is a grammatical problem with the tenses ('*have known*' versus '*do know*'). While the patient misunderstands the present perfect in turn 3, the doctor's reformulation of his question in the simple present tense in turn 5 contributes to resolving the misunderstanding and results in a relevant answer. Third, the expression '*how long*' is semantically difficult as it contains a metaphor of space ('time is a long line of events'). Fourth, the question '*how long have I known you?*' is rather unusual and would be odd outside this specific bureaucratic context. For someone not familiar with the routine of witnessing someone's identity, that question must have come unexpectedly. Expectation is also at the heart of the fifth cause of the misunderstanding: the patient lacks the institutional knowledge that the GP must have known him for a minimum period in order to sign the passport form. As that regulation is not made explicit, the patient obviously has to make quite a jump from having been asked his name to being asked for the length of time he has been known to the GP.

The mundane misunderstanding presented in this example turns out to be quite complex on closer inspection and to result from multiple factors. However, all the factors have their root in language (pronunciation, grammar, semantics) and lack of shared contextual knowledge. Cultural values play no role whatsoever in this misunderstanding nor in any of the many other misunderstandings recorded by the researchers. In fact, all the causes of misunderstanding which the researchers observed except for one are present in this example. The only cause of misunderstandings which the researchers identified and which is not apparent in this example is presentation style. Presentation style problems included patients who said very little about what their problem was or patients who overloaded the interaction with numerous topics, which seemed unconnected to the GP. Interestingly, the GPs misunderstood more often than the patients. The authors recommend awareness-raising for GPs and training in identifying miscommunication resulting from different ways of using language. They sum up their findings as follows:

> Communication textbooks exhort doctors to encourage more talk and to listen better, but such prescriptions are modelled on monolingual, monocultural consultations, where ordinary talk itself is not the problem. GPs need to make rapid assessments of patients' competence in English; they need to acknowledge the difficulties

patients may have in communicating in English and the resourcefulness that patients display in attempting to convey their intent in limited English; they also need to accept that patients may have a systematically different way of presenting themselves and relating to the doctor; and they need to develop strategies for preventing and managing misunderstandings. Although there is now much debate and many recommendations relating to working in an ethnically diverse society, education and training communication programs have not developed more linguistically sensitive and culturally flexible approaches for the thousands of consultations, every day, with patients who do not speak a standard or local variety of English. (Roberts et al. 2005: 474)

The conversations recorded by Roberts et al. (2005) were only conducted in English. However, it is not uncommon for interactions to be much more complex, as Duchêne and Piller (2011) show in their analysis of interactions at the counter of a tourist information centre in a city in the German-speaking part of Switzerland. In a typical interaction, within the space of only a few minutes, a travel agent there engages in the following communicative acts:

1. She speaks with a customer face to face in English.
2. She checks her computer database for an available room; the database is in Standard German.
3. She picks up the phone and calls a hotel in order to book a room for the customer. She speaks with the hotel receptionist in Swiss German.
4. Immediately after that she places another call to the tourism authority's back office, which is unconnected to the customer she is serving at the moment. Again they speak in Swiss German.
5. She returns to the customer who is standing at her counter and explains in English that the room he wants to book is not available for the full booking period.
6. She turns around and speaks to one of her colleagues about the problem in Swiss German.
7. She phones the hotel again and negotiates a solution in Swiss German.
8. She enters booking details into the online database in Standard German.
9. She speaks again to the customer in English and writes out some details for him on a form that has a map and some printed information in Standard German, French, English and Italian.
10. As the customer leaves, she picks up the phone to the back office again to return to the other problem she is dealing with.

All this took place in the space of a little under ten minutes. During the course of her working day, three of which were audio-recorded by the researchers, in addition to the languages apparent in this interaction the agent also used French in spoken interactions. She wrote e-mails in Standard German and English, and often used drawings on maps to communicate with customers to overcome misunderstandings and communicative problems.

Paying close attention to actual interactions not only reminds us of the importance of natural language and the complexity of human interactions; it also demonstrates that interactants sometimes simply do not want to understand each other and that misunderstandings arise not only because of linguistic or cultural differences, but also because people fight and argue. Put differently, in interactions there are often simply different interests at stake and interactants may not actually want to understand each other. Intercultural communication research often creates the impression that if we just knew how to overcome our linguistic and cultural differences, we would get on just fine with each other.

Now consider the following interaction, which was recorded at the transit counter of Swiss Airlines at Zurich International Airport in September 2006.[2] A passenger en route from London to Hong Kong has just left her plane during a scheduled stop. She wants to change her ticket so that she can fly the next day because her partner will be flying from Zurich to Hong Kong via Frankfurt the following day and she wants to be with him. However, while it is possible to rebook her ticket category for the direct flight the following day (basically the same one she has just left), she cannot be rebooked onto the alternative route via Frankfurt. She approaches the transit desk to seek rebooking and to complain. 'P' stands for the passenger and 'T1' and 'T2' for the agents who work at the transit desk. 'M' is their manager. The passenger's first language is French and the transit agents' first language is Swiss German:

P: parlez-vous Français? [*do you speak French?*][3]
T1:   non. [*'no.'*]
P: or English?
T1:   English, ja. ['English, *yes.*']
P: so uhm my partner uhm-
T1:   yes, you've got your ticket. [inaudible] okay, so your partner
         flies erm tomorrow erm via Frankfurt to Hong Kong
P: uhmhu
T1:   but we've just checked your ticket and erm it's actually this-
         this fare it's not possible to change.
P: oh no, no, I don't wanna hear that!

T1: okay, I will just check for that-

P: uhmhu! I just missed the flight for that! So the person told me that everything was okay! So now I am not gonna hear something that my fare or whatever.

T2: ya, but for you it was okay.

P: so what's the problem?

T2: for you it was okay, you have been on the plane! It was okay for you.

P: but they!

T2: it's your OWN DECISION not to travel-

P: no, they didn't tell me that the fare wouldn't apply! Then I would think differently! and no, come on, just like be reasonable!

T2: come on, yes please, sorry! Okay? What I can do- we rebook you via Frankfurt that's not possible with your ticket, I can offer you to make a free change of reservation on the direct flight tomorrow night   [(inaudible)

P: [no, then I wanna take this flight!

T2: that's too late definitely now.

P: this is the worst airplane in the world and we do fly a LOT, believe me!

T2: ya, I do believe you.

P: and Mister Surname, Mister Surname is a gold senator whatever with this [airline's name] thing, whatever, so I think this is just unacceptable and ah I don't know, it's probably the last time we fly [airline's name], Mr Surname flies every weekend with [airline's name], every single fucking weekend!

T2: it was your decision.

P: no! Because they didn't tell me, they didn't tell me! she told me, no, listen! Listen to me! She told me-

T2: not like this Ma'am, please!

P: ex- excuse me, she told me-

T2: ma'am that's too [(inaudible)

P: [that person- that person told me I asked her CHECK THAT THE FLIGHT IS OK FOR ME? I mean, think reasonably,
[I would not change my-

T2: [but you even had your seat!

P: I wanna see your manager! I mean excuse me, excuse me but listen I was about to make this flight, okay?

T2: yes!

P: I didn't make it because I wanted to fly with him, if she told

me you can't fly with him, you have to fly tomorrow night
and where as it is tomorrow afternoon, what do you think I
would have done, do you think I would have waited here?

T2:   yeah, but you asked not to fly!

P: no but come on! IS THERE SOMEONE WITH A BRAIN
HERE? No but come on, but this-

T2:   next one please!

P: no, come on, please it's stupid. I mean- do you? I mean are
you outside of this!

T2:   you will have to deal with him, Ma'am, sorry!

P: no this is ridiculous, ah okay, we are gonna wait for him and
discuss this-

T2:   ja, and then we just have a look, hum, okay?

M: okay, may I ask you to come with me please?

P: oh my God! This is the worst air- air company!

There is plenty of evidence of conversational trouble in this example:
frequent interruptions and overlaps, talking at cross-purposes, failure to
provide a relevant response, the use of rude expressions and insults, and
interlocutors giving up on the conversation. While the interaction takes
place in English as a lingua franca, it is not really talk itself that is the
problem, and even less so cultural difference. The problem in this conversation is due to the fact that the passenger wants something that the status
of her ticket and the airline's policy does not allow.

In sum, interactional sociolinguistics is an empirical approach to intercultural communication that investigates the details of interactions in
order to uncover how misunderstandings actually play out in real interactions. Empirical sociolinguistics research as it is conducted in the tradition
of interactional sociolinguistics and related ethnographic approaches only
uses data from actual naturally occurring conversations. Such data and
their analysis provide a constant reality check lest we mistake language
problems for cultural problems.

STATE LANGUAGE REGIMES

Interactional sociolinguistics shows us that language use is a form of practice and that language choices are implicit in practice: choices become
normalised and GPs in London do not really make a conscious language
choice for each new consultation, even if they have to make on-the-spot
assessments of the linguistic proficiency of their interlocutors. Travel
agents in Switzerland make an initial language assessment (implicit or

explicit) within a range of normalised choices, predominantly English, French, Swiss and Standard German. However, language choice is not only a matter of practice but also one of ideology. Language ideology refers to beliefs about language, the ideas we hold about what good language is and what 'the right thing to do' linguistically is. Language ideologies undergird language use but the purpose of language ideologies is not really linguistic but social: they serve to legitimise the social order and therefore they are always interested, multiple and contested (Piller 2015). In other words, language ideologies are in some people's interests more so than others, and we make our linguistic choices within these common-sense beliefs about what kind of language is good, right, moral or beautiful; and, of course, these beliefs are not only beliefs about language but also about speakers.

Linguistic choices are embedded within language ideologies which valorise some languages over others and some speakers over others. For instance, a few years ago I had a conversation with a young Iranian woman who had grown up bilingually in Persian and Azeri. Azeri is closely related to Turkish and she had taught herself how to read Turkish. Additionally, she had studied Arabic as a foreign language. I was very impressed and, with the expansive map of the areas where these languages are spoken, basically all of the Middle East and Central Asia, before my mental eye, I said: 'Wow, so many languages. You can communicate wherever you go from the Bosporus to Xinjiang.' However, my enthusiastic admiration was cut short when she responded, 'Who cares, if you don't speak English?' The example explains the process of language ideologies and the ways in which they valorise different languages differently quite clearly: proficiency in three widely spoken languages is discounted and considered less valuable than proficiency in the global language English. The example also shows that language ideologies make us overlook the obvious, such as the fact that in her part of the world – we had that conversation in Tehran – you cannot get by on a daily basis without Persian but you certainly can without English. Indeed, the continued spread of English is partly based on the way in which ever more people come to believe that they 'need' English, as I will discuss further below.

In the same way that language ideologies valorise different languages differently, they also valorise different speakers differently. Just think of a middle-class white American who has learnt Spanish as a foreign language in comparison with an illegal immigrant from Latin America who has learnt English as an additional language. In a hypothetical example, they could both have exactly the same kind of bilingual English–Spanish proficiency, and yet the US American's bilingualism will most likely be seen in terms of a bonus ('she knows how to speak another language') while the

Latin American's bilingualism will most likely be framed as deficit ('he's a non-native speaker of English', 'his English isn't very good').

Critical empirical sociolinguistics engaging with language ideologies is methodologically grounded in ethnography in the same way that inter-actional sociolinguistics is. Additionally, it draws heavily from another tradition, the political economy of language. Research into the political economy of language is most closely associated with the work of sociologist Pierre Bourdieu (1930–2002). Bourdieu argues that the valorisation of a particular linguistic practice in a particular social space or a particular institution automatically enhances or restricts access to that space or that institution on the basis of having the right sort of linguistic proficiency.

> The competence adequate to produce sentences that are likely to be understood may be quite inadequate to produce sentences that are likely to be *listened to*, likely to be recognized as *acceptable* in all the situations in which there is occasion to speak. [. . .] social acceptability is not reducible to mere grammaticality. Speakers lacking the legitimate competence are *de facto* excluded from the social domains in which this competence is required, or are condemned to silence. (Bourdieu 1991: 55; emphasis in the original)

Above we saw that doctors pay less attention to patients with limited proficiency in English, and in this context it became apparent that language choice and understanding are indeed very much a matter of what is 'acceptable' in intercultural communication: what our language ideologies enable us to accept, within a particular social space or institution. In addition to healthcare, the law is a highly regimented social space and I will therefore now turn to multilingualism in legal contexts to further explain language ideologies and the ways they play out in intercultural communication in a multilingual world. I will draw on examples from Puerto Rico and Australia.

Puerto Rico is an unincorporated territory of the USA. The main language of Puerto Rico is Spanish although everyone learns English in school. However, English instruction is not necessarily to high levels and according to one newspaper report, ninety-one per cent of Puerto Ricans 'do not master English' (Prensa Asociada 2009). While 'mastery' is not necessarily an objective proficiency level, the figure does suggest that overall English proficiency levels among the majority of Puerto Ricans are not very high. As the island is unincorporated US territory, the language of the federal courts of Puerto Rico is English despite the fact that the vast majority of the inhabitants speak Spanish and that their proficiency levels in English are low. This means that defendants may have their right to a fair trial violated if they do not understand what is going on in the court. In other cases, they may have their right to be tried by a jury of their own peers violated as Pousada (2008) explains. The mandatory use of English in the federal courts of Puerto Rico means that jury service is in effect restricted to upper-class Puerto Ricans as only they have the required levels of proficiency in English. While there is nothing in the law that directly says that eligibility for jury service requires upper-class status, the fact that high levels of proficiency in Standard English only occur among this group, as a direct result of educational privilege, means that language mediates against access to jury service for the vast majority of Spanish-speaking Puerto Ricans.

The newspaper article mentioned above (Prensa Asociada 2009) is devoted to the case of Carlos Ayala López, a young Puerto Rican man who stood trial for murder. During his trial he had difficulty in understanding what was going on, the witnesses found it difficult to make themselves understood, and at times the defendant may have assented to propositions he did not really understand and where in effect he did not know what it was that he was agreeing to. What this means in detail can be gleaned from a court case in Australia that has caused international concern about Australia's justice system and strained Australia's relationship with Japan. In 1992, Chika Honda arrived at Melbourne Airport as a Japanese tourist on what was supposed to be a five-day trip. When heroin was discovered in her suitcase and that of four other members of her tour, they were detained at the airport. The provision of interpreters for non-English-speaking suspects is a legal requirement in Australia. However, the necessity to question five Japanese-speaking suspects at once meant that five interpreters were needed at the same time. Even in a city the size of Melbourne, and for a language such as Japanese, which is the most widely learnt foreign language in Australia, the language of a significant immigrant community and the language of one of Australia's major trading partners, this proved to be difficult. Only one accredited interpreter was available, two interviews were interpreted by paraprofessionals (accredited to translator level), and the accreditation status of two interpreters was unknown, and was no longer retrievable when the issue of interpreter qualifications became a topic of concern during the ensuing trial. In a detailed investigation of the recordings of the cautions ('cautions' are the Australian equivalent of the Miranda warnings in the USA) being read to and interpreted for the five suspects, Nakane (2007a) identified a range of linguistic problems, which even the accredited translators could not handle adequately. First, the police officers delivered the cautions in segments that were too long for the interpreters to interpret accurately. Second, the police officers made arbitrary decisions about turn boundaries, which resulted in omissions in the interpretations. Third, the importance of comprehension checks was underestimated, both by the police officers and by the interpreters. Fourth, the police officers showed no awareness that the transformation of a written text into interpreted dialogic speech might be difficult. Finally, the police officers treated the cautions as 'rituals' rather than 'real' communication. As a result of these shortcomings, some of the suspects failed to understand that they were under arrest and considered their situation less serious than it was, including failing to seek immediate assistance from their embassy. Chika Honda was convicted of drug smuggling and sentenced to up to fifteen years in prison. She served ten-and-a-half of these in a Melbourne jail and was repatriated to Japan in 2003. Chika Honda has always maintained her innocence and became the subject of a documentary theatre performance after her release (Kanamori, 2012). The argument that a miscarriage of justice may have occurred rests on the misunderstandings that first became apparent during the cautions and also marred the remainder of the judicial process.

In order to make the cautions less problematic in intercultural contexts, a group of linguists has issued a set of guidelines that includes seven recommendations (Eades and Pavlenko 2015): police should use a standardised version in plain English; police should have available standardised versions in other languages; interpreter availability should be mentioned at the beginning of the interview; each right should be mentioned separately; yes-no questions should be avoided; there should be a requirement for the interviewee to restate their understanding in their own words; and all interviews should be video-recorded.

The state-sanctioned and state-imposed use of English in Puerto Rico may have violated Carlos Ayala López's right to a fair trial. The state-sanctioned negligence and trivialisation of languages other than English and of translating and interpreting as a profession in Australia may have violated Chika Honda's right to a fair trial. However, the effects of hegemonic language ideologies and their imposition in court goes far beyond individual cases as the research of Diana Eades (2008) shows with reference to Aboriginal Australians before the court. The ways in which Aboriginal defendants and non-Aboriginal legal counsel, magistrates and judges speak English seem, superficially, very similar. So similar in fact that it took Eades' painstaking work over many years to raise awareness that there even was a problem. On the face of it, Aboriginal defendants and non-Aboriginal legal counsel, magistrates and judges all speak English. However, the fact that Aboriginal Australians are in effect segregated from the rest of the population and that interaction between the two groups mostly only occurs in institutional settings such as schools or courts means that they have little knowledge of each other's ways of speaking English.

Non-Aboriginal Australians are not familiar with the pronunciations, lexical and grammatical choices, and discourse and pragmatic conventions of Aboriginal Australians and the latter are unfamiliar with the conventions obtaining in mainstream institutions such as the court. I do not need to point out that being unfamiliar with Aboriginal ways of speaking hardly ever hurts non-Aboriginal Australians in any way while the converse is not true. In fact, ignorance of each other's ways of speaking and doing things with language coupled with the hegemonic role of Standard English in effect means that language has become a form of neo-colonial control that keeps Aboriginal Australians in their place. The state imposes Standard English and there is a widely shared language ideology that Standard English is the 'natural' way of expressing oneself before a court. Coupled with Aboriginal people's frequent ignorance of Standard English, this language ideology means that Aboriginal people before the law are oftentimes effectively barred from giving evidence, from presenting their character in a clear and detailed way, and generally from engaging in court proceedings as a meaningful interaction. Aboriginal voices are being silenced because both parties are ignorant of each other's varieties and the linguistic and cultural expectations that prevail in court. Eades (2008: 339) ends with a stark question which is relevant to all intercultural communication in state-controlled institutions:

> [Can] Aboriginal people ever expect justice in cases of police abuse, or [. . .] will they continue to be taken for a ride by the criminal justice system? [. . .] Can we expect an end to neo-colonial control over Aboriginal people without far-reaching changes to courtroom rules of evidence?

It is part of the power of hegemonic control through language ideologies that even those disadvantaged by those ideologies come to accept them. Bourdieu (1991: 62) explains that the social mechanisms at work in transmitting language work in a double way: on the one hand, they ensure that relatively few people actually know the legitimate language. In our examples, more than ninety per cent of Puerto Ricans do not have sufficient proficiency in English, and relatively few Australians, whether they are Aboriginal or not, know the legal terminology used by barristers. However, while knowledge of the legitimate language is limited (for example, it takes many years of specialised tertiary study to learn how to speak like a barrister), recognition of the legitimate language, on the other hand, is almost universal. That means that even if Puerto Ricans do not speak English, they recognise it as 'the power code'. The same is true of Aboriginal Australians. In effect, this means that speakers who lack 'the power code' – whatever language or language variety that may be in any given context – misrecognise their problems as a result of their own deficiencies rather than as a result of prevailing language ideologies. This leaves them vulnerable not only to state control, as we have seen in this section, but also to exploitative commercial practices, as we will explore in the next.

COMMERCIAL LANGUAGE REGIMES

In her ethnography with young Japanese women who had come to Australia to learn English, Kimie Takahashi (2013) reports an interview she had with Eika, one of her participants. At the time of the interview Eika was in her early thirties but the researcher asked her about her language learning experiences as a teenager back in Japan. Instead of speaking of English classes in high school as one might expect, Eika remembers how she and a classmate were huge fans of Tom Cruise at the time. So, they actually practised English by writing a fan letter to Tom Cruise. Writing a letter in English, a foreign language they had not yet studied for very long, was a big deal for these girls. They were so exhilarated by their efforts (which included approaching their high-school English teacher outside of class time to ask her to proofread the letter) that they fully expected that those efforts would result in a response from Tom Cruise. They imagined that the Hollywood star would be so moved by their hard work that he would invite them to Hollywood. In anticipation of that invitation they practised some more English, namely introductions in front of the mirror:

Eika:	we were practicing together [laughs]
Kimie:	what, English?
Eika:	yeah, practicing English.
Kimie:	are you kidding me?
Eika:	imagining him in front of us, '*How do you do?*' '*My name is Eika*' [spoken in English] [laughing] we were so stupid then, really. We were. [more laughter] (K. Takahashi 2013: 37f.)[4]

As the researcher found, Eika was no exception. Most of her participants had been very much influenced as teenagers by dreams of meeting white male celebrities such as Hollywood stars Tom Cruise and Brad Pitt or soccer player David Beckham (see also Chapter 9 on intercultural romance). Their fantasies were powerful enough to motivate them to practise English above and beyond the call of high-school duties. For the women Takahashi met in Sydney, their teenage dreams had even carried over into adulthood and had motivated them to seek out the greater proficiency in English that a study-abroad period seemed to offer. They are not alone. In my own research with English-and-German-speaking couples, I met many German women who confessed that, as teenagers and young adults, mediated images of cowboys or British cool had been powerful incentives for them to take their English learning beyond the level afforded by 'School English'. This included seeking out additional practice opportunities with 'native speakers', listening to the radio stations of the American and British forces stationed in Germany, spending time in an English-speaking country as an au pair or exchange student, and also adding 'native English speaker' to the criteria they looked for in potential partners.

For these German and Japanese women, mediated discourses of the desirable cultural other were powerful motivators to improve their English. However, the levels of English they desired were simply not available to them in the ordinary course of affairs through compulsory English-language learning as part of their secondary education. In Bourdieu's terms, their schooling gave them knowledge of 'English as a Foreign Language' or 'School English' as my German participants used to call it. Wider media discourses (including, incidentally, the educational discourses they were part of) taught them to recognise their 'English as a Foreign Language' or 'School English' as inferior to 'Native Speaker English'. Achieving the goal of their desires – that well-recognised but unmastered form of 'native speaker English', or 'being *pera-pera* ('fluent')' as K. Takahashi's (2013) participants called it – held the promise of romantic love and self-transformation.

If your language ideologies are such that they lead you to misrecognise 'native speaker English' as the way to fulfil your dreams and desires, what can you do? You can turn to the market and invest in English-language learning by buying English-language teaching materials, by enrolling in private language schools or by going on a study-abroad tour. The language-teaching market obviously thrives on these language ideologies. At the same time, providers of private language teaching and study abroad also need to feed these ideologies in order to grow their businesses. I will now discuss two case studies from the language-teaching industry to exemplify this point, one from English-conversation schools in Japan, the other from US accent-reduction courses.

Across Asia, the private English-teaching market is big business (e.g., Park 2015; Piller and Cho 2013; Zhang 2011). It is embedded in wider discourses of gendered Western desirability but it is also engaged in reproducing those ideologies as Piller and Takahashi (2006) show. In an investigation of advertising materials for English-language schools these researchers found that images of Western men as charming, attractive, caring, loving and chivalrous emanate from many sources: there are, of course, Hollywood movies and numerous other US cultural products, but, even more importantly, international cultural interconnectedness has reached such levels that these images now also emanate from Japanese cultural products, such as *manga* and *anime*, Japanese pop songs (as opposed to American ones, which are available simultaneously), women's magazines and the advertising for the English-language teaching industry. The researchers found that the selling propositions of English-language teaching businesses continually stressed the power of English to bring about self-transformation. Typical slogans include 'Finding a new self overseas: Change your life through study-abroad in Australia' or 'Australia and New Zealand: Let's start a new life'. Language-learning marketing particularly aimed at women portrays English as a glamorous means of reinventing and empowering one's womanhood, as a woman's indispensable weapon to cope in chauvinistic Japan. Another way to capitalise on the occidental longings of Japanese women that inflects their consumption of English-language learning is to employ English teachers that embody the ideology of 'native speaker English' as Western romance. The teachers portrayed in the advertising and teaching materials under analysis were all conventionally good-looking, well-dressed white men in their twenties or thirties. Professional biographical statements of English teachers in these materials often sound like personal ads, as in this example:

> Teacher Kevin Black. He loves Japanese history and hot springs.
> He frequently visits Hakone. 'My policy is to change my teaching
> method depending on my students. I try to get rid of their fear of
> using English.' He likes going to karaoke, and what's more, he likes
> singing Japanese pop songs like those of *Chemistry* [= a popular
> male J-pop duo]. It's a real surprise. (Quoted in Piller and
> Takahashi 2006: 65)

The portrayal of these English teachers constructs and reinforces the myth of white men as ladies-first gentlemen that is prevalent in Japanese media, particularly women's magazines, where white men are often associated with sophistication, sensitivity and refinement. They are portrayed as handsome, often with blond hair and blue eyes, well educated, well dressed, understated and kind, not so different from the ways in which Hollywood stars and Western musicians are represented in the same media.

In a similar study, Blommaert (2010: 47ff.) explores the marketing discourses of accent-reduction training. Where the Japanese English-teaching industry targetting women creates an association with 'native speaker English' and romance with chivalrous white Prince Charmings, the promotional materials for accent-reduction training create an association between an 'American accent' and upward global mobility and financial success. Acquiring an American accent is presented as clearing the only obstacle that stands between the customer and a better job, a superior income and respect from their imagined successful corporate peers they are aspiring to. One website lists the following benefits of modifying a 'foreign accent' towards an 'American accent':

Clear, understandable speech // Efficient, effective communication // Career opportunities // Improved job performance // Successful public speaking // More confidence (Quoted in Blommaert 2010: 52)

The language ideology underlying materials such as this one is that an 'American accent' is a natural ingredient of professional and personal success, and that speakers with other accents are naturally excluded from such success. The absurdity of the proposition is maybe best illustrated by the fact that some of these materials even target speakers with a 'British accent' for accent modification. I am amused to speculate that a London professional would more likely court ridicule than success if they were to start imitating an American accent in their daily lives.

These language ideologies present fluent native English as an index of romance or an American accent as an index of professional success. Obviously, these types of proficiencies are rare among the target audience of Japanese women in the one instance, and Asian, European and Middle Eastern professionals in the other. However, once the audiences have accepted the nexus and also the idea that consuming language training is the avenue to romance or success, they are in for an unreachable goal. Modifying one's accent is the most difficult aspect of learning another language and some linguists question whether it is possible at all (for an overview see Birdsong 2006). So consumers are aiming for an unreachable goal and in the interest of market expansion their lack of proficiency becomes a self-fulfilling prophesy.

The ways in which the commercialisation of language teaching sets up learners as consumers for failure is explored by Piller, Takahashi and Watanabe (2010) in their analysis of the return on investment in study-abroad programmes. These researchers show that many Japanese and South Koreans who go abroad for an extended period to reach the desired level of English proficiency experience disillusionment, a loss of financial security and an increase in anxiety instead of the magic self-transformation they had expected. For instance, they report the case of a South Korean family who had split up so that their two teenage daughters could be educated in an English-speaking country. While the father stayed behind in South Korea to earn an income, the mother and two daughters resettled in Christchurch in New Zealand. When the father's business ran into financial trouble, they were forced to sell their Christchurch house and consequently faced a visa issue. The havoc that the desire for perfect English can cause briefly hit the headlines when all four members of the family committed suicide in May 2010.

It is tragedies such as this one that demonstrate the full extent of the pernicious effects of language ideologies such as the one that the use of English as global language is natural, neutral and beneficial (Pennycook 2001). Rather than a language or variety having universally the same meaning, language ideologies obviously index different meanings and identities in different contexts. While the Japanese women in K. Takahashi's (2013) research desired intercultural romance through English, some Asian, European and Middle Eastern professionals may pursue success through an American accent; for the split Korean family above, English meant a better education and a better future for their children. Furthermore, language ideologies rarely operate in isolation but come in clusters as Chang's (2004) study of the language ideologies undergirding the private English-language teaching business in Taiwan shows. English-language pre-schools where already toddlers can learn how to speak English constitute a particularly successful, and growing, segment of the English-language teaching market in Taiwan. They thrive on a combination of language ideologies, which include: the belief that the earlier a child starts to learn a second language, the better the outcome; the belief that native speakers of English are ideal language teachers; the belief that language means spoken language, as expressed through accent and fluency in casual conversations; and the belief that American English is superior to all other varieties of English. As in the cases above, this creates a very specific set of linguistic knowledge which is difficult to achieve but which is widely recognised. As above, it creates another growth market with a very successful selling proposition. However, all these case studies suggest that English has become a commodity and language learning a form of consumption. Therefore, the educational paradigm that is traditionally applied to understanding English-language teaching and intercultural communication training no longer fits. Rather, we need to ask whether language learners as consumers do not need to be put in a better position to rationally weigh the costs and benefits of the investment they are making and whether the market does not need to be better regulated to ensure consumer protection and fair trading.

In sum, the state is no longer the sole normative authority in regimenting language hierarchies it used to be, as Blommaert (2010) has pointed out. The hegemonic control of speakers through state language regimes is now complemented by commercial language regimes. Language teaching and intercultural communication have also become sites of financial exploitation.

KEY POINTS

This chapter made the following key points:

- Real language matters in intercultural communication. Multilingualism and linguistic diversity is a ubiquitous sociolinguistic reality and speakers make choices from the languages and language varieties they have access to. These choices are a form of social practice and are embedded in language ideologies and the political economy of language.
- Our linguistic proficiencies constrain the identities we can perform and, at the same time, our embodied identities constrain the ways in which our linguistic performances are perceived.
- In order to understand linguistic choice in intercultural communication we need to pay attention to the micro- and macro-contexts of actual interactions. Micro-analysis of actual interactions shows that misunderstandings in intercultural communication are usually the result of a lack of shared linguistic resources and knowledge.
- Language choice in interactions is informed by the beliefs speakers hold about what the use of a particular language means. These beliefs are part of larger language regimes through which states exert control and commercial providers gain a market advantage.

COUNTERPOINT

Linguistic diversity is a ubiquitous yet widely overlooked fact of life, and diverse language repertoires, trajectories and proficiencies play out in all intercultural communication. Yet most intercultural communication research is published in a highly monolingual English academic form. The same is true of most intercultural communication classrooms where relatively limited and highly normative ways of speaking and writing prevail. What are the consequences of these normative ways of using language in higher education and academic publishing for knowledge production in intercultural communication?

FURTHER READING

Piller (2016b) provides an in-depth examination of the social consequences of linguistic diversity. Eades (2010) is a fine introduction to language and the law, and Angermeyer (2015) provides a detailed sociolinguistic analysis of intercultural communication in small claims courts in New York.

ACTIVITIES

Linguistic autobiographies
Read the linguistic autobiography of a multilingual writer such as Clarke (2004), Sedaris (2000) or Turnbull (2002). These three are the accounts of English speakers learning French in Paris; choose a language and context that interest you – there are many linguistic autobiographies available. You might also want to read Pavlenko's (2001a, 2001b, 2001c) analyses of linguistic autobiographies. Write your own linguistic autobiography. Which languages or language varieties do you speak? How did you learn them and in which contexts do you use them? Can you share any anecdotes where the issue of language choice became particularly salient?

Language ideologies in the linguistic landscape
Language ideology is implicit in practice and the language ideologies of a society find expression in the linguistic landscape. Create a collection of images of official signage (for example, street signs, directions, public warnings, council notices) in your street, suburb or town and analyse the languages used. Which language or languages are valorised? Which languages remain invisible? If it is available, you might want to refer to demographic information about the home languages of the inhabitants of your street, suburb or town and compare the languages spoken by inhabitants with the language(s) displayed on the signs. You might want to refer to some of the blog posts on *Language on the Move* tagged 'linguistic landscape' for models (http://www.languageonthemove.com/tag/linguistic-landscape/). You could also compare your findings with those of other contexts presented there.

Language ideologies in toilet signage
Based on the same premise as above, create a collection of images of public toilet signage in a space that is likely to be frequented by people from different backgrounds (for example, the central station in your city, an airport, the English preparation programme on your campus, and so on). What kinds of identities do the language choices in these signs index

for the toilet users? Compare your findings with those discussed at http://www.languageonthemove.com/toiletology/

Advertising languages

Collect advertisements for English-language tuition. Bring them along to class and discuss them in small groups. Which languages are being advertised? What are the language ideologies apparent in those advertisements? How is the language valorised? What are the imagined interactions that the learner is encouraged to aspire to? Which language ideologies are embedded in those materials?

NOTES

1. The transcript has been adapted from the original and the transcription conventions simplified.
2. Data collected by Alexandre Duchêne for the research project 'Languages, identities and tourism: Towards an understanding of social and linguistic challenges in Switzerland in the context of globalization' (2005–2008) funded by the Swiss National Fund (Project number 108608) as part of a national research programme on Language Diversity and Linguistic Competence in Switzerland (Duchêne and Piller 2011).
3. English translations of non-English speech are provided in italics and within square brackets. Square brackets also include the analyst's comments and mark the beginning of overlapping speech. CAPS mark extra emphasis, spoken in a loud voice.
4. The transcript has been adapted, the original Japanese has been omitted, and the transcription conventions have been simplified.

CHAPTER 6

Intercultural Communication in a Transnational World

CHAPTER OBJECTIVES

This chapter will enable you to:

- Learn about mobility as a central aspect of the human experience and critically examine linguistic and cultural aspects of group belonging.
- Explore linguistic and cultural aspects of inclusion and exclusion in migrant-receiving societies.
- Gain an understanding of the linguistic and cultural barriers to the full and equitable labour-market integration of transnational migrants and their descendants.
- Learn about inclusive language and industrial policies in highly diverse societies.

PEOPLE ON THE MOVE

The previous chapter complicated the 'nation equals culture equals language' formula by focusing on the fact of multilingualism as the normal human experience. This chapter will continue problematising this simplistic formula from yet another angle, namely that of transnational migration: nations are not – and never have been – homogeneous units descending from some primordial national ancestors who lived in strict isolation from other such primordial national, ethnic or cultural groups. Multiculturalism and cultural diversity have always been the normal human experience, even in small-scale pre-industrial societies, as anthropologist Ward Goodenough (1976) has shown. However, despite the ubiquity of migration, some groups are in a privileged relationship to the nation and one way to maintain their privilege while excluding others is through discourses of culture. This chapter therefore approaches the key question of this book of how culture is made relevant by whom in which context for which purposes from yet another perspective: how do cultural discourses serve as tools of inclusion or exclusion from the nation and its resources?

We will begin our enquiry with an overview of how the belonging of people on the move has been constructed through the ages. To begin with, mobility constitutes a characteristic of Homo sapiens. In the same way that our ability to communicate through a complex symbolic system – language – distinguishes us from other animals, our propensity to migrate, most notably exemplified by the great human migration out of Africa about 80,000 years ago, distinguishes us from other hominid species. In fact, it has been argued that it is precisely the combination of language and migration that has resulted in the globally dominant position of our species (Gugliotta 2008). However, human language is characteristically diverse: no two human beings speak in exactly the same way but similar ways of using language – in the form of a common language – constitute a group characteristic.

How the great linguistic diversity of thousands of mutually incomprehensible languages came into being has intrigued humans for millennia. The most famous pre-scientific explanation for the multitude of languages can be found in the biblical Babel myth, which posits divine intervention: God confounded the original universal language as punishment for human ambition. Scientific explanations attribute linguistic diversity to group dispersion: as groups moved away from each other their languages developed differently in different contexts and a specific language became the characteristic of a group that had lived together for a long time. While there undoubtedly is a link between a specific language and a specific group, it is important to keep in mind that the link between language and group is cultural rather than genetic because language transmission from generation to generation is not biological but through learning. Unfortunately, the mistake to assume genetic language transmission is a frequent one: in a fallacy that has been called the 'billiard-ball model' (Heather 2010), migrating groups and their languages are conceived of as bounded entities, closed off to outsiders, who transmit their language fully intact and without any discontinuities from one place to another. In reality, the human story has always been a story of cultural and linguistic contact (Piller 2016a). For instance, the early expansion of Indo-European, one of the most widely-used language groups, was most likely one of recruitment transmission (Anthony 2007): migrating tribal chiefs increased their power base by recruiting new followers. The latter adopted the language of the new elite in exchange for practical benefits, such as access to new technologies. Indo-Europeans were able to seek new territory and recruit followers – who in time became new speakers – because they were able to harness horse-riding and the carted wheel as new means of transport.

For much of human history 'a specific language' would have been nothing more than a mutually intelligible system the boundaries of which were determined by intelligibility, as we saw in Chapter 3. However, linguistic criteria for what constitutes a language such as mutual intelligibility have receded, and political criteria have become inextricably intertwined with linguistic criteria. The key political lens which has shaped our understanding of what constitutes a specific language for the past few centuries has been the modern nation state, as we have already seen. The development of the nation state over the past centuries, at a different pace in different parts of the world, has had a profound influence on the ways in which human mobility and its relationship to group belonging is understood today. It is against the ideological dominance of the nation state that languages, identities and group belonging are constituted, negotiated and contested in migration. Against the ascendancy of the nation state both language and migration have come to be redefined. Migration has become strictly controlled by the nation state: in contrast to the permeable and constantly shifting borderlands of premodern empires, modern state borders are absolute. In fact, the very definition of migration has become tied to the crossing of international borders. The state decides which border crossings are legal and which are illegal, who is allowed to remain on its territory, for how long and under what conditions. State regulations of human mobility are undergirded by ideologies of nativism, cultural belonging, legitimacy or desirability, and 'language' and 'culture' are tied to these beliefs in complex and contextually-specific ways. Individual language use where the traces of language learning and multilingualism are readily apparent – as is usually the case for mobile speakers – is usually considered less legitimate or less authentic than the individual language of less mobile speakers. Furthermore, beliefs about who is a prototypical legitimate member of a nation and who is not shape our perceptions of speakers of the particular language conventionally associated with a particular nation. In short, language becomes an index for identity.

The nation state guides the perception of what the ideal language is and who the ideal speaker is through numerous institutional practices that usually render languages and speakers with long-standing ties to a polity as prototypical citizens, and migrant languages and speakers as problematic. State institutions tie language and migration together in myriad ways mediated by ideologies about legitimate languages and legitimate speakers. These positions are always ideological, and linguistic diversity indexes hierarchical social orders. Individuals may be caught up in the identity positions available to them but they are not determined by them. Individuals accept, negotiate, contest and resist the identity positions available to them in dominant ideologies.

EXCLUSIVE INCLUSION

The challenge faced by most migrants is not only related to the fact that their identities may be constructed as marginal in the new society but also to the basic linguistic fact that they have to learn a new language. Language learning as it is experienced by most adult migrants is vastly different from the kind of controlled language learning in the classroom that is studied in much second language acquisition research. Language learning as an adult migrant presents a dual challenge: you have to learn a new language while communicating in that language and you have to communicate while learning the language (Bremer et al. 2013 [1996]). This dual challenge is a major source of inequality: language is all-pervasive and our daily lives are inevitably conducted through the medium of a particular language. For migrants, the language they are trying to learn is often the medium through which they simultaneously have to sustain themselves as workers, citizens, neighbours, parents, patients, consumers and the many other social roles people play.

How exactly does migrants' linguistic difference mediate belonging? The sociologist Rogers Brubaker (2014) offers a framework for thinking systematically about this question by comparing language and religion. 'Religion' serves as a proxy for non-linguistic cultural difference here. Brubaker identifies four domains where difference may be turned into inequality: the political and institutional domain; the economic domain; the cultural and symbolic domain; and the domain of informal social relationships.

In the political and institutional domain, language is inescapable but modern liberal states are relatively neutral vis-à-vis religion. In fact, religious discrimination is widely prohibited where linguistic discrimination is seen as perfectly legitimate. Linguistic discrimination is a result of the fact that migrants as adult language learners are usually confronted with the inescapable fact that institutions operate exclusively in one single language (or in some cases a small set of legitimate languages): this constitutes, eo ipso, a massive advantage for speakers of the institutional language and a massive disadvantage for people who do not speak the institutional language or who do not speak it well.

In the economic domain similar considerations apply: proficiency in the language in which an economic activity occurs is a precondition for participation in that economic activity in a way that religion is not. Speakers of an economically powerful language enjoy an economic advantage because they do not have to invest in learning that language. Furthermore, language learning is a complex – and hence costly – undertaking that may make it difficult to acquire the kind of linguistic proficiency that has high economic value. By contrast, membership of a powerful religion is usually not as directly economically useful as language proficiency is. Furthermore, joining a powerful religion requires a smaller investment. For instance, it is much easier for a non-Christian to convert to Christianity than it is for a non-native speaker of English to acquire high-level proficiency in English.

The cultural and symbolic domain works differently. This domain includes all the discursive and symbolic processes through which respect, prestige, honour – in short symbolic value – is conferred. Here, language is less affected than religion because the 'content' of a language is much thinner than that of a religion. That means that negative stereotypes about language tend to be relatively mild in comparison to negative stereotypes about religion. While many people object to the specific tenets of a particular religion, very few people object to the specific grammatical structures or means of expression of a particular language. For instance, the widespread stigmatisation of Islam in contemporary media discourses simply has no equivalent in negative stereotypes about any language, even if people may be afraid of Arabic as a proxy of Islam.

Informal social relationships also have a significant bearing on inequality, and can work through exclusion and through inclusion. Processes of social exclusion may disadvantage members of certain religions or speakers of certain languages. Examples include differential treatment of minorities on the rental market or attacks against minorities on public transport (see Piller 2016b, for examples). Both members of religious minorities and speakers of minority languages are vulnerable to such 'everyday exclusions'. Informal social relationships also mediate inequality through inclusion in that social circles tend to form around shared identities; and social networks, friendship circles or marriage opportunities are often based on shared identities. Again, religion and language work differently here. Preferences for religion-internal networks is dogma in some religions while preferences for the formation of language-internal networks tend to be much weaker.

In sum, linguistic and religious difference both mediate inclusion and exclusion in diverse societies but they do so in clearly distinct ways:

> The major sources of religious inequality derive from religion's
> thicker cultural, normative and political content, while the major

sources of linguistic inequality come from the pervasiveness of
language and from the increasingly and inescapably 'languaged'
nature of political, economic and cultural life in the modern world.
(Brubaker 2014: 23)

In response to the observation that language constitutes a formidable
barrier to migrant incorporation, immigrant countries such as Australia
and Canada have made a high level of linguistic proficiency in English
a precondition for entry in their skilled migration visa categories. The
rationale for this selection is that skilled and well-educated migrants, who
fill labour shortages, are good for the economy and will find it easy to
integrate into their new society. However, social inclusion is more than
the promotion of economic well-being and also includes a sense of community participation and belonging. The latter is much more complex and
migrants' language skills and high levels of education do not necessarily
translate into a sense of belonging and inclusion, as we will now examine
with a case study of Jewish migrants from the former Soviet Union in
Germany (Roberman 2015a, 2015b). Based on a year-long ethnographic
project to examine the migration and settlement experiences of this group,
the researcher, Sveta Roberman, developed the concept of 'inclusive
exclusion' in response to observations such as these:

> I kept sensing a peculiar atmosphere, intangible and hard to
> describe, that pervades the lives of many, an aura of dissatisfaction
> and restlessness that borders on – or has become – apathy and
> resignation, articulated in an often-expressed sentiment: 'We are
> kind of existing here, not really living.' (Roberman 2015a: 744)

The people Roberman conducted her research with are Jewish migrants
from the former Soviet Union, mostly from Russia and Ukraine, who
settled in Germany in the 1990s and early 2000s. About 220,000 Soviet
Jews were admitted during that period in the hope that these migrants
would contribute to a revival of Jewish cultural and religious life in
Germany (Kramer 2009). For the reunified Germany, accepting substantial numbers of Jewish migrants was yet another step on the long
road of atonement for the Holocaust. Around eighty per cent of these
migrants were tertiary-educated and had established professional careers
in the Soviet Union. Most of them were secular and, because 'Jew' was
an ethnic and not a religious category in the Soviet Union, only about a
third of these migrants ended up joining Jewish religious communities
in Germany (Shcherbatova and Plessentin 2013). In fact, in contrast to
Soviet Jews migrating to Israel or the USA, those coming to Germany

were probably least motivated by ideological reasons; and Roberman's participants did not hesitate to explain that they had migrated for economic reasons, in search of a better life.

This context seems ideal to examine the social inclusion of migrants: a highly-educated migrant group, a high degree of cultural similarity between migrants and hosts, and public desire on the part of the destination society to embrace this particular migrant group. If social inclusion is conceived as economic participation and cultural recognition, Roberman's participants had little to complain of:

> When speaking about their encounters with the host country, my
> interviewees were not troubled by their economic situation; they
> felt secure and protected in that sphere of their lives. Neither did
> they complain about the lack of possibilities for the articulation of
> their Russian or Jewish identities: the former could be practiced at
> the range of Russian cultural centers, clubs, and libraries, while the
> latter could be actualized and maintained within Jewish communal
> centers and organizations. Even the constraint they faced in
> political participation, because many immigrants lacked full
> citizenship, was hardly an issue for my interviewees. (Roberman
> 2015a: 747)

Migration had enabled the participants to partake of Western economic affluence, they had received significant, though not always full, legal and political citizenship rights, and, as a group, cultural recognition. What was missing was access to regular, stable and meaningful employment. Participants who, at the time of migration, had been in their mid-thirties or older, found it extremely difficult to find employment commensurate with their education, skills and experience. This was not for lack of trying. Participants were deeply influenced by the Soviet work ethos and extremely resourceful in their attempts to find work. The German state also helped with the provision of language and training courses and a suite of short-term work and internship programmes designed to help migrants transition into full-time regular employment. During that time they were supported by welfare and a range of casual short-term jobs, including state-sponsored employment schemes. Olga, a qualified and experienced teacher, for instance, arrived in Germany when she was forty years old. Her qualifications were not recognised and she was involved in various retraining schemes. She also held various casual jobs as an attendant in an aged-care home and as a social worker. When she turned fifty without having achieved regular standard employment, she was officially 'removed' from the labour market and declared an 'early retiree'. Being unable to

find regular employment meant that the participants struggled to construct a coherent life-story and to see meaning in their migration, as was
the case for Olga:

> I was sitting in her apartment as she tried to compose a coherent
> narrative of the 10-year period of her life in Germany. But that
> seemed to be an unachievable task: the flow of her life narrative
> stopped at the point of emigration. What followed were fragmented
> facts that she resisted bringing together into a meaningful story,
> seeing little achievement or sense in her 10-year migration
> experience. (Roberman 2015a: 752)

Another participant, Mark, who had been a cameraman in Kiev and was
fifty-three years old when he arrived in Germany had given up looking for
work after six years and lived on welfare. He said, 'Once I had some objectives in life, I aspired to something, I had some plans, [. . .] Today, I wake
up in the morning, and I have one and the same question to ask myself:
what do I do today?' (quoted in Roberman 2015a: 754). Like others in his
situation, he filled his life with surfing the Internet, watching TV, attending doctor's appointments and, above all, shopping. Some developed
elaborate routes to stretch out daily grocery shopping, others threw themselves into the pursuit of specials and sales. While these activities fill time,
in the long run they breed a deep sense of isolation and loneliness. Being
an anonymous shopper trapped them in the position of social strangers.

At one level, consumption spaces are some of the least discriminatory
spaces imaginable; one participant made this point with regard to language
proficiency:

> One does not need language in the supermarket. The system is itself
> interested to sell you the thing, and the system finds its way to do
> it; they succeed in selling it to you in any way. It does not matter
> what language you speak. (Quoted in Roberman 2015a: 756)

At the same time, this participant makes the point that consumption
spaces are spaces of extreme dislocation. In the supermarket or shopping mall it does not matter who you are. In fact, it does not even matter
that you are there. Being reduced to filling their time with consumption
resulted in a sharp feeling of *nevostrebovannost* ('uselessness', 'redundancy',
'feeling like unclaimed luggage'). One participant compared her situation to that of cows who are allowed to graze on lush green pastures but
nobody ever bothers to come and milk them. In short, participants were
free to consume: they had achieved a comfortable and economically secure

existence through their migration. However, their access to resources of real value – stable and meaningful work – was constrained. In this context, the freedom to consume condemned them to consume. Consumption did not result in a sense of dignity and self-worth, it did not allow them to forge coherent positive life-stories and it did not provide them with a sense of belonging. While included economically, legally and culturally, their participation is ultimately constrained – a condition Roberman calls 'exclusive inclusion': our economic system is characterised by over-production and there is the regular need to dispose of surplus goods. Consequently, even relatively poor members of affluent consumer societies, such as Roberman's irregularly employed and/or welfare-dependent interviewees, are readily included in the sphere of consumption. By contrast, stable and regular employment is in short supply. Exclusion from this scare and valuable resource continues to be a powerful way to reproduce social hierarchies. Disadvantaged groups of local people may be similarly excluded but migrants are particularly vulnerable on post-industrial labour markets. As Roberman (2015a: 759) concludes:

> Exclusive inclusion is a much more civilized, camouflaged form of exclusion. It seems to be mild. But, in spite of its apparent mildness, exclusive inclusion, which limits access to social resources of real value and to participation in the arenas of social recognition and belonging, is no less destructive in the ways it undermines the excluded individual's world, threatens humanness, and strains the social fabric as a whole.

JOBS WITH ACCENTS

As Roberman's case study demonstrates, access to meaningful employment is a key aspect of successful migrant settlement and social inclusion. However, data even from countries with such well-established migration programmes as Australia and Canada show that the incidence of unemployment and underemployment of transnational migrants is much higher than that of the native-born population. In Australia, for instance, even during the period of low unemployment and labour and skills' shortages that characterised much of the first decade of the twenty-first century, the unemployment rate of recent migrants was considerably higher than that of the Australian-born population. Furthermore, there were significant differences between different origin groups, and migrants from North Africa were least likely to be employed ('The Place of Migrants in Contemporary Australia' 2014). It is also important to note that statistics such as these reflect only unemployment and not underemployment. In Canada, research published by Statistics Canada 'now confirms a persistent and growing gap between immigrant and native-born incomes that is no longer projected to converge at all' (Creese and Wiebe 2012: 57).

These findings are particularly disturbing in countries such as Australia and Canada because they have long prided themselves in their migration programmes and multiculturalism. In contrast to most other countries that have received significant numbers of transnational migrants in recent history, Australia and Canada have defined themselves as immigrant nations for almost a century (Green and Green 2004; Jupp 2007). Furthermore, in comparison with the USA, another country where immigration is part of the national imagery, Australia and Canada have consciously adopted and experimented with state intervention to facilitate social inclusion, including language programmes. In both national contexts, discrimination on the basis of race and/or national origin as the basis of exclusion from the labour market has become unspeakable and unimaginable, and settlement and language-training services are designed to help newcomers become employable. However, evidence of racial discrimination under the guise of culture and language proficiency continues to persist. I will now discuss two case studies of discrimination in the Australian and Canadian labour markets before addressing the question of the purposes of covert discrimination in these contexts.

In Australia, discrimination against transnational migrants in the workplace is well documented. A study of low-paid work, for instance, found:

> Discrimination on cultural grounds is not an uncommon
> experience for low-paid workers, especially from their managers.
> Discrimination on cultural grounds manifested in many ways,
> including being refused promotion, being limited in the types of
> work they were allowed to perform, intimidation to work harder
> and longer, abusive behaviour, manipulation of student and 'guest
> workers' seeking citizenship points, and favouring Australian-born
> employees for higher positions and wages. (Masterman-Smith and
> Pocock 2008: 44f.)

There is often an assumption that such discrimination is due to lack of language proficiency, that is, migrants are not un- or underemployed because they are being discriminated against, but rather because their English is not good enough to meet job requirements. However, their difficulties remain, even if they have relative proficiency in the language, as a report to the Victorian Equal Opportunity and Human Rights Commission points out (Berman 2008). Furthermore, there is a substantial wage gap between similarly qualified native-born and migrant workers: for instance, among Australian-born with a postgraduate degree fifty-five per cent are in the highest income bracket and nine per cent are in the lowest; by contrast, among overseas-born with a postgraduate degree only thirty-eight per cent were in the highest income bracket but nineteen per cent were in the lowest ('The Place of Migrants in Contemporary Australia' 2014).

Overall, the English proficiency of migrants to Australia is actually high as evidence of English proficiency is a prerequisite in most visa classes, and for many the path to permanent residency and citizenship includes tertiary study at an Australian university. Furthermore, migrants who enter in a visa stream that does not have an English requirement (that is, humanitarian entrants, family reunion migrants, and the dependants of skilled and business migrants) are entitled to free English-language tuition if they have less than 'functional English'. Given such relatively high levels of English proficiency, it is obvious that in most instances of the discrimination reported above it cannot be factual language proficiency – an individual property of the second-language speaker – that leads to exclusion, but rather linguistic and cultural stereotyping on the part of employers.

In order to understand how linguistic and cultural stereotyping works, let's speculate a little on the following what-if questions: Would George Michael have achieved fame as a music star if his name was Georgios Kyriacos Panayiotou? Would Kirk Douglas be a Hollywood legend if his name was Issur Danielovitch? Would Bob Dylan have reached his status as a global cultural icon if his name was Robert Zimmerman? None of these names is made up but Georgios Kyriacos Panayiotou, Issur Danielovitch and Robert Zimmerman are the actual birth names of these stars. It is, of course, impossible to know how their careers would have played out if they had not chosen to change their names but it is fair to assume that the answer to these questions is 'not likely'.

Short Anglo names such as George Michael, Kirk Douglas or Bob Dylan somehow sound more appealing as the names of global music and film starts than the long Greek, Eastern European or German names these men received at their births. Names can signal group membership and the stereotypes associated with ethnic minorities are usually less favourable than those associated with the dominant group. Stereotyping on the basis of names goes some way to explain why migrants may have a harder time finding jobs than the native-born: employers may assume that an applicant with a name that signals a migrant background is not a good fit for their organisation. That stereotypes based on names indeed raise the entry bar to employment for some minority groups has been evidenced in a number of field experiments. In a recent German study, for instance, a total of 1,474 identical application letters that only differed in name and photo of the applicant were sent in response to job ads for administrative assistants (Weichselbaumer 2016). When the fictitious applicant was identified with a German name, 'Sandra Bauer', she was invited for interview in response to 18.8 per cent of her applications. When she was identified with a Turkish name, 'Meryem Öztürk', that figure was 13.5 per cent and when 'Meryem Öztürk' was further wearing a headscarf in her photo such positive feedback was as low as 4.2 per cent.[1] Similar results have been obtained in similar field experiments in a range of national contexts (for an overview see Piller 2016b).

In contexts where it is customary to append a photo of the applicant to job applications, as it is in Germany, employers may have two stimuli that trigger a stereotype, as in the example where the fictitious applicant with the Turkish name and the headscarf as a signal of Muslim identity was least likely to be called back for interview. Appearance may trigger even more powerful stereotypes than names, even if it is based not on a photo but on actual interaction, where looks are easily confounded with language proficiency. In order to explain how the confusion between reacting to a racial stereotype and making a language proficiency judgement work, I will need to take you into the world of experimental acoustics. Researchers of auditory perception have for a long time known that it is possible to hear with our eyes and see with our ears. McGurk and MacDonald (1976) showed that if normal-hearing adults in experimental conditions heard repeated utterances of the syllable 'ba' while simultaneously watching someone make the lip movements for 'ga', the auditory and visual input actually got fused in their brains and they reported hearing 'da'. [d] is produced half-way between [b] and [g] and hearing 'da' is something like a compromise between your ears and your eyes.[2] I am sure you will find this an eye-opening experiment but you might well ask: What does multimodal perception in experimental acoustics have to do with intercultural communication, and specifically with the idea that random language proficiency assessments are a form of racism in disguise? Well, the connection is that our brains make similar compromises when it comes to language proficiency and race, as US research has shown (Rubin 1992; Rubin and Smith 1990). In these studies, the researchers audio-recorded a science lecture aimed at undergraduate students. The speaker on the tape was a native speaker of American English speaking in a Standard American-English accent. The lecture was then played to two different groups of undergraduate students at a US university. In one case, the lecture was accompanied by the picture of a Caucasian woman and in the other, it was accompanied by the picture of an Asian woman. This served to create the impression that a Caucasian woman was speaking in one instance and an Asian woman in another. Both women were shown in the same pose and had been rated as similarly attractive. So, we have one audio-recorded lecture spoken in Standard American English and two different visual signals: a Caucasian lecturer versus an Asian lecturer. Can you guess where this is headed? Right! The students who saw the Asian lecturer heard a 'foreign', 'non-native' or 'Asian' accent although none was present in the auditory signal. What is more, the perceived accent of the perceived Asian lecturer led to reduced comprehension. The students rated the quality of the lecture and the quality of their learning experience much lower when they thought it was delivered by a speaker with a foreign accent. The students must have thought they were making an objective assessment of accented-ness, linguistic proficiency and their learning experience when, in reality, their brains were making a compromise between the expectations created by the embodied identities of the lecturers they saw in front of them and the lecture they heard. Experiments such as these confirm what English speakers of colour have always known, namely that the ways in which they are seen may inflect the ways in which they are heard. Djité (2006: 1f.) provides a memorable anecdote when he writes about an experience that he had at a time when he was the only black African lecturer at the University of Sydney:

> A few years ago, I acted as a language consultant for a large law firm in Sydney. During the life of the project – some six months – I communicated with the firm only by telephone, fax and e-mails, in French and English. I had never met any lawyer or clerical staff from the firm in person. At the completion of the project, I was told that the secretary of one of the senior partners would come to my office and pick up the document I had drafted for them. On the day, I left the door of my office wide open, waiting for the secretary. When she arrived, she knocked at the door and asked to see Dr . . . I got up, greeted her, invited her into the office and asked whether she was here to pick up a document for the law firm (holding the document in my hand). She then said, 'Yes, but I'd like to speak to Dr . . .'. I answered 'I am Dr . . .'. The secretary suddenly turned very pale. I asked her if anything was wrong, and she answered, 'No, not at all. You look far too young to be a doctor.'

Of course, the principle of multimodal perception, of moulding what we hear in the image of what we see, works for white speakers of English, too. However, white speakers usually have the privilege of ignoring the principle as it works in their favour. White native speakers of English are privileged to live with the illusion that their accents are neutral, standard and natural. Even white speakers who use English as an additional language, such as myself, do well out of these perceptual compromises between our voices and our embodied identities because if anything it makes us sound less accented. Indeed, German speakers of English as an additional language often engage in passing-for-a-native-speaker performances (Piller 2002b). Another example of white privilege when it comes to the intersection of voice and embodied identity comes from Colic-Peisker (2005). This researcher found that, in Australia, migrants from the former Yugoslavia were not subjected to 'prejudicial gazes' in public spaces. Australia is factually a multi-ethnic country but continues to be imaged as an Anglo-Saxon one. Being white allowed migrants from the former Yugoslavia to hide their migrant status if they so wished or as long as they remained silent. While this might seem trivial, it can be a considerable luxury, as a Sudanese-born Australian once told me: 'Can you imagine how exhausting it is to be a migrant 24/7?' Conversely, Colic-Peisker's Yugoslavia-born interviewees could pass as non-migrants if they so wished and sometimes their whiteness resulted in little advantages in interactions with strangers, as this story told by a Perth-based taxi driver suggests:

> One day a mature lady entered my cab in South Perth and said: 'I always only call "Black and White Taxis" [a smaller taxi company in Perth] because "Swan Taxis" they're all strangers, Arabs, whoever. [. . .] You cannot talk to them, they speak poor English.' I said, 'Well, my English is not the best either.' She gave me a look sideways and said: 'At least you're the right colour.' (Colic-Peisker 2005: 620)

In sum, discourses of culture and linguistic proficiency can sometimes work to disguise racism. While cultural and linguistic ways of assessing others may seem objective, neutral, natural and value free, they are anything but. These stereotypical judgements based on names and appearance have real-life consequences by excluding 'outsiders' from access to full and equal participation in diverse societies, as research with African migrants in Canada shows. Creese and Wiebe (2012) found that African migrants in Canada experience significant deskilling and downward mobility, which channels them into low-skilled, low-wage jobs well below their educational levels. The researchers interviewed sixty-one migrants from sub-Saharan Africa in Vancouver to uncover their experiences of re-entering the labour market post-migration. Most of their interviewees were tertiary educated, most of them came from Anglophone countries and had been educated in English, and most of them had pre-migration professional experience. And they had one more thing in common: post-migration, they were mostly long-term underemployed. Deskilling played out differently for men and women because the labour market is not only racialised but also gendered. Men's qualifications and experiences were not recognised but there were still jobs for them in the production sector and other blue-collar work. Women's qualifications and experiences were not recognised, either, but, unlike their male counterparts, they did not even have access to blue-collar work, as such work is 'reserved' for men. At the same time, African women did not have access to the lower rungs of the feminised Canadian labour market such as retail and service work, either, because they did not 'look and sound right' for customer service. Consequently, their only options were in cleaning and care work. Thus, the Canadian labour market can be characterised as operating a system of 'economic apartheid', which worked to transform 'skilled migrants' into 'uneducated Africans'. Even if they were reluctant to speak of racism, the fact that attributions of lack of linguistic proficiency were a disguise for something else was obvious to Creese and Wiebe's (2012) interviewees. One of them, Vira from Zimbabwe, for example, explained how she was repeatedly passed over for promotion from a back-office to a front-office role:

> I didn't get the job because I can't, the tone of English they want with the customer service representative. They say their customers want an accent that is clear and like them, which will understand them. But when I talk to them, when I pack things, when I read their things, and I pack and I send it to Calgary, I send it to Minnesota, Missisauga, everything is OK. But when it comes to accent, I am no good [. . .] That's discrimination. They don't want a Black thing in front, that's it. (Quoted in Creese and Wiebe 2012: 70)

Having your accent constantly problematised and focused on can be a source of considerable stress and anxiety and serve to maintain boundaries in the workplace, as Dávila (2008) found in a study of the employment experiences of Latina women in the USA. Although the migrant women in her study were highly educated and spoke English well, they experienced downward occupational mobility and felt they were constantly harassed for their accent. Maria, a university graduate from the Dominican Republic, recounts her experience:

> My boss, she's the wife of the owner. She's always complaining around me because she can't understand me. She says 'I don't know what you are talking about!' Or, 'Say it again' (3 times). It's so rude. Because she doesn't try to understand me either. (Dávila 2008: 365)

Discrimination on the basis of race, ethnicity or national origin is illegal in Australia, Canada and the USA. Furthermore, for all we know, individual employers may consider themselves genuinely non-racist or post-racist. Yet, as the examples above show, discrimination continues to exist. It can continue to exist and even be largely invisible because linguistic discrimination has come to substitute other forms of discrimination. Linguistic discrimination is a common-sense proposition, it seems natural, neutral and objective. It just so happens that these seemingly natural and objective language assessments mean that 'English has a colour', as Creese and Kambere (2003) put it in a clever turn of phrase.

ENHANCING ACCESS

The search for employment and economic opportunities has always held first place among the many reasons why humans choose to migrate, and many migrants measure the success of their migration in economic terms. Likewise, receiving societies tend to measure successful settlement largely in economic terms. Where transnational migrants face the hurdles to meaningful employment and the discrimination in the labour market I discussed above, the success of their migration can be jeopardised at a personal level and the success of a national migration programme can be jeopardised at the societal level. So, what can be done to lift the multiple and complex barriers to migrant inclusion outlined here?

Let's return to the field experiment that pitted a fictitious applicant with a German name against one with a Turkish name (Weichselbaumer 2016). The applicant with the smallest number of positive responses, 'Meryem Öztürk' with a headscarf, received the highest call-back rate from employers whose job ad had explicitly stated that they were an intercultural team or that the company valued diversity. The effect was statistically very small but still seems to suggest that experience with ethnic diversity helps to reduce barriers. This is similar to the experience of women in the workplace: while for the first women the barriers to seeking paid employment, to entering a particular industry, to gaining work at a particular level or to being accepted in a particular workplace are high, they are lowered for other women who follow in their steps.

In order to succeed and overcome gender discrimination, pioneering women in the workplace (be it in paid employment generally, in a particular industry, at a particular level or in a particular company) have had to be 'better' – more qualified, more experienced, more talented, more connected – than their male counterparts.[3] Even in 2016, women's equality in the workplace has not been achieved anywhere in the world – one indicator is the persistent gender pay gap.[4] Nevertheless, women have made their way into the workforce and have overcome incredible obstacles to do so in little over a century. For many individual women, overcoming gender discrimination as an entry barrier has meant that they have had to be better qualified and more experienced than their male competitors in order to get a chance. Does this 'strategy' also work with ethnic discrimination? Does being better qualified and having more experience mean that an applicant with a stigmatised ethnic name receives a positive response as often as a less-qualified applicant with a 'native' name?

Another field experiment study in Sweden was designed to find out exactly that (Arai, Bursell and Nekby 2016). The researchers also used the CVs and application letters of fictitious applicants to respond to job ads for computer specialists, drivers, accountants, high school teachers, and assistant nurses. In the first stage of the experiment, they compared call-back rates for fictitious applicants with an Arabic and a Swedish name; with the unsurprising result that 'Fatima Ahmed' and 'Abdallah Hossein' were invited for interview significantly less often than 'Karolina Svensson' and 'Jonas Söderström.' In a second stage of the experiment, the researchers then systematically enhanced the profile of the applicant with the Arabic name so that he or she was more qualified than their counterpart with the Swedish name. What do you guess happened? Are you betting on employer rationality where the merits of an individual overcome the negative group stereotype or are you a cynic who thinks that bigotry is relatively immune to factual evidence? Well, neither view would be quite right – as always, the results turned out to be more complex: enhanced qualifications did nothing for male applicants with an Arabic name and their Swedish-named counterparts still had better call-back rates despite now being less qualified. For drivers, a 'male' job with the highest call-back rates for all applicants, higher qualifications actually reduced an applicant's chances of being invited for interview. For female applicants, however, their enhanced qualifications 'cancelled' the stigma of having an Arabic name: in the second scenario they were invited for interview as often as their (now less-qualified) counterparts with a Swedish name.

How can these conflicting results be explained? The researchers posit that cultural stereotypes are typically associated with the men of a group and are stronger for men. In other words, negative stereotypes about Middle Eastern men are so strong that superior individual merit does not help to overcome the stigma signalled by an Arabic-sounding name. By contrast, cultural stereotypes associated with women are generally weaker because they are not seen as default representatives of the group in the way men are. Furthermore, cultural stereotypes associated with women are often quite different from the stereotype of men of the same group.

Therefore, superior individual merit may be cancelling out the group stigma in the case of female applicants with an Arabic name.

The lesson from this study is that different employment outcomes of migrants and native-born are partly a result of discrimination at the entry stage. Individual migrants may have relatively little control over those barriers and even 'being better and trying harder' does not necessarily promise success. Rather, it is employers – and members of the dominant group more generally – who need to take up the onus to overcome the persistent 'native' versus 'migrant' divide.

KEY POINTS

This chapter made the following key points:

- Mobility is a normal aspect of the human experience but whether migration results in inclusive or segregated societies depends on a range of linguistic and cultural practices and ideologies that members of sending and receiving groups hold.
- Discourses of culture and language proficiency are sometimes made relevant in transnational migration contexts to serve as a cloak for racism. Such discourses can naturalise discrimination in the guise of objective language assessments.
- Equal employment opportunities are crucial to building inclusive societies but cultural and linguistic stereotypes on the basis of ethnic names or racial appearance may serve as barriers to inclusion for members of minority groups.

COUNTERPOINT

Linguistic and cultural stereotypes about legitimate and authentic group membership are a key aspect of intercultural communication. To some extent it may be unavoidable to rely on stereotypes when we first meet someone new, whether they have a similar or different background from our own. What obligations and responsibilities do we have as individuals, particularly if we are members of socially dominant groups, to engage with others and to contribute to more inclusive and cohesive groups through our personal actions and interactions?

FURTHER READING

Lippi-Green (2012) provides a fascinating introduction to language and discrimination in the USA and Piller (2016b) addresses the intersection of linguistic diversity and social justice in a variety of highly diverse societies around the globe. Roberman (2015b) offers an illuminating case study of the experiences of Soviet Jews in Germany.

ACTIVITIES

Design a stereotype research project
Design an experiment that aims to research the effect of a name or visual stimulus on the perception of a person. Your design should be similar to one of the designs used by Arai et al. (2016), Booth, Leigh and Varganova (2009), Rubin (1992) or Rubin and Smith (1990). Adapt the design to your context and reflect on its methodological affordances and limitations. You do not have to conduct the actual study. Also consider what non-experimental methods you could use to examine the effect of a name or visual stimulus on the perception of a person.

A migrant's story
Interview a migrant to your country about their working life pre- and post-migration. Ask only a few open-ended questions such as 'Can you tell me about your qualifications and work experience before you came here?', 'Can you tell me about your work experience since you've been here? Did you do any further training?', 'I am also curious to hear how you learned English [the local language]?', 'What role does English [the local language] play in your current job?' Audio-record the interview with the interviewee's permission and write an essay where you explore his or her experience with the knowledge you have gained in this chapter. Which aspects fit the pattern? Which do not? Does the interview confirm the overall thrust of the analysis presented here or throw it into question?

NOTES

1. The photographs of the fictitious applicant with different names and with and without headscarf can be viewed at http://www.languageonthemove.com/stereotyped-ethnic-names-as-a-barrier-to-workplace-entry/
2. If possible, I would recommend you actually watch this video to experience the McGurk effect yourself: https://www.youtube.com/watch?v=G-lN8vWm3mo

3. For a portrait of pioneering academic women in anthropology visit http://www. languageonthemove.com/strange-academic-women/ and http://www. languageonthemove.com/what-would-you-do/

4. See https://www.oecd.org/gender/data/genderwagegap.htm

CHAPTER 7

Intercultural Communication at Work

CHAPTER OBJECTIVES

This chapter will enable you to:

- Gain an overview of different approaches to intercultural business communication and how they are shaped by changing forms of globalisation.
- Familiarise yourself with the idea of national cultural values and engage critically with essentialism and overgeneralisations in the intercultural business communication advice literature.
- Identify the linguistic challenges arising from a multilingual workforce and evaluate the relative merit of different corporate language policies.
- Understand corporate intercultural communication as work performed by language workers.
- Explore the practical and theoretical challenges resulting from the changes in intercultural business communication in changing economic contexts.

GLOBALISATION AND INTERCULTURAL BUSINESS COMMUNICATION

In the context of globalisation, talk of intercultural communication has become ubiquitous in contemporary business communication and the importance of preparing business graduates for communication in the global village has become a truism; 'intercultural communication' and 'globalisation' are often mentioned in the same breath. However, 'globalisation' is no more clearly defined than 'intercultural communication' (see Chapter 1). To make this slippery concept in intercultural business communication amenable to a coherent account, I draw on a pithy staging put forward by *New York Times* columnist Thomas Friedman (2006) in his bestselling book about globalisation, *The World is Flat*. There, he distinguishes between three stages of globalisation: Globalisation 1.0, which he says was driven by countries internationalising; Globalisation 2.0, which was driven by companies internationalising; and Globalisation 3.0, which is driven by individuals internationalising themselves. I will therefore organise this chapter around three different phases in intercultural business communication, which coincide rather neatly with Friedman's phases of globalisation. As I demonstrated in Chapter 2, the emergence of the field of intercultural communication studies dates from the 1940s. Researchers were initially focused on comparing the communicative styles of nationals of different countries and, on the basis of those comparisons, making predictions about actual interactions. This phase could be called 'Intercultural Business Communication 1.0' and its most influential author is the Dutch psychologist Geert Hofstede, whose large-scale comparisons of a small set of five cultural values in different countries continue to inspire research in intercultural communication even today. In the 1980s a new focus started to emerge and researchers began to investigate communication in international corporations. It is particularly multinational companies in Central Europe and Scandinavia that have been the locus of research in 'Intercultural Business Communication 2.0'. 'Intercultural Communication 3.0', the most recent phase with the individual as the locus of intercultural communication, has seen the emergence of employees who are specifically employed to communicate interculturally, as is the case with call centre operators, cross-cultural mediators and consultants. While the focuses on nations, companies and individuals emerged at different times, each new focus combined with the previous one and today all three focuses co-exist. Not only do they co-exist, but they also overlap and inform each other.

NATIONAL CULTURAL VALUES

The idea that the nation is the locus of cultural difference is foundational to the intercultural communication literature, as I have shown repeatedly. In addition to having its origin in early American work, as we learnt in Chapter 2, another important source is the work of the Dutch psychologist Geert Hofstede (Hofstede 2001; Hofstede et al. 2010). In the late 1960s and early 1970s, Hofstede worked as a psychologist for IBM and in this role he gained access to data collected from more than 100,000 IBM employees in forty countries on the basis of a questionnaire instrument designed to elicit employee attitudes. Hofstede was particularly interested in collective differences in values, and on the basis of his data from those 100,000+ questionnaires he initially (in the 1980 first edition of Hofstede 2001) distinguished four value orientations: power distance, individualism, masculinity, and uncertainty avoidance. After some further data collection, Hofstede later added two additional dimensions, namely long-term orientation and indulgence.

The 'power distance' index refers to the level of inequality in a society and the degree to which the unequal distribution of power is accepted by members of that society. The 'individualism' index refers to the level of connection in a society and whether individuals are expected to fend for themselves or to act as members of a group. The 'masculinity' index refers to the degree to which gender roles are differentiated in a society. The 'uncertainty avoidance' index refers to the level to which a society accepts uncertainty and ambiguity and to what degree it tries to control uncertainty and ambiguity through the imposition of explicit rules. The 'long-term orientation' index deals with the extent to which a society values thrift and perseverance versus attendance to more short-term goals such as fulfilling social obligations. Finally, the 'indulgence' index measures the degree to which a society allows or represses gratification and 'having fun'.[1]

On the basis of his data collection among IBM employees, Hofstede originally calculated a score on the first four of these indexes for each country in his sample. His research design has since been extended and taken up by others so that there are now scores on all six dimensions available for most countries in the world. Even a cursory glance at Hofstede's websites[2] reveals that they exhibit some typical features of banal nationalism: a drop-down menu of the names of nation states, which lead to a country's 'score diagram' followed by a verbal description of the 'cultural dimensions' of that country. Nation and 'cultural dimensions' are thus presented as a one-to-one match. The national aspect of those cultural dimensions is further reinforced in specific country entries, all of which have the same layout. China, for instance, is described as follows:

> At a score of 20 China is a highly collectivist culture where people act in the interests of the group and not necessarily of themselves. In-group considerations affect hiring and promotions with closer in-groups (such as family) are [sic] getting preferential treatment. Employee commitment to the organization (but not necessarily to the people in the organization) is low. Whereas relationships with colleagues are cooperative for in-groups they are cold or even hostile to out-groups. [. . .] At 66 China is a Masculine society –

success oriented and driven. The need to ensure success can be exemplified by the fact that many Chinese will sacrifice family and leisure priorities to work. Service people (such as hairdressers) will provide services until very late at night. Leisure time is not so important. [. . .] At 30 China has a low score on Uncertainty Avoidance. Truth may be relative though in the immediate social circles there is concern for Truth with a capital T and rules (but not necessarily laws) abound. None the less, adherence to laws and rules may be flexible to suit the actual situation and pragmatism is a fact of life. The Chinese are comfortable with ambiguity; the Chinese language is full of ambiguous meanings that can be difficult for Western people to follow. Chinese are adaptable and entrepreneurial. [. . .] China is a Restrained society as can be seen in its low score of 24 in this dimension [= indulgence]. Societies with a low score in this dimension have a tendency to cynicism and pessimism.[3]

This example exhibits the three basic assumptions underlying Hofstede's work: to begin with, and as I have already pointed out above, the nation state is seen as the locus of culture or, to put it differently, the nation state in which a person lives is the key determinant of their cultural orientation. Second, culture can be reduced to six cultural dimensions – the so-called value orientations – and these value orientations are presented throughout Hofstede's work as the central problem of intercultural communication. Third, these value orientations can be measured and quantified into a precise numeric score.

Hofstede's work has been immensely influential and can be considered foundational to much of contemporary intercultural communication research, particularly in business and management studies, but it has even made its mark in the sociolinguistics of intercultural communication (for example, Bowe and Martin 2007; Clyne 1994). Outside academia the response has been even more enthusiastic and Hofstede's work has spawned a large body of intercultural communication advice. At the same time, Hofstede has also been widely criticised on a number of fronts. Most of this criticism focuses on the details of his data collection and analysis while approving of the overall thrust of his work. I will now introduce some of that specific criticism while arguing throughout that the central problem with Hofstede's work – and, implicitly, much of the work in intercultural communication that shares his assumptions – is actually related to the three underlying assumptions I mentioned above: its banal nationalism, its equation of culture with six value orientations and its quantitative approach.

Typically, academic accounts of Hofstede's work are garnished with a few cautionary remarks against stereotyping, as in the following example from a textbook in political economy:

> Although it is always rather dangerous to classify phenomena into statistical boxes, the categories [identified by Hofstede] seem intuitively reasonable. Most of us would be able to recognize our own national contexts, while also realizing the danger of using simple stereotypes without due care. (Dicken 2015: 180)

It is not quite clear to me how one would use a 'simple stereotype' with 'due care' but the central issue is precisely the fact that Hofstede's country descriptions are 'intuitively reasonable'. Of course they are! They are 'intuitively reasonable' precisely because we have been socialised into them through the discourses and practices of banal nationalism. It is the fact that diagrams with national cultural values are yet another instantiation of the widely circulating discourses of banal nationalism that makes Hofstede's work so appealing. However, restating something that is 'intuitively reasonable' in academic terms does not make it research, nor should 'intuitive appeal' be considered a substitute for critical enquiry in the conduct of research. So, what is wrong with providing an 'intuitively reasonable' account of the 'cultural dimensions' of nations? Two answers: overgeneralisation and essentialism. I will now discuss each of these problems.

Overgeneralisation relates to the fact that findings from one group of people in a country – people employed by IBM in the late 1960s in Hofstede's work – are generalised onto the population as a whole. However, we may well ask what do, say, male, middle-class, educated, professional city dwellers in a country have in common with illiterate, female, landless country dwellers in the same country? The only answer might well be 'nothing much'. These overgeneralisations from a few hundred survey respondents to a whole population of millions of people only make sense if one subscribes to an essentialist view of culture. Methodologically, Hofstede and his followers have made a lot of the size of his original sample. Once one takes a critical look at those numbers, they actually dwindle rapidly:

> In only six of the included countries (Belgium, France, Great Britain, Germany, Japan and Sweden) were the numbers of respondents more than 1,000 in both surveys. In 15 countries (Chile, Columbia, Greece, Hong Kong, Iran, Ireland, Israel, New Zealand, Pakistan, Peru, Philippines, Singapore, Taiwan, Thailand and Turkey) the numbers were less than 200. The first survey in

Pakistan was of 37 IBM employees, the second of 70 employees
[. . .]. (McSweeney 2002: 94)

Hofstede has countered criticisms such as this of his sample size by point-
ing to the fact that all that was needed was homogeneity of the group from
which the data were collected, and if the participants were homogeneous
then even a minimal sample size would be representative. This line of
reasoning only makes sense if one holds an essentialist view of culture, as
Hofstede does. In a catchy phrase, he considers culture 'the software of the
mind [. . .] our mental programming' (Hofstede et al. 2010) rather than,
as most anthropologists do, a social phenomenon that people share (see
Chapter 1).

An essentialist view of culture sees national culture as a stable attribute
of a person in the same way that gender and race are often seen as fairly
stable attributes. Consider the following excerpt from a country profile for
Germany from another intercultural communication advice website; one
that relies heavily on Hofstede's work:

The German thought process is extremely thorough, with each
aspect of a project being examined in great detail. [. . .] German
citizens do not need or expect to be complimented. In Germany, it
is assumed that everything is satisfactory unless the person hears
otherwise. [. . .] Germans are able to consume large quantities of
beer in one evening [. . .].[4]

In this text, the existence of a specific German 'software of the mind' – 'the
German thought process' – is presupposed (see Chapter 1 for a definition).
Indeed, German-ness extends beyond being a trait of the mind to being a
physical characteristic ('Germans are able to consume large quantities of
beer in one evening'). These mental and physical traits of German-ness
are assumed to go hand in hand with German citizenship – it is unclear
where this would leave the hundreds of thousands of German residents
who do not have German citizenship. Indeed, by equating 'German citizens' with 'in Germany', German residents who are not German citizens
are rendered invisible as members of contemporary German society. This
particular country profile thus buys into a view of German national identity as inherited, based on *ius sanguinis*, the law of blood relationships (as
opposed to *ius solis*, the law of residence). Reproducing this particular view
of German citizenship and German identity in a piece of intercultural
business communication advice naturalises one particular view of German
identity – the dominant one – and thus, even if unintentionally, takes
sides in a central political debate of contemporary Germany, the one about

the social, political, cultural and citizenship rights of immigrants and their descendants (e.g., Topçu, Bota and Pham 2012).

Some defenders of Hofstede's work have argued that the discussion of such detail is pointless for the target group of the intercultural business communication advice literature. For instance, an opinion piece by Mikael Søndergaard published on Hofstede's website[5] dismisses McSweeney's (2002) criticism as coming from the academic ivory tower. Søndergaard argues that the key achievement of Hofstede and his followers is the development of a framework that executives can look to for practical implications when doing business in countries other than their own. Well, can they really? How can six cultural dimensions per nation garnished with incidental gossip such as the one that Chinese hairdressers have a great work ethic or Germans can hold their beer be of much practical use to anyone? On the contrary, the assumption that the relationship between culture and the nation works the same the world over will surely make you a less effective intercultural communicator as it blinds you to the cultural variability in human practices, values and relationships. In German business, for instance, companies run by Turkish nationals have become major economic players – in 2012, they employed around 400,000 staff and generated around 40 billion euros in revenue (Cruz 2012). Companies and business people such as these are routinely overlooked in essentialist and overgeneralising work on intercultural business communication that takes the nation as the basic unit of cultural, linguistic and communicative analysis. Intercultural business communication research and advice based on the assumption that there is an essentialist connection between culture and nation is thus neither theoretically sound nor practically useful. As long as the intercultural business communication literature continues to reproduce official ideologies of national belonging, it is nothing more than yet another instantiation of banal nationalism and remains complicit in rendering difference and diversity invisible instead of describing and interpreting it. The centrality of the nation in this line of thinking is cemented not only by ignoring diversity within a nation, but also by maximising differences between nations. Hofstede, for instance, used to have this gloomy quote on his website:[6]

> Culture is more often a source of conflict than of synergy. Cultural differences are a nuisance at best and often a disaster. [. . .] We tend to have a human instinct that 'deep inside' all people are the same – but they are not.

In addition to the essentialism of the research programme for intercultural business communication put forward by Hofstede, there is one more fallacious assumption underlying the idea of national cultural values: the fallacy that culture can be quantified along four, five or six dimensions. Hofstede's cultural dimensions have often been criticised as being Western-centric and lacking validity from an insider perspective. Using Malaysia as an example, Goddard (2006: 15), for instance, argues that the fact that Hofstede claims a high power distance index for Malaysia is entirely meaningless because social relationships are not framed in terms of power in Malay but in terms of *hormat* ('respect'). In addition to the fact that the six cultural dimensions may be meaningless constructs in some cultures, their seemingly exact quantification is also problematic. Personally, I find the precision with which cultural values are supposedly calculated and presented as meaningful almost grotesque ('At 66 China is a Masculine society'). The central methodological problem underlying these figures is the idea that 'culture' can be quantified. Fallacious assumptions inevitably lead to descriptions and analyses that can only be described as wrong, irrespective of the quantity of the data or the sophistication of their statistical analysis. Actually, the problem with false assumptions begins way before the actual analysis: false assumptions lead us to ask the wrong questions – or design meaningless research projects, as the economist Erik S. Reinert (2008: 44) explains:

> If we try to understand other human beings solely through what is quantifiable [. . .] many key aspects are overlooked. In fact, it may be argued through this purely quantitative understanding, the difference between a human being and a big jellyfish consists in a few percentage points of dry matter in favour of the human being.

MULTINATIONAL CORPORATIONS

Where Hofstede and his followers see bounded and stable homogeneous nations, proponents of Intercultural Business Communication 2.0 see 'the diversity of the globalised business community' (Charles 2007: 266). These researchers and practitioners explicitly reject the essentialism of Intercultural Business Communication 1.0 and draw on social constructionism to conceptualise cultural membership. Social-constructionist (or poststructuralist) approaches are characterised by an emphasis on 'doing culture' as opposed to 'having culture' – as memorably expressed in Brian Street's catchphrase 'culture is a verb' (see Chapter 1). This focus on the process of 'doing intercultural communication' usually goes hand in hand with a different methodological orientation. As I explained in the previous section, research into national cultural values typically relies on quantitative methods to collect and analyse data from large populations. Instruments such as multiple-choice questionnaires and large-scale surveys obviously have the advantage of yielding data from a large number of respondents. However, at the same time, these data cannot include but a very limited number of generic items. Researchers in this paradigm will not be able to discover anything that they have not asked. Poststructuralist approaches on the other hand tend to adopt ethnographic methods such as participant observation, recordings of naturally-occurring interactions and semi-structured interviews with participants, or a combination of these. These produce 'rich' data that lend themselves to 'thick descriptions' of local contexts (Geertz 1973). For obvious reasons these approaches are well suited to an exploration of intercultural communication in a specific institutional context such as a company. At the same time, it is also obvious that they would be unsuitable for the description of a national culture.

A key question for Intercultural Business Communication 2.0 is what participants in an interaction actually orient to:

> Instead of imposing outsider categories, linguistic anthropology induces analytic categories that participants either articulate or presuppose in their action, and it insists on evidence that participants themselves are presupposing categories central to the analysis. (Wortham 2003: 2)

Thus, the key analytic question of Intercultural Business Communication 2.0 is no longer how members of different cultures interact. Rather, the key question becomes what categories people in a given context – for instance, employees in a multinational corporation – orient to: What does culture mean to them? What does difference mean? What does communication mean? And do any of these categories actually matter to them? For instance, in research with eight Finnish–Swedish post-merger companies it was found that 'culture', or more specifically cultural differences between Finns and Swedes, was not something that existed outside specific discursive contexts (Vaara 1999, 2000; Vaara et al. 2005). In these companies, 'culture' was selectively used as a discursive resource to explain problems: 'organizational actors often find cultural differences convenient attribution targets. Consequently, failures or unsuccessful experiences are often purposefully attributed to cultural differences, while successes are explained by other factors, such as the management's actions' (Vaara 2000: 105).

The shift in focus from nations to companies has thus also brought with it a theoretical and analytic shift. This has resulted in a further shift in the view of 'communication'. As I explained above, Intercultural Business

Communication 1.0 places a strong emphasis on attitudes, beliefs, values, value orientations and thought patterns. There is also a relatively strong interest in non-verbal communication. However, attention to the role of language use, including multilingual language use, language learning and linguistic proficiency, is relatively underdeveloped (see also Chapter 5). Therefore, some of the most widely read textbooks in intercultural business communication can make strange and surprising reading for a linguist in terms of the way they give short shrift to language and languages. By contrast, a linguist would consider natural languages the most important aspect of human communication, and Intercultural Business Communication 2.0 studies show that language choice and language proficiency clearly matter to social actors, that is, international companies and their employees.

When companies go international – as is the case in cross-border mergers or when an international company sets up a subsidiary in a new market – they basically have three linguistic options (Vandermeeren 1998). They may bring in language professionals, that is, translators and interpreters, to facilitate communication between staff with different linguistic backgrounds. Alternatively, they may rely on some staff members, usually based in the subsidiary, to accommodate speakers of the majority partner's language, in which case communication will be between native speakers and non-native speakers. A third option is the choice of a lingua franca, that is, a link language that is the mother tongue of neither group (Gerritsen and Nickerson 2009). All these options may co-exist within one single company and oftentimes do.

The need for language services can be a significant cost factor as Nekula and Šichová (2004) found in a study of around 400 subsidiaries of Austrian, German and Swiss companies operating in the Czech Republic (out of a total of over 2,000 such subsidiaries operating in the Czech Republic at the time of the research). More than half of these companies had an official company language policy. The majority of the policies decreed the company officially monolingual in German (fifty-five per cent), English (sixteen per cent) or Czech (nine per cent); the remainder were officially bilingual in either English and German (fifteen per cent) or Czech and German (five per cent). However, despite these official language policy decisions, eighteen per cent of all the surveyed companies employed internal translators or interpreters and the percentage increased with the size of the company: of the large companies with more than 500 employees, forty per cent employed language professionals. Additionally, fifty-eight per cent of the surveyed companies regularly outsourced translating and interpreting services to external providers (forty-seven per cent of small companies, sixty-six per cent of medium-sized companies and seventy per cent of large companies). On the basis of their findings, the researchers estimate that the language costs for the 2,000 Czech joint ventures with German-speaking companies must have been 3.3 billion euros between 1989 and 2003. These are the direct costs of using language services only. However, Nekula and Šichová are quick to point out that the indirect costs of language differences in multinational companies are even higher. What the researchers could not calculate are losses resulting from lack of control over external communication, from the non-availability of timely information to production staff, or from negative stereotyping and lack of rapport between staff members from different linguistic backgrounds.

A study of the language practices of the Finnish multinational Kone considered 'softer' language factors whose cost cannot be easily calculated (Marschan, Welch and Welch 1997; Marschan-Piekkari, Welch and Welch 1999a; 1999b). The researchers conducted fieldwork in twenty-five units of the company in ten countries and interviewed a total of 110 employees at top management (24), middle management (57) and operating level (29). Kone's official company language is English but middle management and lower-level employees were not necessarily able to use English. Language was identified as a key concern in internal communication in the multinational company by sixty-five per cent of the interviewees, and they did so from three different perspectives. First, most of the employees saw language as a barrier to both technical and non-technical information exchanges. Language as barrier manifested itself in a number of ways: for instance, employees could not engage in the kind of horizontal relationship-building across units encouraged by the company; or Spanish middle managers had relatively few opportunities to meet with headquarters because Finnish top managers avoided Spain because the staff there were less proficient in English than in any other European country; or staff members with limited English could not attend in-house training courses in Finland. Second, some participants mentioned that language acted as a facilitator. This was true of staff members who were more proficient in English than their peers. Some staff members with English facility accrued significant advantages. For instance, a Spanish operative with good English was sent to represent his unit at training courses and in meetings, even if he did not have functional responsibility for the issue at hand. Third, language was identified as a source of power, with employees proficient in three languages – English as the company language, Finnish as the company's 'home language' and the language of the subsidiary country – being in the most advantageous position of being able to access a wide range of information, to network across the company and to act as a go-between for others.

The power which can accrue to proficient speakers and the disempowering effects of some language choices over others is also apparent in another study of a merger between a Finnish and a Swedish bank (Vaara et al. 2005). When it was decided that the company language would be English, many of the Finnish managers, who were highly proficient in Finnish and Swedish but less so in English, felt like part of their professionalism had been taken away. Marschan-Piekkari et al. (1999b) point out that, in effect, a multinational company's language policy coupled with the proficiencies of staff can result in an alternative 'shadow structure' that de facto supersedes the formal organisational structure of the company.

Currently, there is a global trend for ever more multinational corporations to institute and adopt English as their working language. For instance, in late 2016 iconic German car manufacturer Volkswagen followed other major German corporations such as Lufthansa, Siemens or Adidas and adopted English as their corporate language (Dörner 2016). Meanwhile in Japan, the car manufacturer Honda made the same move and similarly followed a long list of iconic Japanese corporations such as Bridgestone, Uniqlo or Rakuten in adopting English as their corporate language ('Honda Makes English Official' 2015). The argument for English as a corporate language in all these cases is similar to the one made by Hiroshi Mikitani, the founder and CEO of e-commerce giant Rakuten. In his 2013 how-to-do-business advice book *Marketplace 3.0: Rewriting the Rules of Borderless Business*, Mikitani devotes a chapter to explaining his decision to 'Englishnize' his company. He explains that he imposed English so that communication within the company would be faster. English was supposed to improve the speed of communication for a number of reasons. To begin with, Mikitani argues that with an English-only policy the need for linguistic mediation – translating and interpreting – will fall away. Second, as Japanese employees gain confidence in English, they will no longer send e-mails to international subsidiaries but will pick up the phone and call. Finally, Mikitani believes that English communication is faster per se because it is supposed to be a more egalitarian language than Japanese and so employees are forced to stop prevaricating in the face of superiors; the latter belief is a popular language ideology related to the linguistic relativity of Japanese versus English (see Chapter 3). While Mikitani offers many reasons why English as the corporate language seemed like a good idea at the time, he unfortunately does not go into detail as to whether it really worked – whether communication at Rakuten now really is faster than before – or what any of the other consequences of the new corporate language policy were. He does say that Rakuten is now much more widely known because the English-only policy caught the attention of the global media. However, that feat is not really due to its English-only policy per se but to a clever press release about it. The only indicator of how well English at Rakuten is going comes from the claim that ninety per cent of employees had met the language test score required for their level within a year and the remaining ten per cent were excused and given an extension.

Mikitani does not address how the new language policy changed communication and the corporation overall. Did a 'shadow structure' develop in Rakuten where those who were more proficient in English gained an advantage over others who might have been less proficient in English but might have had more technical expertise? Employees who did not meet the required level of English were expected to improve their English language proficiency in their own time. What this means is that the business costs associated with intercultural communication were not actually borne by the company but were socialised to employees, while any profits deriving from the new language policy presumably accrued to the company and its shareholders. That English-only policies in multinational organisations socialise the costs of intercultural communication is explained in a study that compares the costs of the current multilingual provision in the European Union (EU) with the costs that would arise if the EU pursued an English-only policy (Gazzola and Grin 2013). The researchers found that translation and interpreting costs amount to just under one per cent of the EU's annual budget. This is a relatively small cost but could be eliminated if the EU operated only in English. However, the researchers show that the cost would not go away: it would simply be transferred from the institution (which is jointly funded by all members through taxes) to individuals. That individual cost would be substantially different for different individuals depending on their language learning needs: native speakers of English such as the citizens of Great Britain and Ireland would not be paying at all because they already speak English. Around seven per cent of continental Europeans who already speak 'very good' English would not be paying, either. But everyone else – around eighty per cent of Europeans – would be left out of pocket for English-language learning if they wanted to exercise their democratic right to understand what is going on in the European Parliament and to participate in the European project in any other way. The cost to those eighty per cent of Europeans to bring their English up to scratch would be less for some (those who already have 'good' or 'modest' English) and astronomical for those adults who have no English. Turning the language costs associated with intercultural communication from a public expense to a personal language learning expense is, of course, unfair and undemocratic in the case of a supranational state-like organisation such as the EU. In the case of a multinational corporation, it is unethical. Language training costs are business costs and should be borne by the business. Given the high cost of language learning, English-only corporate policies only make sense in contexts where employees already speak English well or very well or where the cost of language training is found to be less than the profits expected to accrue from the policy.

While it is generally assumed that an English-only language policy is profitable in today's globalised world, this is in fact not necessarily true and all kinds of alternative language policies may make sense depending on the business context. The importance of paying close attention to context is evidenced from a study that surprisingly finds that in some circumstances a competitive advantage may even result from *not* knowing English in a global business environment (Coe, Johns and Ward 2012). The researchers investigated the global spread of transnational staffing corporations. With the international rise of neoliberal workplace relations and the widespread demise of regular work over the past decades, temping firms have become a lucrative market internationally. Globally, the temporary staffing market is worth many billions of dollars, with the USA, the UK and Japan being the three largest national markets. This huge market is firmly in the hands of a relatively small number of transnational corporations all of which originate in the USA or Western Europe. In 2008, the three largest players internationally were Adecco, Manpower and Randstad. Adecco, which originates in Switzerland, generated 30.2 billion USD in foreign revenue (ninety-seven per cent of its total) by operating in fifty-nine countries. Manpower, which originates in the USA, generated 19.6 billion USD in foreign revenue (ninety-one per cent of its total) by operating in eighty-two countries. Randstad, which originates in the Netherlands, generated 18.2 billion USD in foreign revenue (seventy-eight per cent of its total) by operating in fifty countries. Temporary staffing is obviously big business; big global business.

In this context, the Japanese temporary staffing market (worth 14.7 billion USD in 2008) constitutes an anomaly: it is not dominated by transnational corporations but by national ones. Coe et al. (2012) investigate why the big global players have failed to significantly penetrate the world's fastest-growing and third-most lucrative market. They argue that transnational staffing corporations have failed in Japan on three levels: gaining market entry; gaining business once established; and securing business on an ongoing basis. On each level, language and culture played a role. In terms of gaining market entry, transnationals have no advantage if they start from scratch ('greenfield entry') because national competitors are well established. As one interviewee explained:

They might think that Japan is a very big market, but it is a not new market . . . it is different here. This is not an English speaking country and it has a long history, and a very different culture. (Coe et al. 2012: 37)

Failing greenfield entry, acquisitions of domestic companies are the other key strategy to gain international market entry. Acquisitions strategies, too, have not been going well in an industry heavily dependent on services and communications. The success of a temping agency depends heavily on its good relationships with the companies it is sending workers to and with the actual workers on its books. As it turns out, expatriate managers, who are typically installed in acquisitions and direct subsidiaries, simply are not as good at developing and maintaining these relationships as their Japanese counterparts. Most clients of a temping agency in Japan prefer to do business with a Japanese person. The way multinational staffing corporations thrive internationally is by entering into global contracts with other multinational corporations (e.g., Staffing Company A has a global contract with Hospitality Company B to supply all their cleaning staff globally). However, that strategy does not work well in the Japanese market, either. Apart from the fact that there are relatively fewer transnational corporations operating in Japan to begin with, even if a global contract is in place, the lack of local networks means that transnational companies often could not actually fulfil their global contract in Japan, as another interviewee explained:

> There is a problem with global contracts because Japan is not an English-speaking country. So, when the foreign company A has a global contract with Manpower . . . for instance Pasona [= 2nd largest national temping agency] has been doing the staffing for company A, but because of the global contract they have to switch to Manpower, but Manpower cannot find the 200 skilled English speakers that they need. So, a company might have a global contract, but they might not be able to switch from Pasona to Manpower. (Coe et al. 2012: 39)

In an industry such as temporary staffing, where the 'service' (i.e., supply of workers) is 'produced' and 'consumed' locally, it is hard to see what transnational companies can actually add in value to the ways in which the service is rendered. On the contrary, they lack a crucial ingredient which their Japanese competitors have: an emphasis on building long-term relationships and trust between clients and companies. The researchers conclude that as Japanese clients value long-term relationships and trust over universal branding and globally uniform business practices, there are obvious limits to the expansion potential of multinational corporations. In this context, *not* speaking English and not engaging in intercultural communication may actually grant national operators in the temporary staffing industry in the Japanese market a competitive edge. Surprising as this finding may be, it demonstrates yet again the paradoxical importance of careful attention to the specific 'local' context in order to understand 'global' intercultural communication.

DOING LANGUAGE AND CULTURE WORK

Friedman (2006) sees Globalisation 3.0 as characterised by individuals 'going global' and competing – and collaborating – globally. Indeed, the research I featured in the previous section portrays individuals within companies whose linguistic repertoires provide them with challenges or opportunities within their organisations. Intercultural Business Communication 3.0 is furthermore characterised by the commodification of language and communication skills (M. Heller and Duchêne 2012). Multilingual proficiency, communicative facility and cultural authenticity have become key aspects of some individuals' business activities, and their access to economic resources has come to be played out on the terrain of intercultural business communication. For employees in the multinational company Kone described in the previous section, intercultural competence in the form of proficiency in English, Finnish and the local language worked to their advantage – in terms of increased networking opportunities, accelerated promotion or enhanced access to information. Lack of proficiency in English, on the other hand, denied other individuals access to those same resources. Intercultural communication skills in the form of multilingual proficiency can thus be converted into economic gain. Intercultural Business Communication 3.0 research has responded to these new challenges by adopting theoretical approaches informed by the political economy of language. These draw on the work of the sociologist Pierre Bourdieu (1991) to explore how linguistic and cultural capital can be transformed into economic capital in the context of Globalisation 3.0 (see also Chapters 3 and 5).

How have language and communicative abilities come to be tied to the ability of individuals to engage in business activities? In an economy characterised by agriculture, primary extraction and production it does not really matter what the language background of workers is and what other languages they may or may not speak (M. Heller 2010). Indeed, factory workers are sometimes banned from speaking at work at all because speech is viewed as idle and detrimental to productivity (Boutet 2008). Meat workers, for example, may be too busy to keep up with the conveyor belt to engage in communication beyond the bare minimum or may feel too tired and exhausted by their heavy workload to speak (Piller and Lising 2014). Cleaners, on the other hand, may find that their work consists of such isolated and lonely tasks that they have no opportunity to communicate simply because they hardly ever meet anyone in the course of their work (Strömmer 2016). However, there are also jobs that are quite different and where key activities centre on knowledge, information and services. In such jobs, language and communication may constitute a central aspect of the work to be performed. The term 'language work' describes jobs where a substantial aspect of the work consists of language-related tasks. Examples include language teaching, translating and interpreting or call centre work. The term 'language work' is modelled on the term 'emotional labour' introduced by the sociologist Arlie R. Hochschild (2012a). In her book *The Managed Heart*, which was originally published in 1983, Hochschild describes the job demands on flight attendants to be friendly, even with aggressive, overly demanding or obnoxious customers, as emotional labour. Jobs that involve at least some linguistic, cultural and communicative labour have increased dramatically in recent years as part of the expanding service economy. Where Hochschild's US flight attendants of the late 1970s and early 1980s 'only' had to be friendly in their native lingua-culture, many of today's flight attendants have to be friendly in many languages as they simultaneously perform cultural authenticity. In research with Japanese flight attendants flying for an Australian low-cost carrier, Piller and Takahashi (2013) found that – despite the glamourous image of flight attendants – the work flight attendants have to perform is low skilled, physically demanding, increasingly poorly paid and offers hardly any structured further training or career progression. Nonetheless, many discourses – both fictional and non-fictional – conspire to maintain the flight-attendant glamour of a bygone era. Consequently, aspiring candidates had to invest heavily to gain entry into this job. All the research participants had invested many years of their lives in perfecting their English and their customer service skills to the levels that made them eligible to be considered for work with their employer. In addition to a desire for English and the West that shaped their careers prior to gaining access to their jobs, it was their proficiency in Japanese that was most immediately relevant during the selection process. They were employed by their employer because their linguistic, cultural, national and racial identities offered a fit with their employer's expansion strategy into Asian markets, particularly the Japanese market. At the same time, the recognition that they had been hired for their generic identity attributes rather than their personal achievements served to instil a sense of precariousness and insecurity. It was a constant reminder that there were many younger competitors with exactly the same attributes who could be hired in locations with lower wages and less stringent labour laws than Japan and Australia. Finally, while their identities as Asians and as speakers of Japanese were an asset on international routes, they were a liability within Australia, where they were constructed as deficient speakers of English who, simultaneously, had to conform to their company's English-only policy at all times.

In addition to flight attendants, call centre workers have come to be seen as the paradigmatic linguistic and cultural labourers of our time. Many people think of India when they think of call centres. India, with its recently installed long-distance fibre cables, comparatively low wages and its pool of well-educated English speakers, experienced a boom in call centres in the early years of the twenty-first century. In Indian call centres, work typically consists of taking calls from or making calls to North America for a range of global companies: inbound calls usually deal with service enquiries such as computer problems, credit card statements or travel bookings, and outbound calls are typically made to market a product or service (Mirchandani 2004, 2015; Pal and Buzzanell 2008). These researchers found that call centre work becomes intimately tied up with operators' identities: all of the workers interviewed had received accent-reduction classes, which were meant to 'neutralise' their Indian accents so that they would be understood by their American clients. In addition they adopted English names and were required to familiarise themselves and stay up to date with everyday knowledge of the American middle class. One call centre operator said: 'We have cross-cultural training. Even little things like Starbucks, Central Park . . . the nitty gritties like that are important' (Pal and Buzzanell 2008: 44f.). Training was also provided in the actual scripting of an interaction and a high level of standardisation was imposed on the interactions that operators could engage in with clients. The level of regulation of interactions is apparent in the following account by another operator:

> This is our script, we have to go through this. Thank you for choosing [name of American company]. My name is Tanya [assigned pseudonym]. May I have your first and last name. Thank you. May I call you by your first name? Thank you very much. How are you doing today? . . . These are the typical statements that we have to say – Great. Thank you. Excellent. Wonderful job. These are the power words. We have to use those words in our scripts. (Mirchandani 2004: 361)

Operators found that the high level of scripting of interactions removed their autonomy, deskilled their work and made it tedious. However, it was not only in the workplace that call centre operators took on new identities; their job had a significant impact on their identities outside of work as well. Due to the time difference between India and North America, call centre operators mostly work night shifts and this fact severely constrains their family and home life: rather than socialising with family and friends during 'normal' hours, the workers' social activities revolved around the workplace, sometimes to such an extent that they described their colleagues as family and their workplace as home.

Call centre jobs are sometimes touted as wonderful opportunities for Indian graduates to advance in the global economy. However, most of the research participants expressed cynicism about their work, which they considered to be a dead end and 'not a career' and which they were treating as providing them with pocket money while pursuing tertiary education. They were very aware that North American call centre operators with significantly lower qualifications earned a much higher salary and expressed resentment at business practices which they considered exploitative. Just like the Japanese flight attendants interviewed by Piller and Takahashi (2013), most of the Indian call centre operators were planning to leave call centre work as soon as they were ready to start a family or as soon as a better job opportunity came up.

The sense of call centre work as lacking career prospects also emerges in a very different context – a multilingual tourism call centre in Switzerland providing online and telephone booking services for Swiss and foreign tourists (Duchêne 2009). However, this call centre was explicitly presented as 'special': not a 'run-of-the-mill' call centre but a high-quality centre providing professional services. That rhetoric notwithstanding, employees did not need any background in tourism or even specialist knowledge of Switzerland in order to be hired. The key prerequisite was multilingual proficiency, particularly in English, French, German and another language (Dutch, Italian or Spanish). Once in the job, employees were constructed as offering superior services (vis-à-vis outsourced call centres in the developing world and vis-à-vis computerised services) and as offering authentic services. The 'authenticity' of their work derived from the fact that they lived in Switzerland, that their languages, particularly German, had a Swiss accent, and that they could draw on personal experience when marketing a destination. One of the main challenges of performing linguistic and cultural work in that context arises when customers challenge the authenticity of the performance. It was the non-native speakers of French who found their ability to speak French challenged most often in this context, as one of the workers, a native Italian speaker from the Italian-speaking part of Switzerland, who also worked in English, French, German and Spanish, explained:

[A]nd sometimes it is very little that you say like you say *bonjour ça va, comme ça* [hi how are you like that] and then they already tell you that *non je veux parler avec quelqu'un qui parle français* [no I

want to speak to someone who speaks French] [. . .] and then I tell
them that I speak French, but they insist that this is not the case
and then ok, then you have to refer them to [name of native-
French-speaking colleague]. (Duchêne 2009: 44)

Just as it is the job of flight attendants to be friendly even with obnoxious
customers, it is the job of call centre workers to accommodate the obnoxious linguistic ideologies of their customers.

From a corporate perspective, a key difference can be observed between
Intercultural Business Communication 2.0 and Intercultural Business
Communication 3.0: where multilingualism and cultural diversity were a
challenge, an obstacle and a cost factor for the multinational corporations
examined above, they have become a means of increasing efficiency and
flexibility and of enhancing profits in the sectors described in this section.
Indeed, the boom in language and communication work has reached such
a peak that the demand for bi- and multilingual workers with the right skill
set is far outstripping supply. O'Neill (2015) tells the story of Guatemalan
call centre workers, where language work and state control combine unlike
anywhere else to conflate old and new regimes of state and corporate
governance to produce 'ideal' workers. As part of attempts to 'near-shore'
US call centres into closer time and cultural zones, call centres in Central
America have been expanding in recent years. In Guatemala, new networks, favourable telecommunications and tax laws, and the availability
of well-educated Spanish-English bilinguals attracted many call centre
service providers from around 2005 onwards. In fact, the country attracted
so many employers that there was a danger that the industry would go
bust due to a lack of bilingual workers, as had happened in Panama and
Costa Rica. To prevent this, recruiters in Guatemala came up with a new
supply mechanism that it is difficult to call anything but cynical: the children of undocumented migrants who are deported from the USA back
to Guatemala in ever-increasing numbers – and who have 'perfect' US
accents and cultural understanding – are met by recruiters directly at the
airport, providing an ongoing supply chain 'forever tainted by the ironic
story of refugees turned deportees turned underrepresented employees of
an ever-expanding global service economy' (O'Neill 2015: 99).

KEY POINTS

This chapter made the following key points:

- Both intercultural business communication itself and approaches to
  intercultural business communication have changed significantly since

the inception of the field as the overall economic context has changed. Even so, some of the early work, with its focus on national cultural values as shaping international business interactions, continues to be influential today. It is particularly in the intercultural business communication advice literature where banal nationalism continues to flourish.

- Intercultural business communication with a focus on the language challenges faced by multinational corporations has adopted new theoretical and methodological approaches in response to the language challenges faced by those corporations, and has focused on the costs and benefits of multilingualism as well as on questions about how stakeholders orient to linguistic and cultural diversity.
- The latest development in intercultural business communication is the emergence of linguistic and cultural labour as an asset to be deployed by service workers operating in transnational markets.
- Intercultural business communication is best understood from inter-disciplinary, context-sensitive and complex perspectives that engage with real-life local aspects of linguistic and cultural interactions rather than simply positing the importance of the global.

COUNTERPOINT

Intercultural business communication is inevitably tied to shifting views of what globalisation means. In the same way that three different aspects of globalisation can be distinguished depending on whether the main drivers are nations, companies or individuals, three different strands of intercultural business communication can be distinguished depending on whether nations, companies or individuals are considered the locus of intercultural business communication. Of course, these three strands are mostly not as clearly demarcated as my account of three different phases may have suggested. How else could we conceptualise intercultural business communication? What are the affordances and constraints of different approaches?

FURTHER READING

Holmes and Stubbe (2015) provide an excellent overview of sociolinguistic research into workplace talk. The edited collection by Bargiela-Chiappini (2009) offers a wide-ranging collection of contemporary approaches to business communication and B. Meyer and Apfelbaum (2010) collect a number of case studies of multilingualism at work.

ACTIVITIES

Language policy in multinational corporations

Reports about corporate language policies are regularly featured in the media, particularly whenever a major corporation adopts an English-only policy. Collect a set of news items about the corporate language policy of a corporation that interests you and examine the language ideologies that are apparent in the media report or related social media commentary. How is language choice related to national and business interests? Can you find evidence of careful cost-benefit analyses of language choice?

Intercultural service work

Collect opinion pieces, letters to the editor, blog posts or the posts on a 'rant forum' about service work where language plays a role, such as call centre operators or tourism service workers. You might want to refer to this blog post about reviews of the English proficiency of Chinese hotel receptionists for further ideas: http://www.languageonthemove.com/seeing-asians-speaking-english/. On the basis of the data you have collected, write an essay that argues for or against the proposition 'Unfair business practices and economic inequalities are misrecognised as linguistic and cultural differences.' Alternatively, you can do this as a debating group activity with one side arguing for and the other against the proposition.

NOTES

1. More detailed definitions can be found in Hofstede (2001) as well as on Hofstede's website at http://geerthofstede.com/culture-geert-hofstede-gert-jan-hofstede/6d-model-of-national-culture/
2. See https://geert-hofstede.com/ and http://geerthofstede.com/
3. See https://geert-hofstede.com/china.html
4 See http://www.cyborlink.com/besite/germany.htm
5. See http://geert-hofstede.international-business-center.com/Sondergaard.shtml
6. In 2017 the quote no longer featured on either of Hofstede's websites. However, it can still be found widely on the web, often as an inspirational quote used by intercultural communication training providers.

Intercultural Communication for Sale

CHAPTER OBJECTIVES

This chapter will enable you to:

- Gain an overview of intercultural communication in consumer advertising and the ways in which images of linguistic and cultural difference are used to construct a product as desirable.
- Learn about the use of English to connote modern and global consumer identities, and the use of languages other than English to imbue a product with an ethno-cultural stereotype about the group who speak the language.
- Engage critically with the emergence of empty linguistic and cultural forms in commercial discourse.

SELLING ETHNO-CULTURAL STEREOTYPES

In 2010 I had the opportunity to visit Hakone, a small tourist town about an hour's train ride west of Tokyo. Expecting an 'authentic' Japanese experience after having visited global Tokyo, I was more than a little surprised when I found that Hakone station was dominated by Swiss imagery. There was a large billboard of Swiss Tourism with an image of Disentis/Mustér, a small town in Grisons in Eastern Switzerland. The billboard was as much a celebration of the fact that the Hakone Tozan Railway is a sister railway of the Rhaetian Railway operating in Grisons as it was an invitation to visit Switzerland. Even the umlaut in the original German spelling of 'Rhätische Bahn' was there – as was the abundant use of the national colour red, the Swiss Tourism emblem which has the Swiss cross at the heart of an edelweiss, the 'national' flower, and the slogan of Swiss Tourism, 'Get natural'. In close proximity to the billboard, there was a little coffee shop, named 'Cafe St. Moritz' after another famous resort town in Grisons. The Cafe St. Moritz, too, was liberally displaying the Swiss flag, including on table tops designed in the shape of the Swiss cross in a circle.[1]

It has become a truism that in today's globalised world commodified cultural and linguistic symbols and imagery rapidly circulate around the globe and turn up in unexpected places (Appadurai 1996; Hannerz 1996). In the example above, Swiss symbols and the tokenistic use of the German language reference one tourist space (Hakone, Japan) to another (Grisons, Switzerland) and they associate a modest train-station food outlet with the glitz and glamour of St. Moritz. Advertising takes cultural and linguistic symbols and images from one place and uses them in another to create authenticity, to reference an original, and to transfer the positive associations of a cultural or linguistic stereotype onto a product.

Interest in language and cultural mixing in commercial discourse may be as old as advertising itself. Early commentators did not think much of the use of loanwords and borrowings they noticed in shop and product names. For instance, an 1891 German publication, which was so popular that it went through a number of revisions and reprints, featured long lists of non-German words the author found in German advertising and regarded as evidence of the 'linguistic stupidity' of his time (Wustmann 1903). American linguists were similarly scathing about the use of Spanish in American advertisements. Pound (1913: 40) refers to Spanish loanwords in commercial language as 'the motley and audacious terms of our own day, [which] seem capricious and undignified indeed, [compared with] the formal designations created by our ancestors'. Examples of such 'capricious and undignified' advertising language include the Spanish ending '-o' in US brand names such as 'Indestructo' or 'Talk-O-Phone'. The purism of these sentiments sounds decidedly old-fashioned today. However, in the way they produced lists and taxonomies of borrowings and loanwords, they were typical of a trend in linguistics research that kept up for most of the twentieth century. Such collections could have all kinds of different focuses, for example languages of origin of loanwords in advertising or formation pattern. Some of these collections are quite amusing, such as those of linguistic mishaps that occur when a trade name or slogan that is perfectly fine in its original linguistic market acquires a negative or taboo meaning in another linguistic market (Aman 1982; Ricks 1996). Famous examples include the Chevrolet Nova, which read as *no va* ('doesn't move') in the Spanish-speaking world, the Toyota MR2, where MR2, if read out, produces *merde* ('shit') in French, or the Mitsubishi Pajero, with *pajero* meaning 'wank' in some varieties of Latin American Spanish. It is doubtful whether any of these really created major marketing problems, and this kind of cultural and linguistic insensitivity to the target market is definitely a thing of the past in today's climate of diversity marketing. However, even if these so-called brand name bloopers never really hurt sales in a particular market in any major way, the idea that major brands are culturally and linguistically insensitive has widespread appeal and many people enjoy mistranslated advertising to such a degree that even the invention of fictional mistranslations is flourishing. Many of us have heard of or read about the Pepsi slogan 'Come alive with Pepsi' which is said to have been mistranslated into Chinese (or Thai or some other 'exotic' language) as 'Pepsi brings your ancestors back from the dead'. I have often read about this example but never have I seen the offending 'Pepsi brings your ancestors back from the dead' in the original (instead of the English back-translation). Thus, the mistranslation may well be another urban legend, as the entry 'Pepsi in China' on the *All Lies* website suggests.[2] There you can also find a list of invented mistranslations of some of the most famous American slogans. However, regardless of the actual marketing impact of some of the brand name bloopers of the 1950s and 1960s, and regardless of whether some of the bloopers actually happened or not, in the last quarter of the twentieth century the mood started to change. Where different languages and cultures had been a nuisance for marketers seeking to enter new markets, and a problem to overcome in the examples above, they began to be transformed into marketing resources.

Using linguistic and cultural references to languages and cultures other than the national one was pioneered in Japanese advertising, where they were used early on to associate consumer products with the positive identities and ideologies of the linguistic and cultural other. In a ground-breaking study, Harald Haarmann (1989) observed the use of a wide range of European languages in Japanese advertising: English, French, German, Italian, Spanish, Portuguese, and even Latin, Greek, Swedish and Finnish. Haarmann described the use of foreign languages in Japanese advertising as an attempt to associate the advertised product with an ethno-cultural stereotype about the speakers of a particular language. No matter whether the target group can actually understand the meaning of a foreign form or not, they will be able to identify the form as belonging to a particular language. They will then transfer the ethno-cultural stereotype about the group most frequently associated with that language onto the product. In his research in Japan in the 1970s and 1980s, Haarmann (1989: 11) found that stereotypes typically associated with English, for instance, included 'international appreciation, reliability, high quality, confidence, practical use, [and] practical life style', while French was associated with 'high elegance, refined taste, attractiveness, sophisticated life style, fascination and charm'. English was used to imbue products such as alcohol, cars, TV sets, stereos and sportswear with these qualities. French, on the other hand, was reserved for fashion, watches, food and perfumes. In Haarmann's study it was mostly product and shop names where elements from languages other than Japanese were used. He lists examples such as a Tokyo fashion shop named '*la maison de élégance X*', a women's magazine named '*bonita*', a line of children's wear named '*piccolo*', or a skin cream named '*victus*'. None of these indexes of French-ness, Spanish-ness, Italian-ness or Latin-ness are really French, Spanish, Italian or Latin, as Blommaert (2010: 29) points out, using the example of a Japanese chocolate brand with the name 'Nina's derrière'. For a French speaker, 'Nina's derrière' might mean 'Nina's bum' but for a non-speaker of French it might mean 'chic, refined, sophisticated, expensive chocolate'. In other words, brand names which use foreign languages often do not function linguistically but emblematically; it is often irrelevant what their meaning in the original language might be as long as the name indexes an ethno-cultural stereotype.

With the exception of English (to which I will return below), the ethno-cultural stereotypes drawn upon in late twentieth-century Japanese advertising have been surprisingly similar across cultures (see Piller 2003, for an overview). French names have been found to carry connotations of high fashion, refined elegance, chic femininity and sophisticated cuisine in most advertising contexts outside the Francophone world. Outside the German-speaking countries, German is usually used to connote reliability, precision and superior technology. Italian is associated with good food and a positive attitude to life, and Spanish with freedom, adventure and masculinity.

Furthermore, in multilingual advertising the foreign-language item may not only function stereotypically but the form itself may also be a stereotype. In other words, a 'French' brand name may not even be a French word but simply *look like* a French word to a non-speaker of French. As in the example of 'Nina's derrière' above, foreign languages in advertising often sound ludicrously incorrect to actual speakers of the language with which an association is created. While '*derrière*' is an actual French word, sometimes all that is needed to turn an expression into 'French', for instance, are a few accent marks and maybe a *le* or *la*, as in the US-owned and internationally sold hosiery brand 'L'eggs'. 'L'eggs' hosiery was for many years sold in egg-shaped packaging and marketed with the slogan 'Our L'eggs fit your legs'.

The invention of foreign-sounding brand names in advertising is not always as innocuous as it is in the 'French' examples above. With reference to the use of invented Spanish in the USA, Hill (2008) and Zentella (1997) have argued that the reduction of linguistic and cultural complexity which is evident in linguistic stereotypes is a form of racism. They explain that 'Mock Spanish' (Hill's term) or 'chiquitification' (Zentella's term) serves a dual purpose: on the one hand, Mock Spanish such as *no problemo*, *el cheapo* or *muchos smoochos*, which have all moved from commercial discourse into mainstream American discourse, index the white users of these forms as cosmopolitan, authentic and having a sense of humour, in short endowed with a desirable personality. On the other hand, they are part of a larger racist discourse that indirectly indexes Spanish speakers as the undesirable and problematic other, as illustrated by the use of 'bad hombres' instead of 'bad men' by Donald Trump during one of the 2016 election debates (McCann and Bromwich 2016).

> Mock Spanish works to create a particular kind of 'American' identity, a desirable colloquial persona that is informal and easy going, with an all-important sense of humour and a hint – not too much, but just the right non-threatening amount – of cosmopolitanism, acquaintance with another language and culture. At the same time that Mock Spanish helps to constitute this identity, it assigns Spanish and its speakers to a zone of foreignness and disorder, richly fleshed out with denigrating stereotypes. (Hill 2008: 128f.)

Multilingualism in advertising may seem like a way of valuing diversity as the positive characteristics of another national, linguistic, cultural or racial group are transferred onto a product. However, even a positive stereotype ultimately serves to reinforce national, linguistic, cultural and racial boundaries. The ways in which stereotypical language use plays out in everyday interaction is described in Rusty Barrett's (2006) ethnography of language use in an Anglo-owned Mexican restaurant in Texas called 'Chalupatown'. Managers and waiting staff in that restaurant were white Anglo-Americans, while kitchen hands and other employees without customer contact were migrants from Latin America. The use of Mock Spanish was a central aspect of creating a Mexican identity for the restaurant. The researcher lists menu items with descriptions such as 'not your *ordinario* hard-shell tacos', 'blended with *fruita fresca*' (note that the Spanish word for 'fruit' is not *fruita* but *fruta*), 'big enough for a *macho* man!' or the use of inverted exclamation marks in English phrases, as in '¡You'll love it!' As part of their routines and to demonstrate their positive attitudes towards Mexican culture, the Anglo managers did not only use English with the Spanish-speaking employees but also liberally mixed Spanish expressions into their English sentences. However, they were completely oblivious to the fact that the way they used 'Spanish' was not 'real'

Spanish that was comprehensible to actual Spanish speakers. Oftentimes, the Spanish speakers were not even aware that supposedly they had been spoken to in Spanish. However, whenever a misunderstanding occurred, it was the Spanish speakers who copped the blame for it, with the English speakers self-righteously feeling they had done everything they could to facilitate communication by employing 'Spanish'; Mock Spanish, in fact. For instance, when orders were not fulfilled because the employees had not understood them, the managers did not consider that their directives might have been confusing but instead blamed the Spanish speakers for being lazy. Overall, the use of Mock Spanish served to give that particular restaurant an 'authentic' Mexican image but, at the same time, to maintain racism in the workplace while obscuring racism and blaming the victim.

ENGLISH FOR SALE

While languages other than English commodify an ethno-cultural stereo-type in commercial discourses of countries where those languages are not dominant, English plays a different role in global advertising. The use of English in the non-English-speaking world connotes a social stereotype of modernity, global elitism and the free market. As befits the status of English as the hyper-central language of globalisation, this social stereo-type is also much more diverse and difficult to sum up than the stereotypes associated with French, German, Italian or Spanish. Haarmann (1989) already noted that in his Japanese advertising corpus languages other than Japanese mostly occurred in shop, business and product names. If an element or elements from a language other than Japanese occurred in other parts of an advertisement or a commercial, such as the slogan or the body copy, that language was almost always English. Examples of extended switches into English from his corpus include slogans such as 'Nice day – nice smoking' and 'One world of Nescafé', or headlines such as 'This is ōbun renji' ('This is an oven range'), where 'This is' is spelled in the Roman script and 'ōbun renji' is spelled in the katakana script. 'Ōbun' and 'renji' are established loanwords from English which are also used in general Japanese.

English is ubiquitous in the commercial discourses of the (so-called) non-English-speaking world. In Germany, for instance, the use of English in the language of advertising (and in the language of the mass media more generally) has been in evidence ever since 1945. The use of English and its relationship with German has also been a matter of intense inter-est. So intense, in fact, that a PhD dissertation investigating the language of print advertising with a special focus on the use of English made for such popular reading that it was reprinted five times (Römer 1976). And the use of English keeps growing. Bajko (1999) observed a three-fold increase in the number of English attestations in his corpus throughout the 1990s, in both absolute and proportional terms. The high incidence of the use of English in advertising in non-English-speaking countries is not unique to Germany and can be observed throughout continental Europe. In a study of advertisements published in the women's magazine *Elle* in 2004, Gerritsen et al. (2007) found that seventy-seven per cent of advertisements published in the Spanish version of *Elle* contained English; as did seventy-three per cent of those published in the Dutch-language Belgian version, seventy-two per cent of those published in the French-language Belgian version, sixty-four per cent of those published in the Netherlands, sixty-three per cent of those published in France, and fifty-seven per cent of those published in Germany. Similar findings have been reported from Ecuador (Alm 2003), Iran (Baumgardner and Brown 2012), Jordan (Hamdan and Hatab 2009), Macedonia (Dimova 2012), Mexico (Baumgardner 2006), Russia (Ustinova and Bhatia 2005), South Korea (J. S. Lee 2006) and Taiwan (Wei-Yu Chen 2006), to name just a few.

In some countries, most famously France, the influx of English into and through commercial discourses has caused significant concern, and there have even been attempts to legislate against the use of English. In the French context, concern about the influx of English loanwords, particularly via advertising, found an early expression in Etiemble's (1964) scathing polemic *Parlez-vous Franglais?* ('Do you speak Frenglish?'). Legislation which came into effect in 1994, the *Loi Toubon*, rules that French has to be used in 'anything having to do with sales, warranties, advertising, the presentation of any goods, trademarks' (Marek 1998: 342). At the time of its introduction this legislation was widely perceived as being aimed against the use of English, although the law does not actually prohibit the use of English, or any other language, but rather prescribes the use of French. This has led to a situation where English is widely used alongside French in the language of advertising (Martin 2005). Thus, the legislation intended to curb the use of English does not seem to have been particularly effective. Some of the advertising copywriters who were interviewed by Martin (2005) even felt that the use of English in French advertising was such a powerful tool that it was better to risk a penalty for using it than to forgo its benefits.

The use of English as a contact language in advertising differs from the use of other languages both in quantitative and in qualitative terms. As pointed out above, English is the most frequently-used language in advertising messages in non-English-speaking countries (after the national language(s), of course). Even more importantly, English does not work exclusively by associating a product with an ethno-cultural stereotype as other languages do. It is only relatively rarely the case that the use of English in advertising in non-English-speaking countries works in a way similar to the use of other languages and indicates an ethno-cultural stereotype. In continental European advertising, for example, English is occasionally used to associate British class with products such as luxury cars or chocolates. Similarly, English may also imbue a product with cowboy spirit and the myth of the American West, as in the international campaign for Marlboro, with its slogan 'Come to Marlboro Country'. Another ethno-cultural stereotype that can be expressed by the use of English is the youth culture, hip hop rebellion and street cred of the black urban US ghetto (for example, brands such as Nike or Tommy Hilfiger). Often these are campaigns for products whose country of origin is the UK or the USA, just as some products for which French is used in international advertising actually originate in France or Switzerland. However, the point of using a foreign language is more often to associate the product with the ethno-cultural stereotype of the country in which the language is spoken, and whether such a relationship exists in actual fact (whether the product is manufactured in or originates from that country) is of minor importance. Country of origin is particularly irrelevant in cases where English is used in advertising, as was demonstrated by Vesterhus (1991). This researcher found that the highest incidence of English loanwords in German car marketing brochures occurred in the materials of Japanese manufacturers. Furthermore, advertising and commercial discourse more generally are, by definition, some of the most creative and dynamic registers, and practices such as the use of English loanwords are constantly evolving and changing. As English spreads, it becomes less and less useful as an ethno-cultural stereotype.

In sum, English is less likely to be used to associate a product with an ethno-cultural stereotype than with a social stereotype. Internationally, English has become a generic symbol of modernity, progress, globalisation and the free market. In advertising and commercial discourse, English is no longer the language of the linguistic and cultural other: it is the language of the modern, young, successful and cosmopolitan bilingual self (Piller 2001).

'GLOBALESE': A GLOBAL NON-LANGUAGE?

Advertising is an enormously influential form of discourse and a major form of global economic activity. A significant proportion of advertising expenditure goes on the creation and maintenance of brands. The 1990s saw the development of all-encompassing 'super-brands' whose value is created not through the product they sell or the service they provide, but rather through their symbolic value. Brands such as Nike, Virgin or Calvin Klein are '"conceptual value-added," which in effect means adding nothing but marketing' (Klein 2001: 15). In the process, an international register of global brand names has emerged. Brand names constitute a 'reasonably consistent register that is formulaic, recognizable, and accessible to as many onlookers-consumers as possible' (Jaworski 2015: 232f.). This register is globally highly uniform and draws on a relatively small number of linguistic forms, mostly from English but also suffixes, umlauts and punctuations marks from a range of other, mostly European, languages.[3] This global brand name register, which Jaworski (2015) calls 'Globalese' is relatively devoid of specific content and thus similar to all the other 'nullities', which the sociologist George Ritzer (2007) sees as characteristic of the globalisation of consumption. Ritzer argues that globalisation is a process in which 'something' is replaced with 'nothing'. 'Nothing' refers to relatively empty forms which are centrally conceived and controlled. The nullities of globalisation identified by Ritzer include non-places, non-things, non-people and non-services. While Ritzer does not pay any attention to the ways in which language intersects with the proliferation of nothing, the proliferation of empty forms – forms devoid of any specific, local content – can only be achieved communicatively, particularly through branding, and one might therefore describe this global brand name register also as a 'non-language'. For example, McDonald's hamburgers – the most widely recognised non-thing, which is at the centre of Ritzer's analysis of globalisation (see also Ritzer 2014) – globally are made of the same ingredients, produced to the same specifications and consumed in the same settings. However, ultimately it is language that achieves the global standardisation and control that is characteristic of global nothings: McDonald's hamburgers are uniformly labelled and the communication processes involved in selling a hamburger are just as centrally conceived and controlled as the product itself – from the shop name, via the menu, down to the actual scripting of server–customer interactions in the outlets of the fast-food chain.

Non-language is a form of communication that is centrally controlled and conceived and which is largely devoid of local specificity. It is language used in non-spaces such as shopping malls or airports to sell non-things such as hamburgers or coffee or non-services such as airport check-in. The corporate control of language at work has been part of the critique of neoliberalism at least since Hochschild's (2012a) sociological enquiry into flight-attendant work was first published in 1983 (see also Chapter 7). However, unlike the focus of Chapter 7, which was on the corporate control of the ways in which employees perform their communicative work, the focus here is slightly different. In addition to attempting the central control of language work, global corporations also exert linguistic control outside the corporation, that is, in public space. The spillover of a corporate-controlled global consumption register into public space may seem like just another aspect of globalisation and consumerism. And it is. However, it also shows the deeply exclusionary and alienating properties of global identities to those who are not within the realm of imagined elite identities of cosmopolitan English speakers, as the following example shows. My mother is a peasant farmer from rural Bavaria in Germany who has active competence only in her Bavarian dialect but not in Standard German, let alone in English. She is in her seventies and has travelled by air twice in her life to visit her nomadic daughter: in 2003 she flew from Munich to Sydney via Singapore and in 2009 she flew from Munich to Abu Dhabi. When she was in Abu Dhabi we had a conversation about how much anxiety and stress airports caused her because they made her feel lost and disoriented. So I tried to be helpful and explained to her the procedure for her return flight: at Abu Dhabi International Airport I would accompany her to customs, and for the restricted area beyond I had hired an escort service to accompany her to the gate. I ended the description of my helpful plan with the assertion that nothing could go wrong at this end in Abu Dhabi, and that there was nothing to worry about at the other end anyway because Munich Airport was back home in Germany and she spoke the language there. My mother did not buy it. Her response was: 'Believe me, I understand just as little at Munich Airport as I do here.' For her, the linguistic landscape of Munich Airport with its multilingual announcements, signage and buzz as well as its global shop names and brands is alienating because it is divorced from the wider linguistic landscape in which the airport is physically located. This may seem like a trivial example. That it is not is demonstrated by the story of Robert Dziekański, who died in 2007 at Vancouver International Airport as a result of being tasered by the Royal Canadian Mounted Police (RCMP) a few hours after he had arrived from his native Poland. Dziekański had never flown before in his life and did not speak any English. Upon disembarking from the plane, Dziekański spent almost ten hours in the restricted arrivals area, presumably waiting to be met by his mother, who had migrated to Canada a few years earlier. Without knowledge of English or of how to navigate the arrivals section of an international airport, Dziekański presumably was unaware that it would be impossible for his mother to enter the restricted area. Security cameras were not working so it is unclear how he spent those ten hours but security personnel did not notice him nor did anyone make any attempt to communicate with him. When he finally approached immigration after ten hours, the immigration officer who conferred landed immigrant status on him described him as follows:

> Visibly fatigued and somewhat dishevelled showing signs of impatience consistent with behaviour displayed after a long flight and frustrations due to lack of English language skills. At no time did he display any signs of behaviour that would be cause for concern. (Kooner 2007: 2)

The immigration officer recognised his lack of English proficiency but could not help him out by bringing in a Polish interpreter because of staffing shortages on the evening shift. We can only assume that Dziekański became fundamentally disoriented during those ten hours because soon after he had cleared immigration, Dziekański became very agitated in front of a set of automatic doors. As a consequence, the RCMP were called in to deal with him. They shot him from behind with a taser gun multiple times and he was pinned to the floor by four officers. Within minutes, Robert Dziekański died. The death of Robert Dziekański was videoed by another traveller and triggered national and international outrage when it made the rounds on *YouTube*. A coronial inquest later found that his death was a homicide ('Death of Polish Man Tasered by RCMP was a Homicide, BC Coroners Rule' 2013).

Airports are discursively constructed as spaces of consumption where cosmopolitan frequent flyers who are confident in English and maybe some other prestigious languages, too, circulate. The images of airports centre on the consumption of high-end brands and the elite consumption of leisure or business travel, as Thurlow and Jaworski (2010) show in their analysis of the identities of travellers constructed in in-flight magazines and frequent-flyer programmes. There is also another reality of airports, of course: in addition to the many workers who work at an airport (see Chapter 7), airports are also spaces frequented by many travellers who cannot afford the high-end brands, who do not travel by air often, who are unfamiliar with the global brand register and who may not speak English or another language with enough clout to figure in airport signage and announcements. Robert Dziekański might still be alive if airports were not only laden with consumption signage but if the difference between the restricted and non-restricted arrivals area at an international airport had been communicated to him in a way he could understand.

In sum, global brand names constitute a corporate-controlled global consumption register divorced from the physical space surrounding it and linked to other hubs of globalisation around the world. The emergence of this global non-language and corporate attempts at public language management have not gone unchallenged. Reactions to McDonald's efforts to have the term 'McJob' removed from the *Merriam-Webster's Collegiate Dictionary* in 2003 and the *Oxford English Dictionary* (*OED*) in 2007 constitute an example. The *OED* definition of 'McJob', which McDonald's took issue with, is 'an unstimulating, low-paid job with few prospects, esp. one created by the expansion of the service sector' (*OED*, s.v. 'McJob'). McDonald's, by contrast, argued that a 'McJob' should be redefined so as to 'reflect a job that is stimulating, rewarding [. . .] and offers skills that last a lifetime' (Thompson 2007). McDonald's exerted political pressure on the dictionaries but stopped short of testing the matter in court ('A New McDefinition?' 2007). McDonald's has, however, repeatedly resorted to litigation in order to keep control over its brand image as in litigation over the use of the prefix 'Mc-'. McDonald's has won injunctions against the use of 'McBagels' and 'McSleep' as brand names. Coulthard (2005) describes the 'McSleep' case in some detail: Quality Inns wanted to create a basic hotel chain brand under the 'McSleep' label. They argued that their choice was motivated by reference to the stereotype of Scottish frugality. McDonald's, by contrast, contended that Quality Inns was attempting to draw on the goodwill of the McDonald's brand. Furthermore, they pointed to their efforts in creating a 'McLanguage'. 'McLanguage' is taught by Ronald McDonald, the clown character that is the corporation's mascot, when he encourages children to 'Mc-ise' their vocabulary by adding the prefix 'Mc' to generic words. Examples include 'McFries', 'McFish', 'McShakes' or 'McBest'. The linguist expert witness at the trial, Roger Shuy, used corpus linguistic evidence to show that the 'Mc-' prefix was indeed widely used generically and had come to mean 'basic, convenient, inexpensive and standardised' (Coulthard 2005: 41). McDonalds, by contrast, used market research to show that consumers associated the 'Mc-' prefix with McDonald's. The court gave greater weight to the latter testimony and accorded the fast-food chain control over the prefix in the commercial domain.

'Globalese' is a form of English, as is most apparent outside Anglophone countries, where its imposition constitutes not only the imposition of a particular corporate style but also of that style in a foreign language. While 'McLanguage' is devoid of local content, centrally controlled and globally standardised, it is globally standardised in an American-led fashion. Indeed, commercial globalisation by and large is a Western-led phenomenon even if counter-examples such as Japanese-led 'pink globalisation' in the form of the 'Hello Kitty' phenomenon can be found. However, 'a Japanese product such as Hello Kitty remains more of a product, and less a bearer of life-style or national identity than Coca-Cola, McDonald's, or Starbucks' (Yano 2013: 14).

Global corporations are, in fact, increasingly seeking to avoid the association of 'McDonaldisation' with Americanisation. One way of doing so is to move away from the exclusive use of English. In 2002 McDonald's, for instance, ran an advertising campaign in Australia which featured a commercial set in Italy, with the characters using a few Italian words and having a heavy Italian accent in their English (Piller 2003). In yet another example of spreading diversity marketing, McDonald's incorporated Pokémon characters into their advertising in Japan.[4] In a further intriguing twist these Pokémon characters were actually proposing to teach young McDonald's consumers English, a prized commodity in Japan's hot English-language learning market (see Chapter 5). Diversity marketing constitutes a symbolic move away from Americanisation, Westernisation and English dominance:

> Today the buzzword in global marketing isn't selling America to the world, but bringing a kind of market masala to everyone in the world. [. . .] the pitch is less Marlboro Man, more Ricky Martin: a bilingual mix of North and South, some Latin, some R&B, all couched in global party lyrics. This ethnic-food-court approach creates a One World placelessness, a global mall in which corporations are able to sell a single product in numerous countries without triggering the cries of 'Coca-Colonization.' (Klein 2001: 131f.)

At a time when the values, tastes and industrial practices of American brands are being exported to every corner of the globe, there is a simultaneous attempt to distance these brands – symbolically – from America. One way of doing so is through the use of languages other than English in advertising. As bell hooks (1992: 21) has argued: 'within commodity culture, ethnicity becomes spice, seasoning that can liven up the dull dish that is mainstream white culture'. The same is true of intercultural advertising!

KEY POINTS

This chapter made the following key points:

* Advertising and commercial discourse more generally is a key space where culture is made relevant for the purpose of enhancing the market value and desirability of a product or service.
* A key means to achieve such intercultural commodification is through

the use of languages other than the national one in the branding and advertising of a product for sale.

- If languages other than English are used in advertising and branding outside their national contexts, they are used to connote an ethno-cultural stereotype. These stereotypes serve to maintain national and racial boundaries and can sometimes constitute a smokescreen for covert racism as in the case of Mock Spanish.
- When English is used in advertising in non-English-speaking countries, rarely is it intended to connote an ethno-cultural stereotype and much more often a social stereotype where bilingualism in English and the national language is used to index modern, cosmopolitan, professional and successful identities.
- The language of brands is tightly controlled by the corporations that own the brand. The central control of the brand language has resulted in a uniform global consumer register. This register uses resources from English and a limited range of other languages to index diversity in a uniform manner.

COUNTERPOINT

It has been one of the arguments of this chapter that multilingual advertising indexes heterogeneity and thereby obscures both the fact that commercial globalisation is largely Western-led and that corporate profits depend on relatively homogeneous global consumption practices. However, I have also shown that, in addition to cultural imperialism and neoliberal control, global advertising indexes modernity, progress, freedom and hedonistic pleasure. How can this tension be reconciled and what are the consequences of this tension for attempts to resist global corporate control?

FURTHER READING

Hannerz (1996) and Ritzer (2007, 2014) offer highly readable explorations of the global flows of commodified cultural symbols. Hannerz explores the global circuits of cultural commodification from the perspective of an ethnographer and Ritzer from the perspective of a sociologist. Klein (2001) provides a pungent critique of super-brands as the 'common language of the global village'.

ACTIVITIES

Multilingual advertising

Watch out for a television commercial currently screening in which a language other than the national language of your country is used. How does the foreign language appear? As accent, words or longer expressions? Where in the commercial does it appear? Is it spoken or written? Who uses it (the narrator or a character)? What kinds of meanings and associations are created through the use of the foreign language? You might want to compare your notes with those of your peers doing the same activity with another commercial.

English in global advertising

Use one edition of an international women's magazine of your choice published in a non-English-speaking country of your choice. Collect all advertisements that are larger than half a page in size and replicate the analysis by Gerritsen et al. (2007). Discuss the similarities and differences between your findings and those of Gerritsen et al. You can expand this research project by using more editions, including editions from different points in time or from different countries.

Global branding

Visit the front page of the global and various national websites of a brand of your choice. Which elements are the same across the various sites? Which are different?

NOTES

1. Images of Swiss-themed Hakone station are available at http://www. languageonthemove.com/finding-switzerland-in-japan/
2. See http://www.all-lies.com/legends/business/products/pepsiinchina.shtml
3. For a range of example images see Jaworski (2015).
4. See http://www.mcd-holdings.co.jp/news/2009/promotion/promo1008b.html

CHAPTER 9

Intercultural Romance

This chapter will enable you to:

- Gain an overview of research into intermarriage and intercultural romance and the discursive construction of intercultural desire in orientalist discourses, including on mail-order bride websites.
- Engage critically with the complex intersections between practices, ideologies and material bases in intercultural communication in the context of love, romance and sexuality.

LOVE GOES GLOBAL

Throughout this book we have repeatedly seen that intercultural communication is often considered problematic. At the same time, it may be celebrated as we saw in the exploration of the commodification of intercultural communication in advertising in the previous chapter. This chapter is devoted to another form of the celebration of cultural difference and diversity, where the cultural other is romanticised and constructed as an object of romantic and sexual desire.

A German woman whom I asked in the late 1990s how she had met her American husband responded, 'I always wanted to marry a cowboy!' (Piller 2008). In saying that, she was – consciously or unconsciously – echoing the lyrics of a pop song that had topped the charts in Germany back in the 1960s when she was a child:

I want a cowboy for a husband // I want a cowboy for a husband // It has nothing to do with the way he shoots // Rather, it has to do with the way he kisses // I want a cowboy for a husband.[1]

A South Korean man who was asked why he was looking for a Vietnamese wife responded 'They will be obedient and good to my parents' (H. M. Kim 2007: 114). In saying that, he was echoing the words found in the promotional materials of international marriage brokers and local governments, which run an international marriage campaign in South Korea. The campaign – with the slogan 'Giving rural bachelors a chance to marry' – has the aim of rejuvenating South Korea's aging society.

These two exchanges occurred in two widely different contexts, yet they are bound together by the pursuit of the most personal desires of love, romance, intimacy and family through intercultural communication. Each exchange makes culture relevant, and stereotypical images of the cultural other have become enmeshed with intimate personal desires – which we oftentimes regard as deeply individual. Furthermore, in each case, the stereotype was no match for reality. Natalie's[2] American husband was anything but a cowboy: a native of the East Coast rather than the 'Wild West' where cowboys are supposed to roam, he is college educated, holds a humanities degree and works in a skilled trade in an arts-related business. So, in addition to being an individual expression of romantic desire, her comment is also an instantiation of wider discourses in which the USA is represented stereotypically as the 'Wild West' and American men as cowboys. Such discourses would have permeated much of Natalie's youth: in addition to the pop song *I want to marry a cowboy*, just think of the Western movie genre, which has been broadcast from Hollywood around the world and has become part of the cultural make-up of people from Germany to Thailand (as we saw in Chapter 4). The advertising industry's Marlboro Man and his countless clones are another international source of the myth of the cowboy as an expression of quintessential American masculinity: rugged, self-reliant, with a clear sense of right and wrong, non-domesticated but romantic and loyal to the right woman.

As for the Korean man quoted by H. M. Kim (2007), I do not know whether his dream of finding an obedient Vietnamese wife who would be good to his parents came true. However, the researcher reports many cases in which the dreams rural Korean men harbour about their prospective international brides were disappointed. While the discourses of the international marriage brokers highlight the obedience and filial piety of Vietnamese women, these women actually have grown up in a socialist state and consider nuclear families the norm. Nor are the Korean extended families into which they marry necessarily very lovable, with some of the foreign women reporting being abused and beaten by their in-laws. Many of the international brides interviewed by H. M. Kim actually desired to live up to the images of Asian femininity that their South Korean husbands held of them. However, they did not see Asian femininity, domesticity and professional motherhood as something that was inherent in their natures. Rather, they expected that the South Korean men they married would be well-enough-off to enable them to lead lives of devout femininity, domesticity and motherhood. One international wife from Mongolia, for instance, said:

> There are many cases in Mongolia in which young people in their early twenties just give birth to children and get married without any preparation. The reason I chose a Korean man is because I heard that they buy houses and everything before marriage, and they have a strong sense of responsibility. I have heard that the men coming over to get married are old because it takes a long time to get prepared. I believed that as a mother, I would be able to raise children at home while my husband supports the family. (Quoted in H. M. Kim 2007: 115)

Unfortunately, it turned out that her older Korean husband was not 'prepared' either: he had left the workforce, lacked the material resources to support a family, was poorly educated and was violent. However, expecting that being 'a good wife' would come naturally to a woman from Mongolia allowed him to place the blame for their failing marriage on his wife.

Around the world, the incidence of international marriages increased dramatically since the second-half of the twentieth century. In Europe, marriages involving partners with different nationalities accounted for 21.6 per cent of all marriages and 17.7 per cent of all divorces in 2006–2007 (Lanzieri 2011). In the same year in Japan, marriages involving a Japanese and non-Japanese partner peaked at 6.11 per cent of all marriages ('A Look at International Marriage in Japan' 2015). Although international marriage statistics are patchy and there are no statistics for non-marital relationships, we can assume that these figures are indicative of a wider trend, and that love, romance and family have indeed gone global. As the examples above have shown, this does not just mean that an increasing number of people from different cultural, national, racial or linguistic backgrounds enter into an intimate relationship; it also means that discourses of love, romance, gender and sexuality have become enmeshed with cultural discourses. Culture is made relevant in the emotional lives of many people and has come to inflect love and desire.

Despite increasing intermarriage rates, most societies around the world continue to portray endogamous relationships – marriage within one's own group – as the norm, and intermarriage as the exception from the norm that is in need of explanation. By contrast, only a relatively small number of societies have traditionally practised exogamy. Examples of traditional societies that consider intermarriage the norm include the Tucanoan in the Vaupés region in the North-West Amazon Basin of Brazil and Colombia (J. E. Jackson 1983). The Tucanoan have a strong taboo against endogamy, and group membership is defined on the basis of language. Residence is patrilocal and language usage is bilingual in a pattern where each partner speaks their 'native' language and receives the partner's 'native' language back. A child grows up hearing the father's language spoken widely, but also the language of the mother, and those of other female relatives, all of whom would be in-married. Thus, children grow up multilingual but consider their father's language their 'native' language. Tucanoan traditions thus provide guidance in matters of marriage, family and parenting, as do most traditional societies.

By contrast, intercultural and multilingual couples in societies where exogamy is not traditional and may even be considered deviant usually do not have such clear guidance to draw on as they navigate their relationship, parenting and family obligations – a conundrum that has given rise to a new sub-genre of intercultural communication advice: intercultural relationship and parenting advice. In addition to such materials, people also have available to them discourses of the cultural other to guide them, particularly in the early days of an intercultural relationship or as they ponder engaging in one. As I have argued again and again here, intercultural communication is a result not of the identities of interactants but of discursive framing. This is obviously true for intimate intercultural communication as well. Partners in an intimate relationship do not engage in intercultural communication by virtue of the fact that they come from different national and/or linguistic backgrounds, but by virtue of what they orient to. Intimate intercultural communication results from partners orienting to cultural difference, doing culture and constructing culture as a category. This is much more likely to happen in the early stages of a relationship or even before they engage in such a relationship. Partners from different backgrounds usually find themselves progressively less likely to frame their communication as intercultural as their relationship becomes more established. In research with bilingual couples I found that these couples engage in a significant amount of communicative work to construct themselves as similar and/or to attribute differences to individual character rather than to culture (Piller 2002a). The English- and German-speaking couples whose conversations I explored used strategies such as the following to construct similarity and deconstruct difference: they minimised difference between Americans, Britons and Germans by maximising difference with other national and cultural backgrounds with comments such as 'it's not like you're Arabian or anything'. In another example, an American woman described her German husband as 'not that bad' in contrast to relationships with people from 'Africa and all over the place'. Another strategy to stress commonality was to focus on non-national aspects of their identities such as a shared love of music, professional identities or similar class backgrounds. Similarly, Visson (1998: 102) found in her study of Russian–American marriages that partners initially tended to see themselves as individuals but their spouses in cultural terms, 'as products of a "foreign" culture'.

Not only are discourses about the cultural other fundamental to understanding intimate intercultural communication, they are also at the heart of the increased incidence of intercultural relationships. On the face of it, it is the rise in international mobility that brings people from different backgrounds together and enhances their chances to meet and form relationships. However, and maybe even more importantly, the rise in international relationships is linked to increased international media flows which bring desires and dreams of emotional and sexual fulfilment with the cultural other within the (imagined) reach of ever more people. Today, unprecedented numbers of people are moving across international boundaries, be it for the purposes of study, employment, pleasure or to seek refuge. Obviously, this increased international mobility increases the chances for people to meet and find a partner from elsewhere. For instance, the European university exchange programme Erasmus has been credited with bringing ever more international couples together as young adults go on exchange at a time in their lives when they are looking for a life partner (Lüdke 2016). If not on student exchange, others meet while one or both partners is working abroad, serving in the military or travelling. In addition to the fact that increased international mobility for a range of purposes creates chances for cross-cultural intimate relationships to emerge, people may actually engage in international travel with the express aim of entering into an intimate relationship, as is the case in romance and prostitution travel. The ubiquity of romanticised and sexualised images of the cultural other – be it images of rugged American cowboy masculinity or images of demure and obedient Asian femininity – has resulted in a multiplication of intercultural desires.

LOVE MAKES THE WORLD GO ROUND

In a blog post about an encounter between a Japanese-Western couple and a homeless Japanese man in Tokyo, Kimie Takahashi (2010) reports how the man takes exception to the English practice of saying 'I love you' in romantic contexts: 'They [= Western men] say "I love you, I love you" and the [Japanese] women love it. It's stupid. If love is there, you don't have to say it.' The man has good reason to be cross with Western-style romance because its pervasive influence makes him an undesirable partner in the local romantic market: 'How can I find a partner when women here watch stupid American romantic movies and expect me to say "I love you"?'

Love and marriage have obviously different meanings in different cultures and the expression of love, romance and desire differs across cultures. The view which has come to dominate the concepts of love and marriage globally is of marriage as a relationship based on choice, romantic love and companionship. Although in many parts of the world such a view has come to predominate as 'natural', it is a recent development, even in the West, where romance and companionship in marriage came to dominate or completely replace views of marriage as a system of familial and financial obligations only during the nineteenth and twentieth centuries (Hirsch and Wardlow 2006). These scholars show that the transformation of love and marriage has gone hand in hand with changes in identity. While kinship relationships used to be central to human identity making (and in many parts of the world continue to be), individuality has now come to hold a central place in our views of who we are. Our identities and loves have changed in the material context of the monetisation of our daily needs and a burgeoning consumer society. Our lives and emotions have changed at different speeds but in interconnected ways to the degree that we can now speak of a global romantic system which is predicated upon material inequalities and discourses of the romantic other. The global romantic system is undergirded not only by material inequalities but also by ideological ones where romantic love has come to be seen as morally superior to other forms of love and care. As Rebhun (1999: 5) writes with reference to lovers in Caruaru, the city in the Pernambuco region of Brazil where she conducted research into the impact of rapid social and economic change on love, marriage and emotions more generally:

> The practice of romance reflects a prestigious involvement with the 'West,' its economic domination, its glorious cultural heritage, its prestige, and its modernity, especially regarding romance as expressed in marriages for love celebrated by women in white dresses and men in dress suits, attended by identically dressed witnesses and blessed by church and state ceremonies.

Notions of prestigious 'Western modern romance' make themselves felt in the emotional lives – and concomitantly the social and economic lives –

even of people seemingly removed from its influence or opposing it as the homeless Japanese man quoted above does. It seemed to that man that the pervasiveness of romantic ideas about love reduced his chances in the relationship market as the women in his circle looked to find more 'romantic men'. His conundrum is not unique: half a world away, in the United Arab Emirates, there was a media panic at around the same time about soaring divorce rates, which were attributed to the 'Noor factor' (Elass 2009). '*Noor*' is the Arabic-language title of the Turkish soap opera *Gümüş* featuring a romantic relationship between the two main characters, Noor and her husband Mohannad. Dubbed into Arabic, '*Noor*' was immensely successful throughout the Arab world, particularly with women (Abu Rahhal 2008). The Mohannad character frequently uses terms of endearment with his wife, tells her how much he loves her and flirts with her in 'the flowery language of the Levant' (Elass 2009). The soap opera was dubbed in Syria, and Levantine Arabic apparently sounds very 'flowery' and romantic to Gulf Arabs. According to Elass, the soap opera raised the romantic expectations of Gulf Arab women to such a level that some of them took the step of divorcing their 'unromantic' husbands, who did not use terms of endearment, profess their love, flirt nor have a 'flowery' Levantine accent.

I will now describe two case studies as examples of the global circuits of love and the material and discursive differences and inequalities in which they are embedded. The first example considers expressions of romantic love by Filipina women married to Japanese men in rural Japan (Faier 2007, 2009), and the second example considers the rejection of romantic love by ex-Soviet women in Istanbul (Bloch 2011). In both cases, the women's emotional lives are embedded in state control and visa regimes as well as media discourses about them, about intercultural romance and about romance in general. Both researchers also write in a context where migrant women who engage in sexual relationships with local men are both demonised as threats to tradition and propriety as well as seen predominantly as victims of human trafficking and global sexual exploitation.

When Filipina women married to Japanese men in Kiso in rural Japan get together, they often profess their love for their husband to each other as Lieba Faier observed in her fieldwork. The following incident is typical:

Malou [one of the Filipina women] rarely spoke English, but that evening she announced with characteristic drama, 'My husband is the best!' She then drew her arms to her chest in a sweeping gesture and continued, 'I love my husband! I love-love-love my husband!' Chuckling at Malou's performance, the other woman confirmed

this: Yes, Malou loved her husband. He was the best. She was
lucky. (Faier 2007: 156)

Performances such as these were part of these women's ways of doing
intercultural love and making sense of their global lives. To begin with,
public professions of love had been inculcated in the women before they
departed the Philippines for Japan to work as entertainers in hostess bars.
It is the key role of a hostess to do 'being loving' and to help male customers have a good time. As their remuneration there is mostly commission
based, they had a strong financial incentive to act in a loving manner, to
do 'being loving'. As almost all of the women in Faier's research had met
their future husbands while they worked in a hostess bar, their training
and work experience had turned the public performance of love and the
display of affection into something like second nature for these women.
They drew on cultural stereotypes of Filipinas as more romantic, loving
and caring than women of any other nationality, particularly Japanese
women, in order to naturalise the performances of love they engaged
in. These cultural stereotypes enabled their performances of love in the
hostess bar and their professions of love for their husbands to be much
more than artifice. Indeed, all the women rejected artifice or deception
as immoral. Perceptions of them as 'cheap' women, their association in
the public mind – both in Japan and the Philippines – with prostitution,
and widespread assumptions that they had only married a Japanese man
for financial gain presented daily challenges to these women. One way to
overcome, or at least challenge, such negative stereotyping was by telling
stories of love at first sight and making public professions of love. Despite
these strong incentives to perform love – for financial gain, to maintain
respectability, as a challenge to negative stereotypes – it would be wrong to
assume that all husbands inspired such love.

> Love was linked to a man's ability to financially and emotionally
> support his wife; to the small, daily kindnesses he showed her; and
> perhaps, above all, to the degree to which he supported her desire
> to send money to, and visit, her family abroad. Thus, when women
> asserted that they loved their husbands, they gestured to forms of
> intimacy and subjectivity that enabled the transnationalities of their
> lives. They suggested that love was not only a product of their
> migration to Japan but also of their ability to maintain their ties to
> the Philippines. (Faier 2007: 157)

Like the Filipina women Faier met in rural Japan, the ex-Soviet women
Alexia Bloch met in Istanbul had left their homes due to the collapse of

local economies in the wake of the insertion of the former Soviet Union into the global capitalist economy. Their encounters with local Turkish men also occurred against state pressures and visa regimes. The Filipina women had entered Japan on six-month entertainer visas and unless they married that category was their only visa option, inevitably pressuring them to consider marriage to a Japanese national. Often, ex-Soviet women come to Turkey on one- or two-month tourist visas and then overstay. While they have more possibilities to re-enter Turkey if deported than Filipinas have to re-enter Japan, their status is inevitably precarious and for them, too, marriage to a Turkish national is the only means of regularising their status. However, while the social and economic backgrounds to their migrations may be similar, their emotional experience is quite different, not least because the gender and sexual stereotypes against which Russian-speaking women from the former Soviet Republics and Turkish men meet are quite different from those against which Filipina women and Japanese men meet. Ex-Soviet women and Turkish men rarely enter into genuine marriages but rather into relationships where an ex-Soviet woman becomes the mistress or 'kept woman' of a Turkish 'patron'. Part of the arrangement of 'keeping a woman' may include arranging and paying for a fake marriage between her and someone else, though. From the perspective of Turkish men, marriage is impossible because they are mostly older and are already married to a woman who is the mother of their children. Marriage is not desirable, either, because it would mean divorce from their current wife and a concomitant loss of respectability. By contrast, keeping a mistress is traditionally sanctioned and actually brings an increase in male status. Furthermore, as local Turkish women are unlikely to be available as mistresses, ex-Soviet women make desirable mistresses, particularly as they are constructed as 'beautiful, smart, caring and without complexes around sex', as one Turkish man said (quoted in Bloch 2011: 5). Such stereotyping of Russian women has a long tradition in Turkey and goes back as far as the early palace harems of the Ottoman Empire in the thirteenth century. From the perspective of the women, too, a mistress relationship is deemed more desirable as it allows them to 'keep their freedom', not 'sell out' to a man as a wife does to her husband, and it leaves them in a better negotiating position when it comes to the financial benefits of the relationship. As was the case for the Filipina women, supporting their families back home was of paramount importance to the women in Bloch's study and the desirability of a potential partner was closely related to his ability and willingness to provide such support. The women's emotional experience of love in this transnational context is embedded in these social and economic inequalities as well as in the gendered and sexualised discourses of the cultural other I have just described. One woman described the love she feels for her Turkish partner as follows: 'He is like my brother, father and boyfriend, all in one; this is much more than I could ever have imagined, and it is what I needed living in this foreign country, all alone with no family or anything' (quoted in Bloch 2011: 2).

As these two case studies demonstrate, love and romance in transnational contexts are not universal emotions but are discursively constructed in specific material and cultural contexts. The material contexts are those of gendered global inequalities and the cultural contexts are those of discourses of the other that, too, are gendered. In both contexts, the construction of love and romance is predicated upon gendered flows of people and discourses to make love go around on a global circuit.

MAIL-ORDER BRIDE WEBSITES

Nowhere is the metaphor of the global circuit of love more apparent than in the discourse of mail-order bride websites. Kojima (2001) analyses the mail-order bride industry as a system for the global division of reproductive labour. Women in industrialised countries have been successful on an individual level in freeing themselves from the imperative to marry and have children, but they have not succeeded in changing the underlying system of capitalism and patriarchy that depends upon gendered unpaid work for social and human reproduction. Consequently, the gap is being filled by migrant wives and mothers. The mail-order bride industry is starkly gendered and cultured: men from the global north go on 'romance tours' to choose an overseas bride, while women from the global south migrate to join their overseas husbands and take up residency with them. A 'romance tour' is a form of package tourism where a mail-order bride agency organises for a client to meet a number of available women in a given destination with the aim of marriage. The package typically includes airfare and accommodation, arranged meetings with individual women or parties with a number of women, marriage contracts and legal assistance, and wedding arrangements. Instead of or in addition to individual introductions, agencies also organise 'socials' for the men to attend along with a number of local women seeking marriage.

The modern mail-order bride industry began in the early 1970s with personal ads and printed mail-order catalogues (O'Rourke 2002). However, it was only with the spread of Internet access that the industry started to boom. The genre of the personal ad has changed dramatically with the new medium. Personal ads are no longer a minimalist genre where the advertiser has to be concise because they are paying per word or even per letter as used to be the case with the print medium (Bruthiaux 1996). Web-based

personal ads typically include a closed list of attributes (age, physical meas-
urements, ethnicity, religion, smoking status, and so on) plus a photo, and
two or more open-ended sections where the advertiser can describe themselves and their desired other. Nor do prospective partners have to rely
solely on the personal ad as most dating sites now also offer instantaneous
chat facilities. Sites either operate a membership system (where the men
pay for access to the data of all the women advertising on a site) or allow
the client to purchase the contact details of the women they are interested
in on a case-by-case basis. The latter facility is called 'add to shopping cart'
on some sites (Piller 2007). The liberalisation of the telephone market and
the emergence of Internet-based communication services have also meant
that even the frequent and long international telephone calls necessary to
conduct a romantic relationship have become widely affordable.

While mail-order bride sites have a poor reputation and sometimes
function as shopfronts for organised crime, women are quite savvy in using
the medium. An ethnography of Chinese and Filipina women engaged
in correspondence relationships with American men, for instance, found
them to be making careful and informed choices, even if broader social
and economic constraints may limit those choices (Constable 2003). The
choices that are available on mail-order bride websites are discursively constructed within a system of gendered and cultured identity options, which
is basically populated by four character types (Piller 2007). First, there
are 'Western men' who seek women from elsewhere. These men are the
principal characters of mail-order bride websites, together with the second
type, non-Western women. Non-Western women are usually referred to
with a specific nationality term ('Filipina', 'Thai', 'Colombian', 'Russian',
and so on). The third identity option is that of 'Western women', who are
not agents on these sites but objects of dissatisfaction for Western men
and the foil against which non-Western women shine. The fourth identity
option that is available in this system is reserved for non-Western men.
These hardly figure, but if they do they are discounted as 'men here' who
are problematic for various reasons.

Let's examine these four identity options which emerge on mail-order
bride websites in some more detail by drawing on the concept of 'member
categorisations'. The term member categorisation comes from ethnometh-
odolgy, an approach to sociology that takes a bottom-up approach to
understanding social organisation by basing analyses of social life on the
social terms in use in a group for members and outsiders instead of more
abstract social categories taken from social theory (Francis and Hester
2004). For instance, one website has the following slogan: 'Western Man
+ Filipina = Happiness. You do not have to be good with Algebra to know
that is a winning equation!!'[3] The categories 'Western man' and 'Filipina'

are member categorisations used on the site and thus can be assumed to be meaningful to the users of the site. The example also provides evidence for the fact that users of this website (be they 'Western men' or 'Filipinas') approach each other (initially) in cultural categories, that is as representatives of their respective cultures. 'Western men' on these sites look for a partner from abroad because of their dissatisfaction with 'Western women':

> We, as men, are more and more wanting to step back from the types of women we meet now. With many women taking on the 'me first' feminist agenda and the man continuing to take a back seat to her desire for power and control many men are turned off by this and look back to having a more traditional woman as our partner.

Negative representations of 'Western women' are pervasive on these websites and their frequency testifies to the fact that the writers see endogamy as the norm, and feel they need to justify their search for a foreign partner. 'Western women' are represented as selfish, aggressive and materialistic. Statements such as this one abound:

> I know many of you are tired of the U.S. or Canadian singles scene like I was. You know . . . insincere girls who like to play games or expect constant material gifts. But these Asian ladies are honest, faithful, rarely lose their figures as they age, are extremely supportive, and care more about your heart than your wallet. [. . .] Don't settle for a demanding and unappreciative woman. The age of the internet has opened up a whole new world of opportunity. It's time you meet the woman you truly deserve! Life is too short to settle for a '6' when you can have a '10'!

Much of what is said about 'Western women' is said by implication, through contrasting them, implicitly or explicitly, with women from elsewhere, as in 'they rarely lose their figures as they age', which implies that Western women do. By contrast, 'Filipinas', 'Russian women', 'Thai women' or women of any other non-Western nationality that a website may be devoted to are constructed as everything that 'Western women' are not, or are no longer. They are the ideal of conventional femininity: beautiful, petite, devoted, religious, obedient, submissive and sexy. Previous research has shown that orientalist images dominate the images of Asian women in the West, and particularly in the USA (Uchida 1998). The image of Asian women is dominated by the 'Madame Butterfly', or, more recently, the 'Miss Saigon' stereotype, which portrays Asian women as exotic, sexually available, submissive, obedient, domestic, sweet and passive. Generalisations about Filipinas found in an analysis of six different mail-order bride websites largely coincided with these stereotypes (Mooring 2004). The following example is typical:

> Why choose a Filipina? Women from the Philippines are noted for their beauty, grace, charm and loyalty. With their sweet nature and shy smiles, Filipina ladies possess an inner beauty that most men find irresistible. Filipina women are by their nature family-orientated, resourceful and devoted. What's more, English is one of the official languages of the Philippines, so communication is straightforward, and as the majority of Filipina ladies are Christian, cultural compatibility is easier than some other Asian countries.

While this excerpt is from a site devoted to Filipina women, the stereotypes of traditional femininity are surprisingly similar on websites for all kinds of nationalities and the attributes are often virtually identical. This leads to the need to insert a 'unique selling proposition' into the stereotypes so as to defend the 'Filipina brand' against competitors from other nations. The strongest 'selling points' of Filipina women vis-à-vis other Asian women, for instance, are their ability in English and their Christianity, although some examples such as this one go even further:

> We are different from most Asian cultures. We are loyal to family unit more than country. We are comfortable loving and marrying men of other race, while most Asians 'lose face' if marry outside their own culture. [. . .] Marry a Filipina, and you not have to eat with chopsticks or bow all time.

The same competition can be observed on Russian mail-order bride websites, where Russian women are positioned vis-à-vis Asian women: 'Western men see Russian women as more mature and usually more educated than their Asian counterparts.' However, their main competitive edge seems to be their race: Russian women are similarly exoticised as Asian women, but they have the added bonus of being white: they 'have a European face but the patience of an Asian'. In sum, 'here are exotic white women who know their place' as an Australian newspaper article put it a few years ago (Phelan 2000).

A niggling problem in these discourses of the gendered cultural self and other is of course the fact that there must be a marriage market in the Philippines or in Russia, too. Therefore, the men in the women's home country are frequently denigrated as emasculated losers as in this example:

The ladies we feature are not 'just trying to get to the USA', they are looking for a responsible life-mate – very difficult to find in modern Russian society. Most Russian men age 30–50 have a very hard time adjusting to a free-trade economy. Because of the sharp increase in regional wars, alcoholism, smoking, stress and suicide the media reports average life expectancy of Russian male to be 54, whereas female life expectancy is well into the 70. There are currently over 20 million more females then males living in the territory of the former USSR.

In sum, the gendered culturist discourses of mail-order bride websites displace inequality onto culture. Economic globalisation and its attendant neoliberal ideologies of the free market have widened rather than narrowed the gap between rich and poor on this globe. At the same time that the economic pressures on families in the global south increase, the global media bring images of consumerism to almost every household in the world, in a kind a 'material striptease' (Ehrenreich and Hochschild 2002). One of the consequences of neoliberal economic regimes in conjunction with the iconisation of consumerism is an increase in international work migration, particularly of women. Female work migrants perform typical 'women's work', that is, reproductive work such as domestic work, child care and elder care, sex work, including the prototypical combination of all these, namely being a wife. What used to be a gender divide – domestic work – is being replaced by a class and race divide that is also gendered, or to put it differently, the emotional, sexual and reproductive labour of being a wife is being outsourced from the global north to the global south in the same way that the production of sneakers, plastic toys and computer chips has been outsourced. However, the very nature of our conceptions of romantic and intimate relationships entails that they not be recognised as work, that is, the work is invisible (Oakley 1974). The current boom in mail-order brides is thus based on material global inequalities but in order to 'work' as an illusion of romantic love it needs to be cloaked in cultural terms.

KEY POINTS

This chapter made the following key points:

- The intercultural has become deeply embedded in emotional experiences of love, romance, marriage and sexuality as discourses of the cultural other construct desires in a globalised world.

- Love, romance, marriage and sexuality are deeply social experiences and differ across cultures. The challenge today is to understand and explore not only the diversity of human emotional experience, but also human emotional experience as an object in motion on the global circuits of love.
- Intercultural romance is predicated upon discourses of the cultural other which make the cultural other desirable at the same time that they are founded in gendered global material inequalities.
- Mail-order bride websites are important sites on which intercultural love and romance are constructed and kept in circulation.

COUNTERPOINT

Intercultural love and romance are embedded in cultural discourses of the self and other that produce intercultural desires. Particularly, when people from different cultural backgrounds first meet they may see each other partly through the lens of national, cultural or ethnic stereotypes. At the same time, discourses of contemporary love are deeply individual and often predicated on the idea of meeting the uniquely right person. This chapter has shown how these tensions are managed by a range of people in a range of discourses and in a wide variety of global contexts. Can you observe these tensions in your own life? How do you manage them?

FURTHER READING

Every student of intercultural communication should have read Edward Said's (1978) foundational work *Orientalism*. There are many fascinating ethnographies of the transnational circuits of love and romance and Constable (2003) and Faier (2009) are particularly relevant to the discussions of this chapter.

ACTIVITIES

Intimate outsourcing

Discuss the metaphor of 'intimate outsourcing'. What are the strengths of the metaphor? How does it enhance our understanding of the global circuits of love? What are its weaknesses? What does it hide and obscure? Read sociologist Arlie Russell Hochschild's (2012b) examination of *The Outsourced Self* to take your debate further.

Mail-order bride websites

Choose five to ten mail-order bride websites designed to advertise for women of a particular national background and analyse their mission statements for gendered and cultured discourses. Are the four membership categories discussed above ('Western men', 'Western women', 'Filipinas/Russian/Thai women' and so on, 'non-Western men') also in evidence? Are there others? What are the attributes of the membership categories? How are their relationships discursively constructed?

Intercultural personal ads

Collect a corpus of personal ads of men or women who advertise on a mail-order bride website. How do they deploy culture to portray themselves and the desired other? For a more substantial research project, use the same analytic categories as R. H. Jones (2000) and relate the context-specific nature of your findings to those of that analysis.

NOTES

1. English translation from http://lyricstranslate.com/en/ich-will-nen-cowboy-als-mann-i-want-cowboy-husband.html
2. All names of research participants, both in the research of others and in my own, are pseudonyms.
3. All quotes from mail-order bride websites in this section are taken from Piller (2007).

CHAPTER 10

Intercultural Communication in Education

CHAPTER OBJECTIVES

This chapter will enable you to:

- Examine critically how 'culture' comes to hide socio-economic status as an explanation for social inequality.
- Understand how cultural stereotyping mediates student academic outcomes through teacher expectations.
- Explore how students from hybrid, complex or 'atypical' backgrounds are disadvantaged in homogenising school systems.
- Evaluate positive educational approaches aimed at supporting students' cultural and linguistic diversity.

CONFLATING CLASS AND CULTURE

In Chapter 4, I introduced the term 'hidden curriculum' to refer to the things we learn in school although they are not explicitly taught. One of the central contents of the hidden curriculum the world over – and one that may even be explicitly denied in the 'published' curriculum – is that society is organised as a meritocracy: people who are smart and talented, who work hard and are willing to take risks will get ahead in life and they deserve their good fortune because they have earned it. On the other hand, there are people who are not so smart, who are lazy, who do not put in enough effort and lack enterprise. These people will not get far in life, they may end up mired in poverty, as teenage single mums and even engaging in crime. These people, too, deserve their lot in life because of their lack of effort. So the theory goes; but there is one problem with this key message of

the hidden curriculum: it is patently not true and far fewer people 'make it
to the top' than are left behind and, in particular, members of some groups
are much more likely to get ahead than others. This is where another
message of the hidden curriculum comes in: instead of learning that we
live in an unequal socio-economic order that is hierarchically shaped and
has far fewer spots on the top than at the bottom, and that class position
largely determines our chances in life, we learn to see 'culture' as the prime
reason why some groups fare so much worse than others.

Let's examine the conflation of class and culture with a case study of
the schooling of migrant children during the Great Depression era in the
US West Coast states (Theobald and Donato 1990). The authors, Paul
Theobald and Rubén Donato, tell a fascinating tale of the manipulation of
schooling as an efficient way to perpetuate class relationships. By comparing two groups of rural migrants they offer an illuminating analysis of the
intersections of class and 'culture'. The two groups are external migrants
from Mexico and internal migrants from the dust bowl of the Great
Plains' states. One of those states engulfed by disaster during the period
was Oklahoma and the latter group therefore came to be collectively
known by the disparaging term 'Okies'. The plight of these early environmental refugees is epitomised in the story of the fictional Joad family in
John Steinbeck's novel *The Grapes of Wrath* (1939).[1]

In California, schooling for Mexicans had developed in the nineteenth
century in a way that systematically segregated Mexican children, even if
Mexicans were not included in the legal provisions for segregation that
applied to Asians, blacks and Native Americans. In 1920, for instance,
eighty per cent of all Mexican children attended separate 'Mexican
schools' or 'Mexican classrooms'. The justification for segregation was that
Mexican students were 'problem students': they were stereotyped as slow
learners with a language problem and un-American habits and values.
Their racial status was also frequently debated and there were a number of
efforts to have Mexicans classified as 'Indian', which would have legalised
their segregation. Efforts to legalise the segregation of Mexicans were never
successful and so their segregation was achieved through other means such
as the construction of 'Mexican' schools, the gerrymandering of school
attendance zones and internal segregation through tracking. Segregation
coupled with the irregular attendance of families who were seasonal agricultural workers resulted in very early drop-out, and most Mexican children left school without having learnt how to read and write.

In the early 1930s around 250,000 Mexicans, including US citizens,
were deported to Mexico. This created a labour void, which desperate dust
bowl migrants were eager to fill. Like Mexicans, 'Okies' were despised in
California because of their poverty and the burden they were seen to place

on the taxpayer. In contrast to Mexicans, there was no readily-available ideology that would justify their segregation: they were white and English-speaking. 'Okies' disrupted the logic of agricultural work and segregation in California because here were white Americans doing 'non-white work'. This meant that the 'inferiority' of agricultural workers could no longer be used to justify their low wages and abominable working conditions. Theoretically, there were two options to deal with this dilemma:

> Either the conditions and circumstances of agricultural labour would have to improve to meet white standards, or the Okies would have to be shown to be as inferior as Mexican migrants. Regrettably, there was (and is) no place like school for defining inferiority. (Theobald and Donato 1990: 34)

Although race and language were not available as rationales for segregation, the low quality of schooling in Arkansas, Oklahoma and Texas, the states from where these internal migrants came, was. A 1939 survey found that ten per cent of 'Okie' migrant children were as much as four years behind their non-mobile Californian peers. Another twenty per cent were three years behind and forty per cent were two years behind. As a result, school authorities felt compelled to institute 'special' classes for 'Okie' children. The result of segregation was the same as it was for Mexican children: poor attendance, early drop-out and dismal outcomes. A contemporary account explains the inferiority complex schooling instilled in 'Okie' children:

> Year by year, as they grow older, the embarrassment of their ignorance increases; held back sometimes four and five grades, when they enter new schools tall youths of 13 are out of place in classes with small-fry of 7. Bashful at their own backwardness and ashamed of their clothes or 'foreign' accent, they stand out as easy targets for the venomed barbs of their richer and settled schoolmates. 'He's from the country camp, that's what they said of my child on the school ground. Don't you see how it hurts?' one transient mother explained. (Quoted in Theobald and Donato 1990: 35)

That the low quality of schooling in Arkansas, Oklahoma and Texas was nothing but a pretext for segregation is most apparent from the experience of children from the states of the Northern Plains. Dust bowl migrants from the Dakotas predominantly entered Oregon and Washington. These two states had no history of segregation because agriculture was not yet industrialised and therefore there were few Mexican (or other non-white) agricultural workers. Furthermore, the schooling system in the Dakotas was superior to that of Oregon and Washington. Even so, segregated schooling for 'Okie' children developed in the Pacific Northwest, too. Theobald and Donato (1990) conclude that schooling during the period was designed to perpetuate the subordination of agricultural labour. When 'language' and 'culture' fell away as means to legitimise the processing of Mexican children into cheap labour, other legitimation strategies such as 'educational backwardness' were found. It is also worth noting that the animosity towards Mexicans and 'Okies' during the Great Depression was justified by their poverty, by the fact that they were a drain on the public purse. However, the segregated schooling instituted for these two groups was a more expensive educational option than integration would have been. Segregation involved the provision of separate buildings and the hiring of extra teachers. The pay-off for this investment was a docile labour force:

> If the maintenance of a docile, inexpensive labour system required social distance between the children of property owners and the children of harvest labourers, then a slightly inflated budget at the local school was, seemingly, a small price to pay. (Theobald and Donato 1990: 36)

It is also instructive to consider what happened after the Great Depression and World War II: 'Okies' were integrated into the mainstream and took up jobs in production and industry. In fact, today even the term 'Okie' itself has disappeared as a social category. By contrast, Mexicans were forced back into agriculture, and segregated schooling for Mexicans continued into the 1960s. The class position of 'Okies' took precedence over white privilege during a time of economic crisis. However, when the crisis was over, 'Okies' were not barred from class mobility in the same way that Mexicans were. This means that class, in the USA as elsewhere, is most restrictive when it is overlaps with a stigmatised 'race', 'ethnicity' or 'culture'. But in whichever way class is circumscribed, schooling plays a crucial role in legitimising class inequality because the basic principles of school finance, educational objectives and student evaluation are defined by those in power.

One of the rationales for segregating Mexican and 'Okie' children in Californian schools in the first-half of the twentieth century was their supposed backwardness. The idea that some ethnic, racial or cultural groups are smarter than others has not gone away and, in fact, this particular research agenda has attracted renewed attention in recent years. The idea that different ethnic, racial or cultural groups have different cognitive abilities makes sense to some people because embodied differences are often closely matched to different stations in life: in Sydney, for instance, some of the most affluent suburbs are mostly inhabited by white and Asian people while some well-known problem neighbourhoods are mostly inhabited by migrants from the Middle East.[2] However, seeing a connection between 'culture' and cognitive ability is a correlational fallacy that can be fully explained by socio-economic status, as a German study of the cognitive and linguistic abilities of 1,008 pre-schoolers in five different groups demonstrates (Becker 2011). Children in the first group had parents and grandparents who were all born in Germany (the 'native' group). Children in the second group had parents who were both born in Turkey (the 'second generation'). Children in the third group had parents who were both born in Germany but each parent had at least one parent born in Turkey (the 'third generation'). Children in the fourth group had one first-generation and one second-generation Turkish parent (the '2A generation'). Finally, children in the fifth group had one 'native' parent and one first- or second-generation Turkish parent (the 'intermarried' group). The researcher found that the children from the intermarried group outperformed all the other groups on a test of cognitive ability, including the natives. She also found that, with the exception of the intermarried group, all the other 'Turkish' groups performed significantly lower than the 'native' group. Children in the '2A group' – with one first-generation and one second-generation Turkish parent – performed particularly poorly.[3]

These results might, at first blush, seem to provide evidence for a link between 'culture' and cognitive ability. However, once parents' socio-economic status (as measured by their level of education and their occupational status) and educational resources (as measured by the number of books in the home; the frequency of bedtime stories; or the number of visits to the zoo) are controlled, the ethnic differences disappear and the difference between the five groups is reduced to non-significance: 'All group differences regarding children's cognitive skills can be fully explained by families' socioeconomic status and educational resources' (Becker 2011: 447). What seems like an ethnic effect ('children of intermarried couples are smarter' or 'German children are smarter than Turkish children') is, in fact, an effect of socio-economic status and educational resources; in other words, a class effect. However, class maps onto ethnicity, in this case, as elsewhere. The vast majority of Turkish families in the sample, which can be assumed to be representative of Turks in Germany, are poorly educated, work in low-status occupations and have few educational resources at their disposal.

As far as the two 'mixed' groups – '2A' and 'intermarried' – are concerned, a process of negative and positive selection respectively can be assumed to apply. Having a first-generation mother and a second-generation father constitutes some sort of 'double jeopardy' for the child: the mother is much less likely to speak German even than first-generation women married to first-generation men; and the father is even less likely to have completed secondary education than other Turkish second-generation men. As the researcher explains, second-generation men who 'import' brides from the country of origin are likely to be negatively selected on various dimensions, and their 'imported' brides will lack knowledge and resources that are useful to raising a child in the destination country. By contrast, a process of positive selection works in favour of a child with a native and a migrant parent. Not only will the native parent 'automatically' have country-specific knowledge and resources but the migrant parent is likely to be positively selected with regard to level of education, proficiency in German, and general 'openness' and 'integration.' This is particularly true in the case of German-Turkish intermarriages, which are comparatively rare and only account for five per cent of all marriages of first- and second-generation Turks in Germany. In this case intermarriage is an expression of parental cosmopolitanism (see also Chapter 9) and is beneficial for children. Not because there is any intrinsic value in intermarriage but because that is how educational reproduction works: well-educated parents with stable jobs, parents who read to their children and who engage in a wide range of family activities confer an advantage on their children. It is just that the advantages – as well as the injuries – of class are increasingly mapped onto ethnicity, race or 'culture'.

TEACHER EXPECTATIONS

If a group is subject to negative stereotyping a further cultural effect is produced through teacher expectations. Teacher expectations produce self-fulfilling prophecies in student performance: high teacher expectations result in students' higher academic performance and low teacher expectations result in students' lower academic performance. The ways in which teachers treat students affect students' self-concept, motivation, achievement and aspirations. Over time, the performance of high-expectation students will increase and the performance of low-expectation students will decline, until student performance and behaviour closely conforms to what was expected of them in the first place (Rist 2015). The positive effect of teacher expectations on student performance is called the 'Pygmalion effect' and the negative effect is called the 'Golem effect'. Evidence for a Golem effect in teaching was first provided in a 1982 Israeli study, which found 'low-expectancy students of high-bias teachers receiving a more negative treatment and performing less well than any of their peers' (Babad, Inbar and Rosenthal 1982: 473). The transformation of teacher expectations into student academic performance works through four factors, as Robert Rosenthal and Lenore Jacobson explain in their classic *Pygmalion in the Classroom* (1968).

- Climate: Teachers are nicer to students of whom they have high expectations and create a warmer climate for them.
- Input: Teachers teach more material to students of whom they have high expectations.
- Response opportunity: Teachers provide more response opportunities to students of whom they have high expectations and help them shape the answer.
- Feedback: Teachers praise students of whom they have high expectations more and provide them with more detailed and constructive feedback when they get their answer wrong.

In the original study of the Pygmalion effect, Rosenthal and Jacobson (1968) created a positive expectation in teachers by telling them at the beginning of the school year that five randomly selected children in their class had done extraordinarily well on a predictive test of academic aptitude and could therefore be expected to become 'late bloomers' over the course of the year. Once the expectation of high performance had been implanted in the teachers' minds, it turned out that, within the school year, these five randomly selected kids achieved the greatest gains in academic performance in the class, providing clear evidence for a Pygmalion effect.

Ethical experimental research designs to investigate the Golem effect are much more difficult to come up with. Babad et al. (1982) had circumvented the ethical problem by studying teacher trainees who made a one-off assessment that had no consequence for the way other teachers assessed the students or the way in which the students' overall performance was assessed. Beyond artificially inducing high or low expectations of academic talent, the implications of the Pygmalion and Golem effects in diverse schools are clear for students from backgrounds about which group stereotypes exist: if there is a widespread belief in a society that 'native' children have higher academic potential than 'migrant' children, many teachers will share those beliefs; and, by treating 'native' and 'migrant' children differently, they will contribute to the self-fulfilling prophecy that actually turns the belief into a reality.

Evidence that teachers have lower expectations of minority children is not hard to find. A recent Belgian study, for instance, found that three-quarters of all surveyed 674 teachers believed that there was no place for languages other than Dutch in schools in Flanders and that children who spoke a language other than Dutch at home were likely to be poor academic performers (Pulinx, Van Avermaet and Agirdag 2015). Another British study poignantly illustrates the effects of low teacher expectations and shows how formal education can serve to limit, rather than expand, opportunities for teenage migrants (M. Cooke 2008). The researcher, Melanie Cooke, followed three teenage migrants in London schools over a period of six months and observed a pronounced mismatch between their own aspirations and the expectations their teachers had of them. At the time of the research, the three boys were sixteen and seventeen years old. We meet Felek, an unaccompanied refugee from Iraqi Kurdistan, whose family had pooled their resources to smuggle him out of Iraq and across Europe almost two years earlier. We meet Carlos, an asylum seeker from Angola, who had arrived in London with his family about a year earlier. And we meet Santos, a Portuguese national, whose parents are from Angola and Cabo Verde, and who had come to London to live with his grandmother. All three boys are described as having high aspirations: first, they want to learn English and find a place in London where they fit in; something that seems impossibly difficulty to achieve. They are disappointed with the slow progress of their English language development, and they are struggling with the fact that, in the one to two years they have been in London, they have not been able to make a single local friend. Felek has met other Kurds and also spends time with other young asylum seekers from Albania and Somalia. The friendship networks of Carlos and Santos are exclusively with other Portuguese speakers. While they are keen to make friends and find a place where they 'fit', they are frequently harassed by local youths, and conflict and fights are a regular part of their experience.

All three boys had high expectations of their future, and all three saw themselves as studious and academic. Felek, for instance, dreamt of becoming an engineer or a doctor to give back to his family and homeland. However, none of the three had received any guidance regarding educational pathways and, other than 'studying hard', had only the vaguest ideas of how their dreams might be achieved. In short, Felek, Carlos and Santos saw themselves as fundamentally 'good boys', who had been through a lot already, who saw migration to the UK as an opportunity, and who wanted to make the most of this opportunity to further their careers and to make a contribution to society. Unfortunately, that was not how educational policy makers and their teachers saw them.

As regards educational policy, as teenage arrivals they simply fall between the cracks of the educational system. While new arrivals up to the age of 16 years are sent to mainstream schools in the UK, arrivals above this

age are treated as adults and are offered English-language classes designed for adults, from all kinds of backgrounds, who lack basic vocational skills. The classes are designed to teach numeracy, literacy and English to allow graduates to transfer into a vocational course and to become 'job-ready'. Other than English-language training, no pathway that would continue their secondary education is available to them because no one ever seems to have envisaged that teenage migrants might have educational aspirations.

As regards their teachers, they knew next to nothing about their students' life outside the classroom and so drew on stereotypes about Middle Eastern and black male adolescents in their interactions with their students: they saw them as ignorant young men who lacked discipline and who had no past and no future. As one teacher put it: 'they come to this country . . . they get off the plane and they have no idea . . . about anything' (quoted in M. Cooke 2008: 32). The teachers, both of whom were middle-class women, one British Asian and the other white British, in particular reacted to what they saw as the boys' sexism. Carlos and Santos, for instance, had both been banned from interacting with younger girls in the mainstream school to which their English-language programme was attached. Supposedly, this was because the boys had been causing trouble. However, Carlos' and Santos' explanation of the event that led to their ban was quite different: in their account, another young boy, who was also a recent arrival from Angola, one day had gone to school wearing girls' pants. According to Carlos, this is what happened next:

> So those girls noticed he had women's trousers. So they started teasing him. He doesn't speak English very well . . . so the only thing he did was answer back, and because we were in the middle, they blamed us all. And they said if you do anything more, they will throw us out of school. (Quoted in M. Cooke 2008: 29)

This innocuous story contrasts with the teacher's view of Carlos as a 'gangster rapper' and 'the naughtiest of the naughty'. One way to control the boys and to keep at bay the dreaded 'gangster' that the teachers believe to be lurking inside the boys is through sticking strictly to the curriculum and through controlling classroom interactions in minute detail. As a result, valuable opportunities for the boys to find their voice in English were lost. For instance, Felek's class at one point read a text about the refugee journey of an Afghan boy. It was a story that not only Felek but most of the students in the class could relate to well, and some had, in fact, watched a TV show about asylum only the night before. Therefore, they were keen to talk about the text and discuss it. However, the teacher stifled these attempts at discussion and stuck to her lesson plan, which treated the text only as a basis for comprehension exercises, new vocabulary practice, reading aloud, and as a gap-fill exercise. The researcher concludes that school is not a good place for Felek, Carlos and Santos:

> [T]he learners described in this article are, educationally speaking, getting the worst of all worlds, despite the intentions of their teachers. A large part of the blame for this must be laid at the door of policy makers who fail to address ESOL [= English for speakers of other languages] teenagers as whole people with transnational, diasporic complexities and aspirations and who regard teachers as technicians. Blame might also be laid at the door of teacher education, which fails to envisage the potential of education as an arena for social transformation or to encourage teachers to develop as 'transformative intellectuals'. (M. Cooke 2008: 37)

As Western societies are struggling to comprehend why so many young men from immigrant backgrounds are turning 'bad', Cooke's research offers a glimpse of how such large social processes play out in everyday interactions: how students become not what they hope to become but what others expect them to become.

The ways in which cultural stereotypes may shape even minute details of classroom interactions is further demonstrated in Australian research with Japanese university students (Nakane 2007b). Attracting sizable cohorts of international students, particularly from Asia, Australian universities have become sites of intense intercultural interactions in recent decades. In this context, Asian students in general and Japanese students in particular are often stereotyped as being shy and silent. Indeed, when the researcher, Ikuko Nakane, interviewed Japanese overseas students in Australia about their experiences of intercultural communication in the classroom, many of them mentioned that they were afraid to speak up because they lacked confidence in their English. They also said that they did not quite understand the conventions of classroom discussions and thus found it hard to get the timing right: either they did not know when to get their contribution in or they found that their turns were interrupted by more vocal, often local Australian, students. As often they did not know what the expectations of a particular format – such as lecture, tutorial, small group or open class discussion, or student presentation – were, they mostly thought it safer to keep silent than to speak at the wrong moment or say the wrong thing. So, the silence of those Japanese students had very little to do with Japanese cultural traits. It is true that some were intentionally silent because they thought it was inappropriate for a student to challenge their lecturer, for instance. However, most of them expressed a desire to speak more. What kept them from engaging was not Japanese culture but a lack of confidence in their English and limited understanding of Australian university classroom formats. Furthermore, silence was not only something they did ('being silent') but also something that happened to them ('being silenced') when their peers kept interrupting, when their lecturers did not allow time for them to speak up, or when the conversation turned to local topics about which they knew nothing. In this environment, the silence and shyness of Japanese students was a cultural stereotype and a truism that was constantly reinforced through the misinterpretation of actual classroom practices involving everyone in those classrooms, not only the relatively small number of Japanese students.

In addition to interviewing students and lecturers, the research design also involved video-recording a number of units of study in order to gain an understanding not only of what students and teachers said about intercultural communication but also of how they actually did intercultural communication. To account for both perception ('what people think they do') and performance ('what people actually do') is important because our perceptions are not always right, as we learnt in Chapter 6. Sociolinguists like to compare self-reports about language usage to the weather forecast: sometimes it is right and sometimes it is wrong. At the same time, perception informs performance and vice versa. One of the overseas students from Japan in some of the classes recorded by the researcher was a young woman named Aya. Aya was different from most of the other Japanese students in the way she frequently sought out speaking opportunities – indeed, she was the second-most frequent contributor in her classes. With 5.8 seconds, the average length of her turns was very similar to the class average of 6.1 seconds. However, the above-average frequency and average length of her contributions did not do anything to change her teachers' and her peers' perception of her as a 'very quiet' student lacking in interest and engagement. To add insult to injury – on top of not having been accurately observed in the first place – her 'silence' was misjudged not as an expression of limited English proficiency, lack of familiarity with Australian classroom routines or lack of familiarity with local topics, but rather as the stereotypical quality of a Japanese overseas student: of being a shy but also uninterested and disengaged student.

ERASING COMPLEXITY

Instead of engaging with their students as individuals, the educational policy makers and teachers we encountered above were guided by cultural stereotypes: Felek, Carlos and Santos became 'naughty black/Middle

Eastern gangsters' in their UK high school and Aya became a 'shy, silent and disengaged Japanese' in her Australian university. In reality, no one is a walking cultural stereotype, of course. However, schools – like most institutions – are set up to slot people into categories in order to function. Categorising necessarily involves an erasure of complexity, which may have detrimental consequences particularly for 'atypical' students. Such negative consequences may be felt most strongly by students with complex trajectories and hybrid experiences, as I will now illustrate with examples from research with Burmese students in a border high school in China (Li 2017) and with returnee students in schools in Albania (Vathi, Duci and Dhembo 2016).

The rise of China has led to a considerable inflow of international students into China, particularly from neighbouring countries. Against this background, Li Jia (2017) examines the experiences of high school students from Myanmar in a border high school in China's southwestern Yunnan province. The school in which the researcher conducted her fieldwork actively sought to attract students from Myanmar as part of China's soft power project. The educational opportunities offered by the school were particularly attractive to students from the border region rather than from more distant parts of Myanmar. These 'Burmese' students were predominantly ethnically Chinese or members of another minority ethnic group from the region such as Jingphaw, Lhaovo, Lisu or Shan. In fact, not a single one of the thirty plus participants in the study was a member of Myanmar's majority ethnic group, the Bamar. This meant that many of the 'Burmese' students had not actually learnt to read and write or even to speak Burmese. By contrast, many of the 'Burmese' students were native speakers of Chinese and, even if they were not ethnically Chinese, Chinese had loomed large in their lives and they had spent many years studying Chinese. Prior to their migration to China, the students, who used to be marginalised as ethnic minority members in government schools in Myanmar, saw Chinese as a way to empower themselves and they oriented their aspirations for the future towards China. However, this was not how the school saw them: the school saw them as 'Burmese' who had 'natural' Burmese proficiency but needed to be taught Chinese in order to become cultural mediators between the two countries. One 'Burmese' student described his hybrid identity and unexpected aspirations as follows:

> I used to ask my father whether I was Chinese or Burmese. My father said: 'You are Chinese and you are not Burmese'. [. . .] My mother wanted me to come to China to study so that I can be a Chinese and learn to write good Chinese scripts. (Quoted in Li 2017: 197)

While students aspired to an education that would make them more fully Chinese and allow them to settle in China, the school offered no such trajectory. Instead, all the pathways open to the students constructed them as returning to Myanmar, where they were imagined as future cross-cultural mediators. That schools are poorly equipped to deal with 'return' migrants with complex identities is further demonstrated in another study of border education in a region half a world away from Yunnan, namely the Greek-Albanian border region (Vathi et al. 2016). This research demonstrates that it is not only complex identities that schools find difficult but that there is a specific linguistic component to the erasure of complexity. As we saw in Chapter 3, our understanding of the role of language in social life suffers from a particularly intractable problem: that is, the terms we use to speak about language are not often very useful; on the contrary, they are confusing, obscurantist and create problems that we cannot even see because of our limited linguistic imagination. When schools fall prey to applying imaginary language labels to their students, the consequences are severely curtailed educational opportunities, as happened to the Burmese teenagers above and also to Albanian 'returnee' children to which I will now turn.

Albania is one of the poorest countries in Europe and is a country with a very high emigration rate (Barjaba and Barjaba 2015). The preferred international destination of Albanian emigrants is neighbouring Greece. However, as is well known, Greece was hit particularly hard by the 2008 global financial crisis. Within Greece, Albanian migrants were particularly vulnerable and around a quarter of adult Albanians returned from Greece to Albania in the period between 2009 and 2013 (134,544 out of around 600,000 Albanians in Greece). Many of these returnees had school-aged children who needed to transition from a school in Greece to one in Albania. Most of these children were Greek-dominant bilinguals with varying levels of proficiency in Albanian. However, the fact that they are ethnically Albanian means that they are expected to speak Albanian natively, in the same way that their monolingual peers who have only ever been schooled in Albania do. In other words, ethnicity obscures language proficiency.

As a result of this mismatch, the educational experiences of returnee students were mostly negative. Many reported that their language was often the object of ridicule, not only by their peers but even by their teachers. With the exception of a school in the border region which also catered to a local Greek minority, none of the schools in the study was prepared to cater for the specific linguistic needs of returnee students. Measures such as supplementary Albanian classes for this cohort were non-existent. While schools failed to recognise the specific linguistic needs of Greek-dominant bilingual students, they imagined (and addressed) another 'need' they thought returnee students had: they imagined that the returnee students were particularly in need of a patriotic education. The consequence of such well-intentioned efforts to support their 'Albanian-ness' constituted a further source of exclusion: in reality, many of the students missed Greece, considered themselves to have plural identities and had global rather than narrowly national aspirations. While teachers thought they were being supportive by strengthening the students' Albanian identities, returnee students felt deeply alienated when only one aspect of their multiple identities was valued.

There is a widespread assumption that the central problem in the education of migrant students is related to 'culture'. As this study clearly shows, being part of the 'dominant' ethnicity does not protect migrant students from the effects of the linguistic and institutional disjuncture between different national school systems if views of them are clouded by culturist thinking. As a result of this disjuncture, most returnee students experience downward educational mobility: they move into lower grades than those they had attended in Greece and their performance worsens. Some drop out of school altogether. As long as we do not even have the terminology which could disentangle linguistic proficiency from ethnicity and as long as we see students first and foremost as representatives of some 'culture' or other, schools around the world will continue to fail students who do not quite fit the profile we imagine for them.

SUPPORTING DIVERSITY

So far, I have illustrated the cultural dimensions of one of the key findings of contemporary educational research, namely that minority children experience educational disadvantage vis-à-vis their culturally dominant peers. Cultural stereotyping and a mismatch between complex identities and simplistic school expectations play a key role in their educational disadvantage. This mismatch has a specific linguistic dimension in the fact that educational institutions continue to maintain a monolingual habitus while migrant children bring to school the experience of multilingualism. Throughout the world, schools have been extremely slow to adapt to the realities of cultural and linguistic diversity, as we have seen; and the obsession of educational systems with cultural and linguistic homogeneity constitutes one of the great paradoxes of our time. While the benefits of diversity education have been documented in a substantial body of research spanning a number of decades, the implementation of diversity education has been relatively slow, small-scale, discontinuous and often politically controversial (see Piller 2016b). I will now consider two aspects of the question of how to better support students in culturally and linguistically diverse schools: first by introducing a dual immersion programme and, second, by examining links between the school and the home.

Let's begin by visiting dual immersion elementary schools in the Northern German port city of Hamburg (Duarte 2011). Since the early 2000s, that city has been offering dual immersion programmes in Italian, Portuguese, Spanish and Turkish in its public elementary schools. The account on which I draw here, by Joana Duarte, reports only on the Portuguese programme, so in the following I will refer only to the German-Portuguese programme. The aim of these dual immersion programmes is to teach two languages to children who are dominant in German as well as children who are dominant in Portuguese. Therefore, children whose stronger language is German and children whose stronger language is Portuguese are enrolled in roughly equal numbers. Like many dual language immersion programmes, the bilingual programmes under examination have three key aims: first, to develop high-level bilingual proficiencies in German and Portuguese, including the ability to read and write in both languages; second, to achieve at or above grade level in content areas such as mathematics, sciences and social studies; and, third, to develop intercultural competences.

In order to achieve these goals about half of the curriculum is taught bilingually: German and Portuguese language classes are taught contrastively and with a strong focus on linguistic form. Social studies are taught through a team-teaching approach by a German- and a Portuguese-dominant teacher, and music and parts of mathematics are taught by a bilingual teacher who uses both languages. Didactically, there is a strong focus on explicit and contrastive language instruction, and explicit grammar and form-focused instruction is an important feature of all instruction, including subject instruction.

So, how does this kind of programme work for the students? The researchers conducted a three-way comparison of students in the programme with Portuguese bilingual migrant students and native German monolingual students at a 'regular' German elementary school, and also with native Portuguese monolingual students studying in Portugal. To begin with, the students in the bilingual programme significantly outperformed their Portuguese-speaking peers in a 'regular' German elementary school on assessments of academic language proficiency and subject content. Their gains were such that, over the six years of elementary school, the initial condition of linguistic heterogeneity disappeared and their performance was equal to that of monolingual German children after controlling for socio-economic background and individual student cognitive ability. This means that bilingual education in a dual immersion programme can completely erase the educational disadvantage of migrant students. These findings are not unique to this particular programme but have been confirmed elsewhere (Lindholm-Leary 2001, 2013). Comparison with Portuguese students in Portugal showed an additional bonus: Portuguese-speaking migrant children in the programme in Hamburg reached proficiency levels in Portuguese that were comparable to those of monolingual Portuguese children in Portugal.

Migrant children are disadvantaged in monolingual schools because they face the double task of learning a new language and new subject content simultaneously, and they do so in the presence of native-born monolingual students for whom the educational system is designed, and who thus 'only' face the task of content learning. Where schools level the playing field through the provision of bilingual education – as the Hamburg programmes described here do – they not only overcome language-based educational disadvantage but also enable both migrant and non-migrant children to accumulate cultural capital by institutionalising and certifying bilingual proficiency.

Against the background that the cultural and linguistic expertise of transnational children is widely dismissed and they are mostly seen in deficient terms, the importance of 'creating room for kids to be experts' (Orellana 2016: 95) cannot be overstated. One area where transnational children may accumulate significant expertise is by acting as linguistic and cultural mediators between the school and the home.

Migration inevitably changes families. As children are usually much quicker than adults to learn new languages and adapt to new circumstances, children and youths often inevitably become mediators between their parents and the host society. While the direction of learning is typically imagined to flow from adults to children, in reality learning is bidirectional and adults learn from children, too. In migrant families, bidirectional learning may be particularly salient as children may be important sources of cultural and linguistic learning for their parents (Motaghi-Tabari 2016). Adults – migrant and local – often feel rather ambiguous about children as linguistic and cultural mediators: Is a child who translates at a parent-teacher interview at school really to be trusted? Parents and teachers may feel apprehensive that the child is not interpreting 'the truth' but may be representing their academic performance in a more favourable light than is actually warranted. Should not children be kept away from medical examinations? Parents and doctors often struggle with the fact that where children act as mediators in a medical encounter they may gain knowledge of their parents' bodies in ways that might be considered inappropriate or premature. And does not the balance of power overall shift in favour of the child? Are migrant parents 'losing control' as the supposedly clear power hierarchy between adult and child breaks down when a migrant adult depends on a child for help to interact in the wider society? The fear that bilingual children might be manipulating their monolingual parents is memorably encapsulated in fiction when the American-born daughter of a Chinese mother in the novel *The Joy Luck Club* shares this childhood memory:

> I often lied to her when I had to translate for her, the endless forms, instructions, notices from school, telephone calls. '*Shemma yisz?* – What meaning? – she asked me when a man at a grocery store yelled at her for opening up jars to smell the insides. I was so embarrassed I told her that Chinese people were not allowed to shop there. When the school sent a notice home about a polio vaccination, I told her the time and place, and added that all students were now required to use metal lunch boxes, since they had discovered old paper bags can carry polio germs. (Tan 1989: 109f.)

Amusing and poignant as this account may be, it is certainly not the full story. Let's hear from the memoir of a real-life former child mediator. In her autobiography titled *Durch die Wand* ('Through the Wall'), Nizaqete Bislimi, a German lawyer shares her story (Bislimi 2015). In fact, Bislimi's story has been well publicised in Germany for a number of years: born in Kosovo in 1979, her Romani family fled to Germany when she was fourteen years old. For the next thirteen years the family did not manage to achieve a secure legal status and lived under the constant threat of deportation. Even so, Bislimi finished high school and graduated as one of the top students in her class. She went on to study law and became a partner in a law firm specialising in migration and citizenship law and also became the president of the German Romani Federation, the national peak body of Romani organisations in Germany.[4] Given the family's precarious legal status over many years, it is not surprising that a typical experience during Bislimi's early years in Germany should have been that she needed to mediate between her mother and their pro bono lawyer. Bislimi was ambitious, determined and, obviously, smart, and learnt German quickly. Even so, *Amtsdeutsch* ('bureaucratic German') and the legal register were beyond the teenager. During one of their meetings with their lawyer, Bislimi said to her mother, 'One day I will understand all this. I promise.' The lawyer explained that the only way for this to happen was for Bislimi to study law. Her career adviser in school had a different idea and recommended that she get married instead of going to university. Bislimi's ambitions clearly did not fit his stereotype of a young

Romani refugee woman from the Balkans. But Bislimi had promised her mother, and she has succeeded.

The anxieties about child mediators mentioned above notwithstanding, Bislimi's experience of deriving strength from acting as a linguistic and cultural mediator for her parents does not seem to be unique. Research with child language brokers has examined cognitive development, academic performance, parent-child relationships, emotional stress and moral development. Acting as a linguistic and cultural mediator had been found to be beneficial for a child's cognitive development. Because linguistic and cultural mediation involves children in more complex situations than they would normally encounter, for instance in legal or medical contexts, child mediators have been found to develop higher problem-solving skills and better decision-making strategies (Morales and Hanson 2005). Mediation may also enhance academic performance, as some studies have found that acting as a linguistic mediator may be associated with higher scores on standardised tests (Dorner, Orellana and Li-Grining 2007). Be that as it may, analysis of recorded parent-teacher interviews where the child interpreted between parent and teacher showed that children certainly did not lie to present their academic performance in a more favourable light than warranted (Sánchez and Orellana 2006). On the contrary, such children were likely to downplay praise from the teacher in translation. Furthermore, despite the common assumption that parents who have to enlist their children's help to communicate outside the family are losing power and status, the evidence suggests otherwise. A US study, for instance, found that language brokering 'may provide opportunities for communication and contact with parents that may contribute to adolescents feeling trusted and needed by parents' (Chao 2006: 295). This experience may actually be beneficial for children's mental health and also for their moral development. As regards the latter, some studies view linguistic and cultural mediation as a form of 'required helpfulness' similar to having to help out with domestic chores, and required helpfulness has been associated with maturity and moral development (Bauer 2013).

None of this should be taken to glorify children as cultural and linguistic mediators. There certainly are situations and contexts where it may be traumatic for children to interpret for their parents. For instance, it may be inappropriate to seek children's assistance with medical interpreting, particularly where violence may be under discussion or where they might gain insights into taboo topics such as their parents' sexuality. In such cases there should always be provision for the services of professional interpreters (see also Chapter 5). However, overall, in migration contexts it is often inevitable that children take on the roles of linguistic and cultural brokers between the adults in their family and the wider society. Given that this is the case, overburdening the activity with all kinds of anxieties is not helpful. In fact, child mediators may 'make it possible for their parents to live, eat, shop and otherwise sustain themselves as workers, citizens and consumers in their host country' (Orellana 2009: 124). Conversely, they provide an important service to the host society which might be struggling to provide professional translators and interpreters in all the contexts in which they might be necessary. For many children, contributing in this way to their families and societies is normal and will give them the strength to succeed against the odds. We should aim to help them with their brokering roles by developing their multilingual proficiencies and skills and by smoothing their paths so that we will be able to see many more success stories like that of Nizaqete Bislimi.

KEY POINTS

This chapter made the following key points:

- Schooling serves the purpose of social reproduction, including the reproduction of a docile and compliant labour force. This purpose of schooling is usually hidden behind discourses of meritocracy, and culturist discourses about subordinate groups may serve to make their unequal schooling publicly acceptable.
- Negative stereotypes about minority groups along with positive stereotypes about dominant groups may shape the way schools are organised. Transformed into teacher expectations, cultural stereotypes may turn into self-fulfilling prophecies.
- Culturist views of students are particularly detrimental to students from hybrid, complex and atypical backgrounds.
- In the interest of the common good, we need to work harder to create school spaces where cultural and linguistic diversity is acknowledged, valued and supported to enable all children to reach their full multilingual and intercultural potential.

COUNTERPOINT

Most readers of this book will be members of educational institutions as students or teachers and will certainly have been members of educational institutions in the past. How do the educational institutions of which you are/were a member compare to the patterns described here? Does your institution reproduce or challenge the social order, or both simultaneously?

Through which discourses and practices does that happen? Does the educational experience of disparate groups differ? How? What efforts are there to support cultural and linguistic diversity? Are these effective and do they benefit all members of the institution? Some diversity initiatives are alienating to members of dominant groups; what can be done to avoid that and to create inclusive multilingual and intercultural spaces that are beneficial to all?

FURTHER READING

Monica Heller (2006) and Luisa Martín Rojo (2010) offer two excellent school ethnographies in highly diverse schools in Toronto, Canada, and Madrid, Spain, respectively. Orellana (2016) introduces a longitudinal educational outreach project in Los Angeles, USA, that engages with the education of children of migration in a highly diverse urban context. Leibold and Chen (2014) provide a broad selection of research into multilingual and multicultural education in China.

ACTIVITIES

Textbook analysis
The culturist stereotyping of educational policy makers, teachers and peers may not be the only stereotyping with which students are confronted in schools. Textbooks can be another important source of stereotyping. Choose a language learning or social science textbook and analyse how linguistic and cultural diversity is represented in the textbook. If you work in pairs and each pair is assigned a specific textbook that is in use in your context, everyone can present their findings and you can compare and contrast how linguistic and cultural diversity is taught in your context. To standardise your analysis, you could model your analysis on Shardakova and Pavlenko (2004).

Teachers' views
In Chapter 5, we encountered junior nurses and doctors who were keen to improve the experience of patients with limited English proficiency but were prevented from doing so due to a range of institutional and systemic constraints (Kenison et al. 2016). Similarly, teachers often find their best intentions stymied by factors outside their control. Interview a teacher or – if you are a teacher yourself – reflect on your experience: What do teachers know about the linguistic and cultural needs of minority students? How

are those needs met in their school and in their classroom? Are they satisfied with the ways minority students are educated in their school or their classroom, or would they like to see change? What can or can't they do to contribute to such change? What are the constraints?

NOTES

1. For images of this great migration visit http://www.languageonthemove.com/children-of-the-harvest-schooling-class-and-race/
2. By using data available from the Australian Bureau of Statistics ('2011 Census Quickstats' 2016; 'Census of Population and Housing: Socio-Economic Indexes for Areas' 2013), population data for socio-economic status can be mapped onto those for 'ancestry', 'country of birth' and 'home language'.
3. A diagram of the results is available at http://www.languageonthemove.com/are-the-children-of-intermarried-couples-smarter/
4. See http://www.bundesromaverband.de/nizaqete-bislimi-vorsitzende-des-bundes-roma-verband-e-v-und-rechtsanwaeltin-in-essen-mit-taetigkeitsschwerpunkt-im-auslaender-und-asylrecht/

CHAPTER 11

Becoming an Intercultural Mediator

CHAPTER OBJECTIVES

This chapter will enable you to:

- Reflect on your own experiences with and roles in intercultural communication.
- Pursue intercultural communication scholarship of your own and design your own intercultural communication research projects.

REINVENTING A NEW COMMON CULTURE

Talk of diversity, even 'super-diversity', leading to inter-, metro-, multi- or trans-cultures is everywhere these days. At the same time, we also see a resurgence of old nationalisms that hanker for some mythical past without migration, globalisation and the mixing and mingling of people they have brought. Insisting on maintaining 'authentic' cultural identities by dominant and subordinate groups alike seems to have reached an impasse that can only lead to more confrontation. Instead of clinging to old cultural identities, unity in diversity is predicated on bridge building and on 'reinventing a new common culture', as Cuban scholar Fernando Ortiz put it in 1940 (quoted in Orellana 2016: 90). How intercultural communication scholarship can contribute to building such a new common culture based on engagement, interaction and service to the common good will be the focus of this final chapter.

Intercultural communication is a field that is home to a lot of goodwill, and many publications explicitly state the aim of intercultural communication research as being to contribute to bridging cultural conflicts, to developing intercultural competence or to contributing to world peace. The good intentions that emanate from numerous intercultural communication texts are best expressed in Deborah Tannen's (1986: 43) oft-quoted dictum: 'The fate of the earth depends on cross-cultural communication.' The rhetoric that a greater understanding of cultural differences will contribute to making the world a better place is embraced by many writers in intercultural communication. However, as I have argued throughout, rather than asking 'How does group X communicate?' there is a much more powerful question to be asked, namely 'Who makes culture relevant to whom in which context for which purposes?' This question is a realist one which embraces an understanding of culture and discourse as ultimately grounded in the material, socio-economic, embodied base of our lives. Culture is sometimes nothing more than a convenient and lazy explanation built on the fallacious misrecognition of material and social inequality as cultural difference: 'it may be wise to keep in mind that many misunderstandings, innocent or not, have their origin in inequality, not just in difference' (Blommaert 2005: 77). Because this is so, becoming an intercultural mediator involves more than the simple acquisition of a set of intercultural 'competences'.

CULTURAL BROKERING

To demonstrate that intercultural mediation is not only a set of competences but is embedded in service to the common good by reinventing a new common culture, let's meet three men who might have been considered sophisticated cultural brokers in their time. The first is Sir John Bagot Glubb (1897–1986), a British colonial office with extensive linguistic and cultural knowledge of the Arab world who devoted his life to 'intercultural communication' with Arabs in the British interest. The other two are Bolad (ca. 1240–1313) and Rashid al-Din (ca. 1250–1318), two thirteenth-century Mongol and Persian statesmen whose friendship and dedication to the common good – as opposed to the narrow interest of their own groups – helped to connect East and West Asia.

Let's start with Sir John Bagot Glubb. As I explained in Chapter 2, intercultural communication training has historically been happening in the halls of power. Military and secret service training academies in particular have produced some of the finest multilinguals and most skilled intercultural communicators. There we met US diplomats trained in the Foreign Service Institute. Here, we will focus on British colonial officials, particularly those serving in the Middle East in the early twentieth century. These men (and a few women) were *Kingmakers* (such is the title of the collection of the biographies on which I draw here (K. E. Meyer and Brysac 2008) and basically invented the modern Middle East. Meyer and Brysac (2008) call their subjects 'kingmakers' because they worked to secure British influence in the Middle East through 'indirect rule'. In the late nineteenth century, 'indirect rule' became a much-hyped strategy of semi-colonial administration, which did not involve full-fledged occupation but rather wielding influence through being the power behind an indigenous autocrat. All the 'kingmakers' were accomplished orientalists, who were highly proficient in Arabic and/or other languages of the region, who spent many years of their lives there and who gained a deep understanding of its peoples and cultures. One of them was John Bagot Glubb, also known as Glubb Pasha, the British commander of the 'Arab Legion', the army of Transjordan (later Jordan) in the early twentieth century (Castlewitz 2006). In his autobiography, Glubb described his intercultural experience as follows:

> I spent thirty-six years living among the Arabs. During the first nineteen of these years, I lived entirely with them, rarely meeting Europeans and sometimes not speaking a word of English for weeks on end. I originally went to Iraq in 1920 as a regular officer of the British Army, seeking fresh fields of adventure and a wider knowledge of the many different forms of modern soldiering. But when I had spent five years among the Arabs, I decided to change the basis of my whole career: I made up my mind to resign my commission in the British Army and devote my life to the Arabs. My decision was largely emotional. I loved them. (Quoted in K. E. Meyer and Brysac 2008: 265)

One of the forms that his 'devotion' and 'love' took was through the fact that he pioneered aerial bombing in Iraq. During World War I, the British had promised a tribal chief in the Hejaz, a region in today's Saudi Arabia, a kingdom. After the war, no suitable kingdom was available for various reasons, including conflicting promises made to others. So, eventually, he was installed in Iraq, which had just been carved out of the Ottoman Empire but where he had no local base whatsoever. As a result, local tribes felt no need to be loyal to their new king nor to pay taxes to support his regime. The fact that Iraq had only recently been invented (by another set of British advisors) as a nation out of three previous Ottoman provinces did not help (Dodge 2003). So, the new Iraqi king and his British backers decided to engage in some stark nation-building: the submission of the Beni Huchaim tribes of Southern Iraq to their new nation and their imported king was to be achieved through terrorising them with aerial bombing. Thus it came to pass that, in 1923, what is today's Southern Iraq became a testing ground for the aerial bombing of civilian populations. In those early days someone needed to map the terrain before any bombing could be undertaken. The only person with the right skill set was Glubb: he had the geographical mapping skills, the military knowledge of operational aspects, and the language and cultural skills to be able to move among the local population. As he notes in his autobiography, on at least two occasions it was the Beni Huchaim tribes' hospitality that enabled him to make the maps that would enable the Royal Air Force (RAF) to bomb them. In addition to mapping the terrain, he was also 'mapping' their social structure by pinpointing those sheiks whose influence among their people would render them particularly 'suitable' for attack.

Glubb was not without sympathy for the tribes: he notes their poverty as well as the fact that to them the central government was nothing but 'a kind of absentee landlord which never concerns itself with them except periodically to demand revenues' (quoted in K. E. Meyer and Brysac 2008: 268). Given his excellent cultural knowledge, he was also well aware that what he was doing was a serious breach of the norms of Arab hospitality (as a matter of fact, any norms of hospitality it would seem to me). The justification Glubb offered for his betrayal was that he did not actually lie to the tribal people. On the contrary, he says he was candid about his purpose and even warned them 'that he, himself, would lead the bombers if they [= the Beni Huchaim tribes] proved recalcitrant' (quoted in K. E. Meyer and Brysac 2008: 268). In the end, that is exactly what happened: Glubb led the enforcement of government policy to use aerial bombing for non-payment of taxes. He praised the strategy as 'extremely efficient' because it demoralised the tribesmen by making them feel helpless and precluded any effective response on their part. Despite Glubb's obvious excellent linguistic and intercultural competence, it obviously demonstrates an extraordinary lack of empathy to consider Glubb's non-lying fair warning. To warn people who have never even seen airplanes, and who have no idea of what a bomb might be, of potential air raids may be technically telling the truth but it is practically meaningless. Not to mention that aerial bombing is obviously an extraordinarily unjust and cruel way of enforcing tax compliance.

In Glubb we encounter a highly competent linguist and intercultural communicator acting immorally and violating basic principles of trust and interpersonal relationships. In the context of the imperial make-over of the Middle East during and after World War I, language and culture teaching were a key aspect of the education of an imperial elite, and intercultural communication was nothing more and nothing less than an aspect of establishing and maintaining imperial control. What was obviously missing was a moral compass that would have enabled the reinvention of a new common culture for the common good.

Before you conclude that there may be a fundamental conflict between self-interest and service to the common good, let's meet two thirteenth-century statesmen who had a healthy dose of both and who took on the roles of cultural brokers as an act of public service. In an age when most of our own political leaders seem to be more inclined towards erecting new borders, strengthening old ones and tearing down bridges, it is instructive to consider the friendship of these two men who helped to connect East and West Asia: the Mongol Bolad and the Persian Rashid al-Din.

Of the two, Rashid al-Din is today the better-known; as the author of the *Jāme' al-Tawārikh* ('Universal History') he is credited with having been 'the first world historian' (Boyle 1971). Rashid al-Din was born around 1250 CE into a Jewish family in Hamadan in northwestern Iran. At the age of twenty-one or thirty (different accounts exist in different sources; see Kamola 2012), he converted to Islam and at around the same time he entered the service of the then-ruler of Iran, the Il-Khan Abaqa (1265–1281) as court physician. Under Abaqa's grandson Il-Khan Ghazan (1295–1304), Rashid al-Din became vizier, one of the most influential roles in the state. Rashid al-Din also served Ghazan's son and successor Öljeitü (1304–1316). After Öljeitü's death he became the victim of a court intrigue and was put to death in 1317, when he was around seventy years old. During his long career he served his kings in many capacities: as physician, head of the royal household, military and general adviser, the mastermind of far-reaching fiscal and agricultural reforms, and, through his writing, as chief ideologue and propagandist of the Il-Khanid dynasty. In short, Rashid al-Din was a power-broker, who did very well for himself and the realm he served.

Thousands of miles to the east, Bolad's career was very similar to that of Rashid al-Din: Bolad was about ten years older than Rashid al-Din and born around 1240 somewhere in Mongolia. His father was a man named Jürki, a member of the Dörben, a Mongolian tribe, who had submitted to Genghis Khan in 1204. Jürki quickly rose through the ranks of the Imperial Guard. In addition to his military distinction as a 'Commander of a Hundred in the Personal Thousand' of Genghis Khan, he also became a *ba'ruchi* ('cook') in the imperial household. While 'cook' may not sound like much of a rank, in the Mongolian system this household position carried great prestige and showed close personal ties with the ruler (Allsen 1996: 8). As a result of his father's position, little Bolad was assigned to the service of Genghis Khan's grandson Kublai Khan at age eight or nine. His education included the military arts and Chinese language and civilisation. Bolad, too, forged a distinguished administrative career at the Yuan court. As he grew older, his duties and assignments included formulating court ceremonies, educating young Mongolians who entered the imperial service, and organising the 'Censorate', the investigative arm of government. He became Head of the Bureau of Agriculture, which he helped establish; took on the role of Vice-Commissioner of Military Affairs; and headed a major anti-corruption investigation. His diverse appointments close to the centre of power at Kublai Khan's court earned him the Chinese title *chengxiang*, 'chancellor'.

In the spring of 1283, Bolad was appointed Kublai Khan's ambassador to the Il-Khanids. The journey from Kublai Khan's capital Khanbaliq (Dadu; modern Beijing) to the Il-Khan's court in Tabriz took more than one year and Bolad and his embassy arrived in late 1284. He was supposed to return to China in 1285 but hostile forces made it impossible for a man of his rank to travel. He therefore stayed in Iran for the final twenty-eight years of his life. In addition to the role of ambassador, Bolad there assumed the role of chief advisor to the Il-Khan. During Öljeitü's reign he became third minister and was in charge of logistics during a number of military campaigns. Active until well into his seventies, Bolad died in 1313 while he was in command of the northern garrisons. Like Rashid al-Din, Bolad was a power-broker. He distinguished himself at not one but two courts. Like Rashid al-Din, Bolad and his family, too, acquired significant wealth in their service to the Mongolian Empire and Yuan dynasty.

Rashid al-Din and Bolad obviously met and became friends at the Il-Khanid court and it is necessary to briefly sketch the broader context of their encounter.[1] After the death of Möngke Khan, a brother of Kublai Khan's, in 1259, the unity of the Mongolian Empire Genghis Khan had forged was permanently broken and the descendants of Genghis Khan fell into various succession wars. Kublai Khan held strong in Yuan China. The Il-Khanid line in Iran, founded by his brother Hülegü, formally acknowledged Kublai Khan's sovereignty. Between these two allies, the Genghizid lines in Central Asia and Russia established various autonomous regional khanates, including the famous Golden Horde. These were at various times allied in various ways, at war with each other in various ways, and, particularly relevant here, often at war with China and Iran.

As nomadic aristocracy ruling two realms with a settled agrarian population and ancient civilisations, the Yuan in China and the Il-Khanids in Iran faced similar sets of issues: How would nomadic warriors be able to rule these complex agrarian societies? Kublai Khan understood early that he would need Chinese support. His own Chinese language skills were not strong and he relied on interpreters in interactions with Chinese advisors (Fuchs 1946). However, he did seek out Chinese advisors and, more importantly, initiated the bilingual and bicultural education of young

Mongolian courtiers such as Bolad. Bolad developed an intercultural disposition and 'his frequent and active support for the recommendations of the emperor's Han advisers indicates that he found much to admire in Chinese civilization' (Allsen 1996: 9).

It is unclear when and how Bolad learnt Persian but on his long trip to Iran and for the first few years there, he was accompanied by an interpreter, a Syriac Christian in the employ of the Mongols, who is known in Chinese sources as *Aixue* and in Persian sources as *Isa kelemchi* ('Jesus the interpreter') (H. Takahashi 2014: 43). The actual linguistic repertoire of Aixue/Isa kelemchi is uncertain; and that is an indicator of the linguistic situation in the Il-Khanate, which was even more complex than that at the Yuan court. The preferred languages of Il-Khan Ghazan, for instance, were Mongolian and Turkish. Additionally, he happily spoke Persian and Arabic with his courtiers. Furthermore, he reportedly understood Hindi, Kashmiri, Tibetan, Khitai, Frankish 'and other languages' (Amitai-Preiss 1996: 27). Rashid Al-Din wrote in Persian, Arabic and Hebrew; from his style, it can be assumed that he also had some knowledge of at least Mongolian, Turkish and Chinese (Findley 2004: 92).

In short, the nomadic Mongolian conquerors, whose strength was military, needed to integrate their culture with that of the ancient settled civilisations of China and Iran in order to maintain the empires they had gained. They did so by fostering a new class of cultural brokers. These could either be drawn from the Mongolian population and raised bilingually and biculturally, as in Bolad's case; or recruited from the local population, as in Rashid al-Din's case. The latter must have been far more numerous because the nomads obviously did not end up imposing their language and culture on either China or Iran. Bolad and Rashid al-Din ended up not 'only' mediating between the nomad conquerors and the settled societies they came to rule, but their friendship is an example of the deep connections between East and West Asia that were forged during that time:

> Their friendship was, without question, a crucial link in the overall exchange process, for Rashid al-Din, a man of varied intellectual interests and tremendous energy, was one of the very few individuals among the Mongols' sedentary subjects who fully appreciated and systematically exploited the cultural possibilities created by the empire. (Allsen 1996: 12)

The *Jāme' al-Tawārikh* presents the culmination of their interactions. These chronicles were the first-ever attempt to write a world history and include information about the Muslim dynasties, the Indians, Jews, Franks, Chinese, Turks and Mongols. Much of what is today known about the history of Central Asia up to the thirteenth century comes from the *Jāme' al-Tawārikh*. This could not have been achieved without extensive collaboration, and Rashid al-Din says about Bolad that he had no rival 'in knowledge of the genealogies of the Turkish tribes and the events of their history, especially that of the Mongols' (quoted in Allsen 1996: 13). Inter alia, Bolad translated information from a now-lost Mongolian source, the *Altan Debter* ('Golden Book'). Access to the *Altan Debter* was forbidden to non-Mongols, and Rashid al-Din even describes how their collaboration proceeded in this case: Bolad, who, as a high-ranking Mongol, had access to the *Altan Debter*, would extract the desired information and then, 'in the morning before taking up administrative chores', dictate the Persian translation of the desired passages to Rashid al-Din (Allsen 1996: 13).

Given the wide-ranging interests and experiences of the two men, it is not surprising that their collaboration was not restricted to history but took in many other fields, too. Principal among these was agriculture. Rashid al-Din also produced an agricultural text (*Āthār va ahyā'*, 'Monuments and Animals'), which shows considerable Chinese influence (Allsen 1996). During this time an agricultural model farm was also established in Tabriz and, on Ghazan's orders, new strains of seeds were solicited from China and India. While the details of these cross-fertilisations have been lost in the shifting sands of time, it 'can be asserted with confidence that a considerable body of information on Chinese agriculture was transmitted to Iran and that Bolad was the principal conduit' (Allsen 1996: 15). The two men also collaborated in the introduction of paper money to Iran, which would have necessitated knowledge of block-printing, only available in China at the time; the translation of medicinal treatises and the implementation of aspects of Chinese medicine in the Tabriz hospital Rashid al-Din had founded; and, of course, food. Rashid al-Din, in fact, developed such a taste for the delights of Chinese cuisine that he had a Chinese chef recruited for his household.

The intense friendship of Bolad and Rashid al-Din is the story of a meeting of like-minded individuals who came together across what might seem a vast chasm of cultural difference. Their wide-ranging interests and intercultural dispositions allowed them to contribute extensively – and deeply – to the fusion of Asian cultures. The results were new heights of achievement in all kinds of spheres of life.

The intercultural friendship and collaboration of Bolad and Rashid al-Din demonstrates that intercultural competence is not a set of context-free competences that can be listed, taught and assessed. Rather cultural brokering is a disposition towards deep engagement that can enrich all involved through the creation of a new common culture. It also demonstrates that, to be truly beneficial, intercultural competence cannot be value free but must be undergirded by a commitment to public service and the common good. Where Glubb's intercultural communication was a one-way street, Bolad's and Rashid al-Din's friendship changed both men and benefited the wider world in which they lived.

BUILDING BRIDGES

Bolad and Rashid al-Din may seem far removed from our experiences and concerns. However, in fact, they too lived in troubled and perilous times. As I was finalising the manuscript for the revised second edition of this book in late 2016, I had many occasions to reflect that 2016 had not been a good year for intercultural understanding as ever more barriers between people had been put up and fortified while bridges and connections were being torn down. As unscrupulous media and politicians stoke ethnic and racial fear and hatred for their personal gain, it is the weakest members of society who suffer most.

For instance, a 2016 survey of more than 10,000 Australians found stark differences in the experiences of discrimination by various groups, as evidenced by responses to the question 'Have you experienced discrimination because of your skin colour, ethnic origin or religion over the last 12 months?' (Markus 2016). More than half of respondents born in Africa reported having experienced discrimination in the past twelve months and those from South Sudan and Zimbabwe were most affected. Most of the experiences of discrimination occurred in interactions where people were made to feel excluded or where they were verbally abused.[2] While 'made to feel like [I] don't belong' may sound relatively mild, nothing could be further from the truth. Qualitative descriptions of what it means to be 'made to feel like [I] don't belong' gathered in focus group interviews are harrowing, as in the excerpt where a young man from South Sudan sums up his experience as 'makes it hell'. This particular young man located his experience of exclusion predominantly in 'white' rather than 'diverse' suburbs, as others did, too:

It's weird . . . when you go to really white places.

If I have to go to . . . the city or . . . somewhere that is . . . white . . . like white-dominated Australia ... I would feel . . . a bit off. I would feel like, 'Oh my god, they're looking at me. They're looking at me. What is she doing here?'

They look at you like you're an alien . . . Everyone was just like . . . 'What are you doing in this area?' (Quoted in Markus 2016: 58)

Conversely, spaces where diversity was the norm had the opposite effect and interviewees reported a sense of belonging to a place just because it was 'diverse':

> I used to live in . . . Berala. Berala's kind of Auburn City Council [= a highly diverse Sydney suburb]. In this area . . . it's like very multicultural, like I could see [the] Arab base, mostly, and then like Asians, and then even Sudanese. There's a lot of Sudanese here. So it's very multicultural. I feel like I fit in here, because it's so multicultural.

> I've got a lot of friends who come from the affluent side of Melbourne and they come from old Australian money and to them, I am like this foreign being because I'm half Asian, I'm half European, but born here . . . When I'm in Broadmeadows [= a highly diverse Melbourne suburb] I'm just normal. (Quoted in Markus 2016: 60)

These examples confirm that spaces where a new common culture is forged feel more inclusive to people who might not traditionally belong. They also confirm that many societies are deeply divided: the anger of rural and deindustrialised communities cut adrift by neoliberal globalisation is readily harnessed against the more concrete scapegoat of minorities, particularly if people have little experience with diversity. Against this context, opportunities for everyday mundane connections that allow people to engage beyond the stereotypes can become a crucial means to overcoming division and exclusion. That this is not just a pious hope is demonstrated in research with African migrants in Australia (Tetteh 2015). There we meet Timothy, a man in his early thirties from Sudan, who lives in rural NSW. According to census statistics, ninety per cent of the inhabitants of the town in which he lives are Australia-born and the largest groups of non-Australia-born have migrated from the UK, New Zealand and South Africa (in this order). So, the town is a 'white space' if you will, and is certainly significantly less diverse than is true for the NSW average, where only sixty-eight per cent of the population are Australia-born. However, in contrast to many other Africans who the researcher met in the course of her research, Timothy, who only completed primary education in Sudan and whose self-assessed English is 'not good', is gainfully employed and working happily for a car parts manufacturer. His employment success is the direct result of a mundane relationship where two people were able to connect beyond mediated stereotypes of the racial other. As Timothy recounts it, one of his white Australian neighbours, Mark, accosted him one day and asked why Africans did not work and relied on welfare. That Africans are 'dole bludgers' and 'welfare cheats' is a racist stereotype many Australians are familiar with from the media and extremist political groups. In fact, it was not only Mark who had been exposed to the stereotype but Timothy, too. However, instead of hunkering down in the face of his neighbour's racism, Timothy set about educating Mark and appealed to the 'typical Australian' sense of a fair go:

> And then one day I will stay here and then he ask me, he say why you you Africa you stay at home and receive money from Centrelink [= Australia's social welfare office], you don't want the job. I tell him no because not like that, we need a job but here it's difficult for us because we are, some people put the application and then they tell me call you back, and nothing. (Quoted in Tetteh 2015: 267)

It turned out that Mark had his heart in the right place and could learn to see beyond the racist stereotype. What Timothy tried to tell him – that Africans faced discrimination in the job market – made sense to him. A few days later he showed up at Timothy's door with an application form and recommended him to the car parts factory, where they have been colleagues ever since. At a time when stereotypes divide us ever more deeply and the temptation to retreat into our own in-group bubble is great, Timothy's and Mark's story reminds us of the power of ordinary people and our mundane everyday interactions as a force for good.

It is no accident that the positive examples of intercultural communication with which I close this book are not of individuals but of relationships. Bolad and Rashid al-Din as well as Timothy and Mark remind us that intercultural competence is not some sort of individual trait but a dedicated interpersonal engagement to reinvent a new common culture that is mutually beneficial.

KEY POINTS

This chapter made the following key points:

- Intercultural communication scholarship should not only be analytic but also engaged and should contribute to serving the common good by actively engaging in cross-cultural mediation.
- An important way to learn about the affordances and constraints of

intercultural mediation is through examining the experiences of other intercultural mediators.

COUNTERPOINT

When the eminent sociolinguist Joshua Fishman (1926–2015) was a little boy his father reportedly regularly asked him 'What did you do for Yiddish today?', and the question became the basis for Fishman's activist scholarship (Spolsky 2017). Activist scholarship remains as important as ever and it is my hope that you will come away from this book inspired to ask yourself regularly what you can do to reinvent a new common culture, to build bridges and to serve as an intercultural mediator.

FURTHER READING

The stories – fictional and non-fictional – of intercultural mediators and their experiences can be immensely inspiring. They will also significantly enrich your understanding of intercultural communication in real life and in context. This book has introduced a wide variety of geographical and historical contexts which you might wish to pursue. Good reads about intercultural mediation which I have not drawn on here include an examination of the role of everyday intercultural interaction in the highly diverse world of medieval Spain (Lowney 2006); the fictional *Ibis* trilogy by Amitav Ghosh set against the nineteenth-century Indian Ocean trade (Ghosh 2008, 2011, 2015); or accounts of the language learning and intercultural mediation experiences of the Jesuit missionaries in China in the seventeenth and eighteenth centuries (Brockey 2007, 2014).

ACTIVITIES

Designing your own research project
Identify a context in which you would like to gain a deeper understanding of the social practice of intercultural communication. What kinds of data do you need to collect to be able to answer these three research questions?

- What kinds of oral, written and computer-mediated communicative practices, particularly in relation to language choice, can be observed?
- What (language) ideologies are implicit in these practices?
- How are these practices, ideologies and discourses tied to cultured

identities? How does 'culture' serve to devalue or valorise some identities over others and produce hierarchical relationships in the context under investigation?

- What contribution to intercultural mediation and the common good will your project make?

Join the conversation

If you would like to pursue further the approaches, methods, sites and politics of intercultural communication introduced here, I cordially invite you to join the conversation at www.languageonthemove.org

NOTES

1. Maps and images are available at http://www.languageonthemove.com/cultural-brokering/
2. A table and interview excerpts are available at http://www.languageonthemove.com/building-bridges-in-a-divided-world/

References

2011 Census Quickstats. (2016). Retrieved from http://www.abs.gov.au/websitedbs/censushome.nsf/home/quickstats

Abu Rahhal, L. (2008, 22 August). Noor, a Soap Opera to Test the Moral Compass. *Menassat*. Retrieved from http://www.menassat.com/?q=en/news-articles/4480-noor-soap-opera-test-moral-compass

Agar, M. (1994). *Language Shock: Understanding the Culture of Conversation*. New York: William Morrow.

Allan, K. (2016). Going Beyond Language: Soft Skilling Cultural Difference and Immigrant Integration in Toronto, Canada. *Multilingua*, 35(6), 617–647. doi: 10.1515/multi-2015-0080

Allsen, T. T. (1996). Biography of a Cultural Broker, Bolad Ch'eng-Hsiang in China and Iran. In J. Raby and T. Fitzherbert (Eds), *The Court of the Il-Khans, 1290–1340* (pp. 7–22). Oxford: Oxford University Press.

Alm, C. O. (2003). English in the Ecuadorian Commercial Context. *World Englishes*, 22(2), 143–158. doi: 10.1111/1467-971x.00284

Aman, R. (1982). Interlingual Taboos in Advertising: How Not to Name Your Product. In R. J. Di Pietro (Ed.), *Linguistics and the Professions: Proceedings of the Second Annual Delaware Symposium on Language Studies* (pp. 215–224). Norwood, NJ: Ablex.

Amitai-Preiss, R. (1996). New Material from the Mamluk Sources for the Biography of Rashid Al-Din. In J. Raby and T. Fitzherbert (Eds), *The Court of the Il-Khans, 1290–1340* (pp. 23–37). Oxford: Oxford University Press.

Anderson, B. (1991). *Imagined Communities: Reflections on the Origin and Spread of Nationalism* (2nd edn). London: Verso.

Ang, I. (2005). Multiculturalism. In T. Bennett, L. Grossberg and M. Morris (Eds), *New Keywords: A Revised Vocabulary of Culture and Society* (pp. 226–229). Oxford: Blackwell.

Angermeyer, P. S. (2015). *Speak English or What? Codeswitching and Interpreter Use in New York City Courts*. New York and Oxford: Oxford University Press.

Anthony, D. W. (2007). *The Horse, the Wheel, and Language: How Bronze-Age Riders from the Eurasian Steppes Shaped the Modern World*. Princeton, NJ: Princeton University Press.

Appadurai, A. (1996). *Modernity at Large: Cultural Dimensions of Globalization*. Minneapolis: University of Minnesota Press.

Arai, M., Bursell, M. and Nekby, L. (2016). The Reverse Gender Gap in Ethnic Discrimination: Employer Stereotypes of Men and Women with Arabic Names. *International Migration Review*, *50*(2), 385–412. doi: 10.1111/imre.12170

Ayres, A. (2009). *Speaking Like a State: Language and Nationalism in Pakistan.* Cambridge: Cambridge University Press.

Babad, E. Y., Inbar, J. and Rosenthal, R. (1982). Pygmalion, Galatea, and the Golem: Investigations of Biased and Unbiased Teachers. *Journal of Educational Psychology*, *74*(4), 459–474. doi: http://dx.doi.org/10.1037/0022-0663.74.4.459

Bailey, B. (2000). Communicative Behavior and Conflict between African-American Customers and Korean Immigrant Retailers in Los Angeles. *Discourse and Society*, *11*(1), 86–108.

Bajko, I. Z. (1999). Fremdwörter in der Deutschen Werbesprache am Beispiel zweier Slogankorpora. [Foreign Words in German Advertising Language, Exemplified by Two Corpora of Slogans]. *Moderna Språk*, *93*(2), 161–171.

Bargiela-Chiappini, F. (Ed.). (2009). *The Handbook of Business Discourse*. Edinburgh: Edinburgh University Press.

Barjaba, K. and Barjaba, J. (2015). Embracing Emigration: The Migration-Development Nexus in Albania. *Migration Policy Institute*. Retrieved from http://www. migrationpolicy.org/article/embracing-emigration-migration-development-nexus-albania

Barnlund, D. C. (1989). *Communicative Styles of Japanese and Americans: Images and Realities*. Belmont, CA: Wadsworth.

Barrett, R. (2006). Language Ideology and Racial Inequality: Competing Functions of Spanish in an Anglo-Owned Mexican Restaurant. *Language in Society*, *35*, 163–204.

Bauer, E. (2013). Reconstructing Moral Identities in Memories of Childhood Language Brokering Experiences. *International Migration*, *51*(5), 205–218. doi: 10.1111/imig.12030

Baumann, G. (1996). *Contesting Culture: Discourses of Identity in Multi-Ethnic London.* Cambridge: Cambridge University Press.

Baumgardner, R. J. (2006). The Appeal of English in Mexican Commerce. *World Englishes*, *25*(2), 251–266. doi: 10.1111/j.0083-2919.2006.00463.x

Baumgardner, R. J. and Brown, K. (2012). English in Iranian Magazine Advertising. *World Englishes*, *31*(3), 292–311. doi: 10.1111/j.1467-971X.2012.01761.x

Becker, B. (2011). Cognitive and Language Skills of Turkish Children in Germany: A Comparison of the Second and Third Generation and Mixed Generational Groups. *International Migration Review*, *45*(2), 426–459. doi: 10.1111/j.1747-7379.2011.00853.x

Begley, P. A. (2015). Communication with Egyptians. In L. A. Samovar, R. E. Porter, E. R. Mcdaniel and C. Sexton Roy (Eds), *Intercultural Communication: A Reader* (pp. 126–132). Boston, MA: Cengage Learning.

Beizai, B. (Dir.) (1989). *Bashu [The Little Stranger]*. International Home Cinema Inc.

Benhabib, S. (2002). *The Claims of Culture: Equality and Diversity in the Global Era.* Princeton, NJ: Princeton University Press.

Bennett, T. (2005). Culture. In T. Bennett, L. Grossberg and M. Morris (Eds), *New Keywords: A Revised Vocabulary of Culture and Society* (2nd edn, pp. 63–69). Oxford: Blackwell.

Bennett, T., Grossberg, L. and Morris, M. (Eds). (2005). *New Keywords: A Revised Vocabulary of Culture and Society* (2nd edn). Oxford: Blackwell.

Bergelson, M. (2015). Russian Cultural Values and Workplace Communication Patterns. In L. A. Samovar, R. E. Porter, E. R. Mcdaniel and C. Sexton Roy (Eds), *Intercultural Communication: A Reader* (pp. 133–140). Boston, MA: Cengage Learning.

Berman, G. (2008). Harnessing Diversity: Addressing Racial and Religious Discrimination in Employment. Melbourne: Victorian Multicultural Commission, Victorian Equal Opportunity & Human Rights Commission.

Billig, M. (1995). *Banal Nationalism*. London: Sage.

Bilton, P. (1999). *The Xenophobe's Guide to the Swiss*. London: Oval Books.

Birdsong, D. (2006). Age and Second Language Acquisition and Processing: A Selective Overview. *Language Learning, 56*, 9–49.

Bishop, H. and Jaworski, A. (2003). 'We Beat 'Em': Nationalism and the Hegemony of Homogeneity in the British Press Reportage of Germany Versus England During Euro 2000. *Discourse and Society, 14*(3), 243–271.

Bislimi, N. (2015). *Durch die Wand: Von der Asylbewerberin zur Rechtsanwältin [Through the Wall: From Asylum Seeker to Lawyer]*. Köln: Dumont Buchverlag.

Bloch, A. (2011). Intimate Circuits: Modernity, Migration and Marriage among Post-Soviet Women in Turkey. *Global Networks, 11*(4), 502–521. doi: 10.1111/j.1471-0374.2011.00303.x

Blommaert, J. (2005). *Discourse: A Critical Introduction*. Cambridge: Cambridge University Press.

Blommaert, J. (2010). *The Sociolinguistics of Globalization*. Cambridge: Cambridge University Press.

Blommaert, J. (2013). *Ethnography, Superdiversity and Linguistic Landscapes: Chronicles of Complexity*. Clevedon: Multilingual Matters.

Blommaert, J. (2015). Commentary: 'Culture' and Superdiversity. *Journal of Multicultural Discourses, 10*(1), 22–24. doi: 10.1080/17447143.2015.1020810

Booth, A., Leigh, A. and Varganova, E. (2009). Does Racial and Ethnic Discrimination Vary across Minority Groups? Evidence from Three Experiments. *Australian Policy Online*. Retrieved from: http://apo.org.au/node/17347

Bourdieu, P. (1991). *Language and Symbolic Power*. Cambridge: Polity.

Boutet, J. (2008). *La vie verbale au travail: des manufactures aux centres d'appels [Language at Work: From Manufacturing to Call Centers]*. Paris: Octares.

Bowe, H. and Martin, K. (2007). *Communication across Cultures: Mutual Understanding in a Global World*. Cambridge: Cambridge University Press.

Boyle, J. A. (1971). Rashīd Al-Dīn: The First World Historian. *Iran, 9*, 19–26. doi: 10.2307/4300435

Bremer, K., Roberts, C., Vasseur, M.-T., Simonot, M. and Broeder, P. (2013 [1996]). *Achieving Understanding: Discourse in Intercultural Encounters*. London: Routledge.

Brockey, L. M. (2007). *Journey to the East: The Jesuit Mission to China, 1579–1724*. Cambridge, MA: Harvard University Press.

Brockey, L. M. (2014). *The Visitor: Andre Palmeiro and the Jesuits in Asia*. Cambridge, MA: Harvard University Press.

Brubaker, R. (2014). Linguistic and Religious Pluralism: Between Difference and Inequality. *Journal of Ethnic and Migration Studies, 41*(1), 3–32. doi: 10.1080/1369183X.2014.925391

Bruthiaux, P. (1996). *The Discourse of Classified Advertising: Exploring the Nature of Linguistic Simplicity*. New York and Oxford: Oxford University Press.

Bryson, L., Finkelstein, L. and MacIver, R. M. (Eds). (1947). *Conference on Science, Philosophy and Religion in Their Relation to the Democratic Way of Life, Columbia University, 1945: Approaches to Group Understanding; Sixth Symposium*. New York: Harper.

Bunker, R. M. and Adair, J. (1959). *The First Look at Strangers*. New Brunswick, NJ, and London: Rutgers University Press.

Caesar, J. (2009 [ca. 50 BCE]). *Commentarii De Bello Gallico [Commentaries on the Gallic War]* (W. A. Mcdevitte and W. S. Bohn, Trans.). Boston, MA: Internet Classics Archive.

Carlisle, E. (1967). *Cultures in Collision: U.S. Corporate Policy and Canadian Subsidiaries.* Ann Arbor, MI: University of Michigan Press.

Castlewitz, D. M. (2006, 6 December). Glubb Pasha and the Arab Legion. *HistoryNet.* Retrieved from http://www.historynet.com/glubb-pasha-and-the-arab-legion.htm

Census of Population and Housing: Socio-Economic Indexes for Areas (SEIFA), Australia, 2011. (2013). Retrieved from http://www.abs.gov.au/ausstats/abs@.nsf/Lookup/2033.0.55.001main+features100212011

Chaney, L. H. and Martin, J. S. (2014). *Intercultural Business Communication* (6th edn). London: Pearson Education.

Chang, J. (2004). *Ideologies of English Language Teaching in Taiwan* (PhD). University of Sydney, Sydney.

Chao, R. K. (2006). The Prevalence and Consequences of Adolescents' Language Brokering for Their Immigrant Parents. In M. H. Bornstein and L. R. Cote (Eds), *Acculturation and Parent-Child Relationships: Measurement and Development* (pp. 271–296). Mahwah, NJ: Lawrence Erlbaum Associates.

Charles, M. (2007). Language Matters in Global Communication: Article Based on Ora Lecture, October 2006. *Journal of Business Communication, 44*(3), 260–282. doi: 10.1177/0021943607302477

A Child's Garden of Verses. (2016). Wikipedia.

Cicero, M. T. (45 BCE). Tusculanae Disputationes [Tusculan Disputations].

Clarke, S. (2004). *A Year in the Merde*. New York: Bloomsbury.

Clyne, M. (1994). *Inter-Cultural Communication at Work*. Cambridge: Cambridge University Press.

Clyne, M. (2005). *Australia's Language Potential*. Sydney: UNSW Press.

Coe, N. M., Johns, J. and Ward, K. (2012). Limits to Expansion: Transnational Corporations and Territorial Embeddedness in the Japanese Temporary Staffing Market. *Global Networks, 12*(1), 1–26. doi: 10.1111/j.1471-0374.2011.00333.x

Colic-Peisker, V. (2005). 'At Least You're the Right Colour': Identity and Social Inclusion of Bosnian Refugees in Australia. *Journal of Ethnic and Migration Studies, 31*(4), 615–638. doi: 10.1080/13691830500109720

Communications Scholar William Gudykunst Dies. (2005, 24 January). *CSUF News & Information.* Retrieved from http://calstate.fullerton.edu/news/2005/116_gudykunst.html

Constable, N. (2003). *Romance on a Global Stage: Pen Pals, Virtual Ethnography, and 'Mail-Order' Marriages*. Berkeley, CA: University of California Press.

Cooke, G. (1962). *As Christians Face Rival Religions: An Interreligious Strategy for Community without Compromise*. New York: Association Press.

Cooke, M. (2008). 'What We Might Become': The Lives, Aspirations, and Education of Young Migrants in the London Area. *Journal of Language, Identity & Education, 7*(1), 22–40.

Coulthard, M. (2005). The Linguist as Expert Witness. *Linguistics & the Human Sciences, 1*(1), 39–58.

Coupland, N. (Ed.). (2010). *The Handbook of Language and Globalization*. Malden, MA and Oxford: Wiley-Blackwell.

Cox, J. W. and Minahan, S. (2004). Unravelling Woomera: Lip Sewing, Morphology and Dystopia. *Journal of Organizational Change Management, 17*(3), 292–301.

Creese, G. and Kambere, E. N. (2003). What Colour is Your English? *Canadian Review of Sociology and Anthropology, 40*(5), 565–573.

Creese, G. and Wiebe, B. (2012). 'Survival Employment': Gender and Deskilling among African Immigrants in Canada. *International Migration, 50*(5), 56–76. doi: 10.1111/j.1468-2435.2009.00531.x

Cross, R. and Hudson, A. (2006). *Beyond Belief: The British Bomb Tests: Australian Veterans Speak Out*. Kent Town, SA: Wakefield Press.

Cruz, J. (2012, 30 July). Deutschtürken sorgen für 400.000 Arbeitsplätze [Turkish-Germans Provide 400,000 Jobs]. *Migration Business*. Retrieved from http://www.migration-business.de/2012/07/8741/

Darnell, S. C. (2014). Orientalism through Sport: Towards a Said-ian Analysis of Imperialism and 'Sport for Development and Peace'. *Sport in Society, 17*(8), 1000–1014. doi: 10.1080/17430437.2013.838349

Dávila, L. T. (2008). Language and Opportunity in the 'Land of Opportunity': Latina Immigrants' Reflections on Language Learning and Professional Mobility. *Journal of Hispanic Higher Education, 7*(4), 356–370.

Death of Polish Man Tasered by RCMP was a Homicide, BC Coroners Rule. (2013, 9 April). *National Post*. Retrieved from http://news.nationalpost.com/news/canada/death-of-polish-man-tasered-by-rcmp-was-a-homicide-bc-coroners-rule

Dicken, P. (2015). *Global Shift: Mapping the Changing Contours of the World Economy* (7th edn). London: Guilford.

Dimova, S. (2012). English in Macedonian Television Commercials. *World Englishes, 31*(1), 15–29. doi: 10.1111/j.1467-971X.2011.01731.x

Djité, P. G. (2006). Shifts in Linguistic Identities in a Global World. *Language Problems and Language Planning, 30*(1), 1–20.

Dodge, T. (2003). *Inventing Iraq: The Failure of Nation-Building and a History Denied*. London: Hurst.

Dörner, A. (2016, 15 December). Congrats, Volkswagen! *Handelsblatt*. Retrieved from http://www.handelsblatt.com/unternehmen/industrie/konzernsprache-wird-englisch-congrats-volkswagen/14982788.html

Dorner, L. M., Orellana, M. F. and Li-Grining, C. P. (2007). 'I Helped My Mom,' and it Helped Me: Translating the Skills of Language Brokers into Improved Standardized Test Scores. *American Journal of Education, 113*(3), 451–478. doi: 10.1086/512740

Dousset, L. (2003). On the Misinterpretation of the Aluridja Kinship System Type (Australian Western Desert). *Social Anthropology, 11*(1), 43–61.

Duarte, J. (2011). Migrants' Educational Success through Innovation: The Case of the Hamburg Bilingual Schools. *International Review of Education/Internationale Zeitschrift für Erziehungswissenschaft/Revue Internationale de l'Education, 57*(5/6), 631–649. doi: 10.2307/41480148

Duchêne, A. (2009). Marketing, Management and Performance: Multilingualism as Commodity in a Tourism Call Centre. *Language Policy, 8*(1), 27–50.

Duchêne, A. and Piller, I. (2011). Mehrsprachigkeit als Wirtschaftsgut: Sprachliche Ideologien und Praktiken in der Tourismusindustrie. [Multilingualism as a Commodity: Linguistic Ideologies and Practices in the Tourism Industry]. In G. Kreis (Ed.), *Babylon Europa: Zur Europäischen Sprachlandschaft [European Babylon: Europe's Linguistic Landscape]* (pp. 135–157). Basel: Schwabe.

Eades, D. (2008). *Courtroom Talk and Neocolonial Control*. Berlin: Mouton de Gruyter.

Eades, D. (2010). *Sociolinguistics and the Legal Process*. Clevedon: Multilingual Matters.

Eades, D. and Pavlenko, A. (2015). Guidelines for Communicating Rights to Non-Native Speakers of English in Australia, England and Wales, and the USA. http://www.une. edu.au/__data/assets/pdf_file/0006/114873/Communication-of-rights.pdf

Ehrenreich, B. and Hochschild, A. R. (Eds). (2002). *Global Woman: Nannies, Maids, and Sex Workers in the New Economy*. New York: Metropolitan Press.

Ehrlich, S. (2001). *Representing Rape: Language and Sexual Consent*. London: Routledge.

El-Najjar, H. A. (2008). *Discrimination against Bidoons, Palestinians, and Other Immigrants in Kuwait*. Paper presented at the American Sociological Association Annual Meeting, Boston, MA. http://citation.allacademic.com/meta/p_mla_apa_research_citation/2/4/2/3/9/p242399_index.html

Elass, R. (2009, 14 February). Love is in the Desert Air – If You Nurture It. *The National*. Retrieved from https://www.pressreader.com/uae/the-national-news/20090214/281586646495348

Elkin, A. P. (1938–1940). Kinship in South Australia. *Oceania, 8, 9, 10*, 419; 452; 441–478, 198–234, 295–349, 369–489.

Errington, J. (2008). *Linguistics in a Colonial World: A Story of Language, Meaning, and Power*. Oxford: Blackwell.

Etiemble, R. (1964). *Parlez-vous Franglais? [Do you Speak Frenglish?]*. Paris: Gallimard.

Faier, L. (2007). Filipina Migrants in Rural Japan and their Professions of Love. *American Ethnologist, 34*(1), 148–162. doi: 10.1525/ae.2007.34.1.148

Faier, L. (2009). *Intimate Encounters: Filipina Women and the Remaking of Rural Japan*. Berkeley, CA: University of California Press.

Farr, M. (2006). *Rancheros in Chicagoacán: Language and Identity in a Transnational Community*. Austin, TX: University of Texas Press.

Farsi: Aval Dabestan [Persian Primer: First Grade]. (N.d.). Tehran: Ministry of Education, Iran.

Findley, C. V. (2004). *The Turks in World History*. New York and Oxford: Oxford University Press.

Flanagan, R. (2008). *Wanting*. Sydney: Knopf.

Flügge, M. (Ed.). (1984). *Heinrich Zille: Fotografien von Berlin um 1900*. Leipzig: VEB Fotokinoverlag.

Foley, W. (1997). *Anthropological Linguistics: An Introduction*. Oxford: Blackwell.

Forji, A. G. (2006, 3 September). Ghana Issues Ultimatum to Int'l Gay Conference. *Ohmy News*. Retrieved from http://english.ohmynews.com/articleview/article_view. asp?no=315045&rel_no=1

Francis, D. and Hester, S. (2004). *An Invitation to Ethnomethodology: Language, Society and Interaction*. London: Sage.

Friedman, T. L. (2006). *The World is Flat: The Globalized World in the Twenty-First Century*. London: Penguin.

Fuchs, W. (1946). Analecta: Zur Mongolischen Übersetzungsliteratur der Yuan-Zeit. *Monumenta Serica, 11*, 33–64.

Galasiński, D. and Jaworski, A. (2003). Representations of Hosts in Travel Writing: *The Guardian* Travel Section. *Journal of Tourism and Cultural Change, 1*(2), 131–149.

Garcia, O. and Li, W. (2013). *Translanguaging: Language, Bilingualism and Education*. Basingstoke: Palgrave.

Gazzola, M. and Grin, F. (2013). Is ELF More Effective and Fair than Translation? An Evaluation of the EU's Multilingual Regime. *International Journal of Applied Linguistics, 23*(1), 93–107. doi: 10.1111/ijal.12014

Geertz, C. (1973). *The Interpretation of Cultures: Selected Essays*. New York: Basic Books.

Geldard, F. A. and Bouman, M. A. (Eds). (1965). *NATO Symposium on Communication Processes, Washington, D.C. 1963*. New York: Macmillan.

Gerritsen, M. and Nickerson, C. (2009). BELF: Business English as a Lingua Franca. In F. Bargiela-Chiappini (Ed.), *The Handbook of Business Discourse* (pp. 180–192). Edinburgh: Edinburgh University Press.

Gerritsen, M., Nickerson, C., Van Hooft, A., Van Meurs, F., Nederstigt, U., Starren, M. and Crijns, R. (2007). English in Product Advertisements in Belgium, France, Germany, the Netherlands and Spain. *World Englishes*, 26(3), 291–315. doi: 10.1111/j.1467-971X.2007.00510.x

Gerver, D. and Sinaiko, H. W. (Eds). (1978). *NATO Symposium on Language Interpretation and Communication, Giorgio Cini Foundation, 1977: Language Interpretation and Communication*. New York: Plenum Press.

Ghanaian Gay Conference Banned. (2006, 1 September). *BBC*. Retrieved from http://news.bbc.co.uk/2/hi/africa/5305658.stm

Ghosh, A. (2008). *Sea of Poppies*. London: John Murray.

Ghosh, A. (2011). *River of Smoke*. London: John Murray.

Ghosh, A. (2015). *Flood of Fire*. London: John Murray.

Goddard, C. (2006). Ethnopragmatics: A New Paradigm. In C. Goddard (Ed.), *Ethnopragmatics: Understanding Discourse in Cultural Context* (pp. 1–30). Berlin and New York: Mouton de Gruyter.

Goddard, C. (2009). Not Taking Yourself Too Seriously in Australian English: Semantic Explications, Cultural Scripts, Corpus Evidence. *Intercultural Pragmatics*, 6(1), 29–53.

Goodenough, W. H. (1976). Multiculturalism as the Normal Human Experience. *Anthropology and Education Quarterly*, 7(4), 4–7.

Green, A. G. and Green, D. (2004). The Goals of Canada's Immigration Policy: A Historical Perspective. *Canadian Journal of Urban Research*, 13(1), 102–139.

Griffiths, M., Qian, D. and Procter, N. G. (2005). Beyond Words: Lessons on Translation, Trust and Meaning. Canberra: Multicultural Mental Health Australia.

Gugliotta, G. (2008). The Great Human Migration: Why Humans Left their African Homeland 80,000 Years Ago to Colonize the World. *Smithsonian Magazine*. Retrieved from http://www.smithsonianmag.com/history/the-great-human-migration-13561/?no-ist

Gumperz, J. J. (1982a). *Discourse Strategies*. Cambridge: Cambridge University Press.

Gumperz, J. J. (Ed.). (1982b). *Language and Social Identity*. Cambridge: Cambridge University Press.

Gumperz, J. J. and Levinson, S. C. (Eds). (1996). *Rethinking Linguistic Relativity*. Cambridge: Cambridge University Press.

Haarmann, H. (1989). *Symbolic Values of Foreign Language Use: From the Japanese Case to a General Sociolinguistic Perspective*. Berlin and New York: Mouton de Gruyter.

Haebich, A. and Delroy, A. (1999). *The Stolen Generations: Separation of Aboriginal Children from Their Families in Western Australia*. Perth: Western Australian Museum.

Hall, E. T. (1959). *The Silent Language*. Garden City, NY: Doubleday.

Hall, E. T. (1960). A Microcultural Analysis of Time. In A. F. C. Wallace (Ed.), *Selected Papers of the Fifth International Congress of Anthropological and Ethnological Sciences, 1956* (pp. 118–122). Philadelphia: University of Pennsylvania Press.

Hall, E. T. (1966). *The Hidden Dimension*. Garden City, NY: Doubleday.

Hall, E. T. and Hall, M. R. (1987). *Hidden Differences: Doing Business with the Japanese*. Garden City, NY: Doubleday.

Hamdan, J. M. and Hatab, W. A. A. (2009). English in the Jordanian Context. *World Englishes, 28*(3), 394–405. doi: 10.1111/j.1467-971X.2009.01599.x

Hannerz, U. (1996). *Transnational Connections: Culture, People, Places*. London: Routledge.

Heather, P. (2010). *Empires and Barbarians: The Fall of Rome and the Birth of Europe*. Oxford and New York: Oxford University Press.

Heller, C. (2009). I Am Mutti. In S. Kamata (Ed.), *Call Me Okaasan: Adventures in Multicultural Mothering* (pp. 124–133). Deadwood, OR: Wyatt-MacKenzie Publishing.

Heller, M. (2006). *Linguistic Minorities and Modernity: A Sociolinguistic Ethnography* (2nd edn). London: Continuum.

Heller, M. (2010). The Commodification of Language. *Annual Review of Anthropology, 39*, 101–114.

Heller, M. and Duchêne, A. (2012). Pride and Profit: Changing Discourses of Language, Capital and Nation-State. In A. Duchêne and M. Heller (Eds), *Language in Late Capitalism: Pride and Profit* (pp. 1–21). New York: Routledge.

Heyes, C. (2002). Identity Politics. In E. N. Zalta (Ed.), *The Stanford Encyclopedia of Philosophy*. Stanford, CA: Stanford University.

Hill, J. H. (2008). *The Everyday Language of White Racism*. Malden, MA: Wiley-Blackwell.

Hirsch, J. S. and Wardlow, H. (Eds). (2006). *Modern Loves: The Anthropology of Romantic Courtship and Companionate Marriage*. Ann Arbor: University of Michigan Press.

Hobsbawm, E. (1990). *Nations and Nationalism Since 1870: Programme, Myth, Reality*. Cambridge: Cambridge University Press.

Hochschild, A. R. (2012a). *The Managed Heart: Commercialization of Human Feeling* (3rd edn). Berkeley: University of California Press.

Hochschild, A. R. (2012b). *The Outsourced Self: What Happens When We Pay Others to Live Our Lives for Us*. New York: Henry Holt and Company.

Hofstede, G. H. (2001). *Culture's Consequences: Comparing Values, Behaviors, Institutions, and Organizations across Nations* (2nd edn). Thousand Oaks, CA: Sage.

Hofstede, G. H., Hofstede, G. J. and Minkov, M. (2010). *Cultures and Organizations: Software of the Mind: Intercultural Cooperation and Its Importance for Survival* (3rd edn). New York: McGraw-Hill.

Holliday, A. (1999). Small Cultures. *Applied Linguistics, 20*(2), 237–264.

Holliday, A., Kullman, J. and Hyde, M. (2017). *Intercultural Communication: An Advanced Resource Book* (3rd edn). London: Routledge.

Holmes, J. and Stubbe, M. (2015). *Power and Politeness in the Workplace: A Sociolinguistic Analysis of Talk at Work* (2nd edn). London: Routledge.

Honda Makes English Official. (2015, 18 July). *The Japan Times*. Retrieved from http://www.japantimes.co.jp/opinion/2015/07/18/editorials/honda-makes-english-official/

hooks, b. (1992). *Black Looks: Race and Representation*. Cambridge, MA: South End Press.

hooks, b. (1994). *Teaching to Transgress: Education as the Practice of Freedom*. New York: Routledge.

Hourani, A. (2005). *A History of the Arab Peoples*. London: Faber and Faber.

Hunt, K. and Taylor, M. (2004). *The Xenophobe's Guide to the Aussies* (2nd edn). London: Oval Books.

Huntington, S. P. (1993). The Clash of Civilizations? *Foreign Affairs, 72*(3), 22–49.

Hymes, D. (1974). *Foundations in Sociolinguistics: An Ethnographic Approach*. Philadelphia: University of Pennsylvania Press.

Hymes, D. (1996). *Ethnography, Linguistics, Narrative Inequality: Toward an Understanding of Voice*. London: Taylor & Francis.

Jackson, A. (2004, 1 June). Aladdin Sisalem Released from Manus Island. *The Age*. Retrieved from http://www.theage.com.au/articles/2004/05/31/1085855499159.html

Jackson, J. E. (1983). *The Fish People: Linguistic Exogamy and Tukanoan Identity in Northwest Amazonia*. Cambridge: Cambridge University Press.

Jain, N. C. (2015). Some Basic Cultural Patterns of India. In L. A. Samovar, R. E. Porter, E. R. Mcdaniel and C. Sexton Roy (Eds), *Intercultural Communication: A Reader* (pp. 121–125). Boston, MA: Cengage Learning.

Jaworski, A. (2015). Globalese: A New Visual-Linguistic Register. *Social Semiotics, 25*(2), 217–235. doi: 10.1080/10350330.2015.1010317

JETRO. (1999). Communicating with Japanese in Business. Tokyo: Japan External Trade Organization.

Jones, R. H. (2000). 'Potato Seeking Rice': Language, Culture, and Identity in Gay Personal Ads in Hong Kong. *International Journal of the Sociology of Language, 143*, 33–61.

Jones, W. J. (1990). *German Kinship Terms (750–1500): Documentation and Analysis*. Berlin: Walter de Gruyter.

Joseph, J. E. (2004). *Language and Identity: National, Ethnic, Religious*. Basingstoke: Palgrave Macmillan.

Jupp, J. (2007). *From White Australia to Woomera: The Story of Australian Immigration*. Melbourne: Cambridge University Press.

Jurji, E. J. (1969). *Religious Pluralism and World Community: Interfaith and Intercultural Communication*. Leiden: E. J. Brill.

Kamola, S. (2012). The Mongol Īlkhāns and their Vizier Rashīd Al-Dīn. *Iranian Studies, 45*(5), 717–721. doi: 10.1080/00210862.2012.702557

Kanamori, M. (2012). Chika: A Documentary Performance. Retrieved from http://mayu.com.au/2012/09/01/chika-a-documentary-performance/

Keegan, W. J. (1984). International Competition: The Japanese Challenge. *Journal of International Business Studies, 15*(3), 189–193.

Kenison, T. C., Madu, A., Krupat, E., Ticona, L., Vargas, I. M. and Green, A. R. (2016). Through the Veil of Language: Exploring the Hidden Curriculum for the Care of Patients with Limited English Proficiency. *Academic Medicine: Journal of the Association of American Medical Colleges* 92(1), 92–100. doi: 10.1097/ACM.0000000000001211.

Kim, H. M. (2007). The State and Migrant Women: Diverging Hopes in the Making of 'Multicultural Families' in Contemporary Korea. *Korea Journal, 47*(4), 100–122.

Kim, S. (2016, 24 December). Manus Island Refugee Turned Away from Clinic for 'Pretending to Be Sick' before Death, Detainee Claims. *ABC News*. Retrieved from http://www.abc.net.au/news/2016-12-24/refugee-turned-away-from-clinic-before-death:-detainee/8147032

Kipling, R. (1899). The White Man's Burden: The United States and the Philippine Islands. The New York Sun, 10 February 1899.

Kirsch, S. (1996). Ethnographic Representation in the Shadows of Development. *Visual Anthropology Review, 12*(2), 96–109. doi: 10.1525/var.1996.12.2.96

Kisch, E. E. (1937). *Landung in Australien [Australian Landfall]*. Amsterdam: Allert de Lange.

Klapproth, D. M. (2004). *Narrative as Social Practice: Anglo-Western and Australian Aboriginal Oral Traditions*. Berlin and New York: Mouton de Gruyter.

Klein, N. (2001). *No Logo*. London: HarperCollins.

Knudsen, B. D. (2016, 26 November). Danish Hygge – Even Danes Don't Realise That, Surprisingly, It Is Not About the Candles. *Your Danish Life*. Retrieved from http://www.yourdanishlife.dk/the-things-you-need-to-know-about-hygge/

Koch, N. (2013). Sport and Soft Authoritarian Nation-Building. *Political Geography, 32*, 42–51. doi: http://dx.doi.org/10.1016/j.polgeo.2012.11.006

Kojima, Y. (2001). In the Business of Cultural Reproduction: Theoretical Implications of the Mail-Order Bride Phenomenon. *Women's Studies International Forum, 24*(2), 199–210.

Kooner, B. (2007). RCMP Taser Incident at Vancouver International Airport. Vancouver, Canada: Canada Border Services Agency.

Kraemer, A. J. (1969). *The Development of Cultural Self-Awareness: Design of a Program of Instruction [United States. Dept. of the Army. Office, Chief of Research and Development. Nato Conference on Special Training for Multilateral Forces]*. Alexandria, VA: George Washington University, Human Resources Research Office.

Kramer, S. J. (2009, 22 September). Zwanzig Jahre Jüdische Zuwanderung nach Deutschland. [Twenty Years of Jewish Immigration to Germany]. *Mediendienst des Zentralrates der Juden in Deutschland*. Retrieved from http://www.zentralratdjuden.de/de/article/2646.zwanzig-jahre-j%C3%BCdische-zuwanderung-nach-deutschland.html

Kramsch, C. (1998). *Language and Culture*. Oxford: Oxford University Press.

Kramsch, C. and Boner, E. (2010). Shadows of Discourse: Intercultural Communication in Global Contexts. In N. Coupland (Ed.), *The Handbook of Language and Globalization* (pp. 495–519). Malden, MA and Oxford: Wiley-Blackwell.

Kress, G. and van Leeuwen, T. (1996). *Reading Images: The Grammar of Visual Design*. London: Routledge.

Kroeber, A. L. and Kluckhohn, C. (1963). *Culture: A Critical Review of Concepts and Definitions*. New York: Vintage.

Kulick, D. (2003). No. *Language and Communication, 23*(2), 139–151.

Lanzieri, G. (2011). *A Comparison of Recent Trends of International Marriages and Divorces in European Countries*. Paper presented at the IUSSP Seminar on Global Perspectives on Marriage and International Migration, Seoul, South Korea. http://www.academia.edu/2565606/A_comparison_of_recent_trends_of_international_marriages_and_divorces_in_European_countries

Lee, J. S. (2006). Linguistic Constructions of Modernity: English Mixing in Korean Television Commercials. *Language in Society, 35*(1), 59–91.

Lee, S. and Li, D. C. S. (2013). Multilingualism in Greater China and the Chinese Language Diaspora. In T. K. Bhatia and W. C. Ritchie (Eds), *The Handbook of Bilingualism and Multilingualism* (pp. 813–842). Oxford: Blackwell.

Leeds-Hurwitz, W. (1990). Notes in the History of Intercultural Communication: The Foreign Service Institute and the Mandate for Intercultural Training. *Quarterly Journal of Speech, 76*(1), 262–281.

Leibold, J. and Chen, Y. (Eds). (2014). *Minority Education in China: Balancing Unity and Diversity in an Era of Critical Pluralism*. Hong Kong: Hong Kong University Press.

Lévi-Strauss, C. (1969). *The Elementary Structures of Kinship* (J. H. Bell, J. R. Von Sturmer and R. Needham, Trans.). Paris: Mouton.

Li, J. (2017). *Social Reproduction and Migrant Education: A Critical Sociolinguistic Ethnography of Burmese Students' Learning Experiences at a Border High School in China* (PhD). Macquarie University.

Lindholm-Leary, K. J. (2001). *Dual Language Education*. Clevedon: Multilingual Matters.

Lindholm-Leary, K. J. (2013). Bilingual and Biliteracy Skills in Young Spanish-Speaking Low-SES Children: Impact of Instructional Language and Primary Language Proficiency. *International Journal of Bilingual Education and Bilingualism*, *17*(2), 144–159. doi: 10.1080/13670050.2013.866625

Lippi-Green, R. (2012). *English with an Accent: Language, Ideology, and Discrimination in the United States* (2nd edn). London: Routledge.

List of Wikipedias. Wikipedia. Retrieved from https://meta.wikimedia.org/wiki/List_of_Wikipedias

Loewenstein, A. (2016, 12 August). Dark Past: So Little Has Changed in Australia's Posture Towards Asylum Seekers. *The Guardian*. Retrieved from https://www.theguardian.com/commentisfree/2016/aug/12/dark-past-so-little-has-changed-in-australias-posture-towards-asylum-seekers

A Look at International Marriage in Japan. (2015, 19 February). *Nippon*. Retrieved from http://www.nippon.com/en/features/h00096/

Lorenzoni, N. and Lewis, B. A. (2004). Service Recovery in the Airline Industry: A Cross-Cultural Comparison of the Attitudes and Behaviors of British and Italian Front-Line Personnel. *Managing Service Quality*, *14*(1), 11–25.

Lowney, C. (2006). *A Vanished World: Muslims, Christians, and Jews in Medieval Spain*. New York and Oxford: Oxford University Press.

Lucy, J. A. (1992). *Language Diversity and Thought: A Reformulation of the Linguistic Relativity Hypothesis*. Cambridge: Cambridge University Press.

Lüdke, S. (2016, 15 August). Wie funktioniert die Liebe, wenn man nicht die gleiche Sprache spricht? [How Does Love Work When Partners Don't Speak the Same Language?]. *bento*. Retrieved from http://www.bento.de/gefuehle/zweisprachige-beziehung-wie-beeinflusst-sprache-die-liebe-775818/

Lynch, J., Ross, M. and Crowley, T. (2002). *The Oceanic Languages*. Richmond, Surrey: Curzon.

Maher, J. C. (2010). Metroethnicities and Metrolanguages. In N. Coupland (Ed.), *The Handbook of Language and Globalization* (pp. 575–591). Malden, MA and Oxford: Wiley-Blackwell.

Marek, Y. (1998). The Philosophy of the French Language Legislation: Internal and International Aspects. In D. A. Kibbee (Ed.), *Language Legislation and Linguistic Rights* (pp. 341–350). Amsterdam: John Benjamins.

Markus, A. (2016). Australians Today: The Australia@2015 Scanlon Foundation Survey. Melbourne: Scanlon Foundation.

Marschan-Piekkari, R., Welch, D. and Welch, L. (1999a). Adopting a Common Corporate Language: IHRM Implications. *The International Journal of Resource Management*, *10*(3), 377–390.

Marschan-Piekkari, R., Welch, D. and Welch, L. (1999b). In the Shadow: The Impact of Language on Structure, Power and Communication in the Multinational. *International Business Review*, *8*(4), 421–440.

Marschan, R., Welch, D. and Welch, L. (1997). Language: The Forgotten Factor in Multinational Management. *European Management Journal*, *15*(5), 591–598.

Martin, E. (2005). *Marketing Identities through Language: English and Global Imagery in French Advertising*. London: Palgrave Macmillan.

Martín Rojo, L. (2010). *Constructing Inequality in Multilingual Classrooms*. Berlin: Mouton de Gruyter.

Masterman-Smith, H. and Pocock, B. (2008). *Living Low Paid: The Dark Side of Prosperous Australia*. Sydney: Allen & Unwin.

Mayers, M. K. (1974). *Christianity Confronts Culture: A Strategy for Cross-Cultural Evangelism*. Grand Rapids, MI: Zondervan.

McCann, E. and Bromwich, J. E. (2016, 20 October). 'Nasty Woman' and 'Bad Hombres': The Real Debate Winners? *New York Times*. Retrieved from http://www.nytimes.com/2016/10/21/us/politics/nasty-woman-and-bad-hombres-the-real-debate-winners.html

McClintock, A. (1995). *Imperial Leather: Race, Gender and Sexuality in the Colonial Contest*. New York: Routledge.

McGurk, H. and MacDonald, J. (1976). Hearing Lips and Seeing Voices. *Nature, 264*, 746–748.

McSweeney, B. (2002). Hofstede's 'Model of National Cultural Differences and Consequences: A Triumph of Faith – a Failure of Analysis. *Human Relations, 55*(1), 89–118.

Melville, I. (1999). *Marketing in Japan*. Oxford: Butterworth-Heinemann.

Menagh, J. (2016a, 5 July). Elderly Woman with Infected Wound Refused to Go to Hospital, Inquest Told. *ABC News*. Retrieved from http://www.abc.net.au/news/2016-07-05/nurse-told-pressure-sore-patient-to-go-hospital-inquest-niceforo/7571788

Menagh, J. (2016b, 4 July). Home Care Examined after 75yo Perth Woman Died with Infected Pressure Wounds. *ABC News*. Retrieved from http://www.abc.net.au/news/2016-07-04/inquest-into-death-of-perth-woman-maria-niceforo-kincare/7567784

Meyer, B. and Apfelbaum, B. (Eds). (2010). *Multilingualism at Work: From Policies to Practices in Public, Medical and Business Settings*. Amsterdam: John Benjamins.

Meyer, K. E. and Brysac, S. B. (2008). *Kingmakers: The Invention of the Modern Middle East*. New York: W.W. Norton & Co.

Mikitani, H. (2013). *Marketplace 3.0: Rewriting the Rules of Borderless Business*. New York: Palgrave Macmillan.

Mirchandani, K. (2004). Practices of Global Capital: Gaps, Cracks and Ironies in Transnational Call Centres in India. *Global Networks, 4*(4), 355–373.

Mirchandani, K. (2015). Flesh in Voice: The No-Touch Embodiment of Transnational Customer Service Workers. *Organization, 22*(6), 909–923. doi: 10.1177/1350508414527779

Moore, A. M. and Barker, G. G. (2012). Confused or Multicultural: Third Culture Individuals' Cultural Identity. *International Journal of Intercultural Relations, 36*(4), 553–562. doi: http://dx.doi.org/10.1016/j.ijintrel.2011.11.002

Moorehead, C. (2006). *Human Cargo: A Journey Among Refugees*. London: Vintage.

Mooring, Y. (2004). *The Discourse of Filipina Mail-Order Bride Websites* (Honours Thesis). University of Sydney, Sydney.

Morales, A. and Hanson, W. E. (2005). Language Brokering: An Integrative Review of the Literature. *Hispanic Journal of Behavioral Sciences, 27*(4), 471–503. doi: 10.1177/0739986305281333

Motaghi-Tabari, S. (2016). *Bidirectional Language Learning in Migrant Families* (PhD). Macquarie University.

Mullaney, T. S. (2011). *Coming to Terms with the Nation: Ethnic Classification in Modern China*. Berkeley, Los Angeles, London: University of California Press.

Müller, M. (2006, 14 November). Nein Sagen und Ja Meinen: Kleines Chinesen-Einmaleins. [Saying No and Meaning Yes: The ABC of Communicating with the Chinese]. *20 minuten*, 31.

Nakane, I. (2007a). Problems in Communicating the Suspect's Rights in Interpreted Police Interviews. *Applied Linguistics, 28*(1), 87–112.

Nakane, I. (2007b). *Silence in Intercultural Communication: Perception and Performance*. Amsterdam: John Benjamins.

Nekula, M. and Šichová, K. (2004). Sprache als Faktor der Wirtschaftlichen Integration. [Language as a Factor in Economic Integration]. *brücken*, *12*, 317–335.

A New McDefinition? (2007, 24 May). *The Guardian*. Retrieved from http://www.guardian.co.uk/commentisfree/2007/may/24/anewmcdefinition

O'Neill, K. L. (2015). *Secure the Soul: Christian Piety and Gang Prevention in Guatemala*. Berkeley, CA: University of California Press.

O'Rourke, K. (2002). To Have and to Hold: A Postmodern Feminist Response to the Mailorder Bride Industry. *Denver Journal of International Law and Policy*, *30*(4), 476–498.

Oakley, A. (1974). *The Sociology of Housework*. Oxford: Martin Robertson.

Oertig-Davidson, M. (2002). *Beyond Chocolate: Understanding Swiss Culture*. Basel: Bergli Books.

Orellana, M. F. (2009). *Translating Childhoods: Immigrant Youth, Language, and Culture*. New Brunswick, NJ, and London: Rutgers University Press.

Orellana, M. F. (2016). *Immigrant Children in Transcultural Spaces: Language, Learning, and Love*. New York: Routledge.

Pal, M. and Buzzanell, P. (2008). The Indian Call Center Experience: A Case Study in Changing Discourses of Identity, Identification, and Career in a Global Context. *Journal of Business Communication*, *45*(1), 31–60. doi: 10.1177/0021943607309348

Papunya School. (2001). *Papunya School Book of Country and History*. Sydney: Allen & Unwin.

Park, J. S.-Y. (2015). Language as Pure Potential. *Journal of Multilingual and Multicultural Development*, *37*(5), 453–466. doi: 10.1080/01434632.2015.1071824

Pasassung, N. (2004). *Teaching English in an 'Acquisition-Poor Environment': An Ethnographic Example of a Remote Indonesian EFL Classroom* (PhD). University of Sydney.

Pavlenko, A. (2001a). 'How Am I to Become a Woman in an American Vein?': Transformations of Gender Performance in Second Language Learning. In A. Pavlenko, A. Blackledge, I. Piller and M. Teutsch-Dwyer (Eds), *Multilingualism, Second Language Learning and Gender* (pp. 133–174). Berlin and New York: Mouton de Gruyter.

Pavlenko, A. (2001b). 'In the World of the Tradition, I Was Unimagined': Negotiation of Identities in Cross-Cultural Autobiographies. *International Journal of Bilingualism*, *5*(3), 317–344.

Pavlenko, A. (2001c). Language Learning Memoirs as a Gendered Genre. *Applied Linguistics*, *22*(2), 213–240.

Peaceful Pacific? (1931, 9 July). *The North Western Courier*. Retrieved from http://trove.nla.gov.au/newspaper/article/138431511

Pennycook, A. (2001). English in the World/the World in English. In A. Burns & C. Coffin (Eds), *Analysing English in a Global Context: A Reader* (pp. 78–89). London: Routledge.

Pennycook, A. (2007). Language, Localization and the Real: Hip-Hop and the Global Spread of Authenticity. *Journal of Language, Identity & Education*, *6*(2), 101–116.

Pennycook, A. and Otsuji, E. (2015). *Metrolingualism: Language in the City*. London: Routledge.

Phelan, A. (2000, 1 April). Reds in the Beds. *Sydney Morning Herald Magazine*, 49–52.

Piller, I. (2001). Identity Constructions in Multilingual Advertising. *Language in Society*, *30*(2), 153–186.

Piller, I. (2002a). *Bilingual Couples Talk: The Discursive Construction of Hybridity.* Amsterdam: John Benjamins.

Piller, I. (2002b). Passing for a Native Speaker: Identity and Success in Second Language Learning. *Journal of Sociolinguistics*, *6*(2), 179–206.

Piller, I. (2003). Advertising as a Site of Language Contact. *Annual Review of Applied Linguistics*, *23*, 170–183.

Piller, I. (2007). Cross-Cultural Communication in Intimate Relationships. In H. Kotthoff and H. Spencer-Oatey (Eds), *Intercultural Communication* (pp. 341–359). Berlin and New York: Mouton de Gruyter.

Piller, I. (2008). 'I Always Wanted to Marry a Cowboy:' Bilingual Couples, Language and Desire. In T. A. Karis and K. D. Killian (Eds), *Intercultural Couples: Exploring Diversity in Intimate Relationships* (pp. 53–70). London: Routledge.

Piller, I. (2015). Language Ideologies. *The International Encyclopedia of Language and Social Interaction*. [Online.] doi: 10.1002/9781118611463.wbielsi140

Piller, I. (2016a). Language and Migration. In I. Piller (Ed.), *Language and Migration (Vol. 1: Languages in Contact)* (pp. 1–20). London: Routledge.

Piller, I. (2016b). *Linguistic Diversity and Social Justice: An Introduction to Applied Sociolinguistics*. Oxford and New York: Oxford University Press.

Piller, I. (2016c). Monolingual Ways of Seeing Multilingualism. *Journal of Multicultural Discourses*, *11*(1), 25–33. doi: 10.1080/17447143.2015.1102921

Piller, I. and Cho, J. (2013). Neoliberalism as Language Policy. *Language in Society*, *42*(1), 23–44.

Piller, I. and Lising, L. (2014). Language, Employment and Settlement: Temporary Meat Workers in Australia. *Multilingua*, *33*(1/2), 35–59.

Piller, I. and Takahashi, K. (2006). A Passion for English: Desire and the Language Market. In A. Pavlenko (Ed.), *Bilingual Minds: Emotional Experience, Expression, and Representation* (pp. 59–83). Clevedon: Multilingual Matters.

Piller, I. and Takahashi, K. (2011). Language, Migration and Human Rights. In R. Wodak, B. Johnstone and P. Kerswill (Eds), *Handbook of Sociolinguistics* (pp. 573–587). London: Sage.

Piller, I. and Takahashi, K. (2013). Language Work Aboard the Low-Cost Airline. In A. Duchêne, M. Moyer and C. Roberts (Eds), *Language, Migration and Social Inequalities: A Critical Sociolinguistic Perspective on Institutions and Work* (pp. 95–117). Clevedon: Multilingual Matters.

Piller, I., Takahashi, K. and Watanabe, Y. (2010). The Dark Side of TESOL: The Hidden Costs of the Consumption of English. *Cross-Cultural Studies*, *20*, 183–201.

The Place of Migrants in Contemporary Australia: A Summary Report. (2014). Canberra: Department of Immigration and Border Protection.

Pound, L. (1913). Word-Coinage and Modern Trade-Names. *Dialect Notes*, *4*(1), 29–41.

Pousada, A. (2008). The Mandatory Use of English in the Federal Court of Puerto Rico. *Centro Journal*, *20*(1), 136–155.

Prensa Asociada. (2009, 24 February). ¿Se Discrimina al usar el Inglés en algunos tribunales de Puerto Rico? [Is the Use of English in Some Puerto Rican Courts Discriminatory?]. *NY Daily News Latino*. Retrieved from http://www.nydailynews. com/latino/espanol/2009/02/25/2009-02-25_se_discrimina_al_usar_el_ingls_en_ alguno-2.html#ixzz12QpzSHty

Pulinx, R., Van Avermaet, P. and Agirdag, O. (2015). Silencing Linguistic Diversity: The

Extent, the Determinants and Consequences of the Monolingual Beliefs of Flemish Teachers. *International Journal of Bilingual Education and Bilingualism.* [Online.] doi: 10.1080/13670050.2015.1102860

Pullum, G. K. (1991). *The Great Eskimo Vocabulary Hoax and Other Irreverent Essays on the Study of Language.* Chicago: University of Chicago Press.

Rampton, B. (2011). Style Contrasts, Migration and Social Class. *Journal of Pragmatics,* 43(5), 1236–1250. doi: http://dx.doi.org/10.1016/j.pragma.2010.08.010

Rebhun, L.-A. (1999). *The Heart Is Unknown Country: Love in the Changing Economy of Northeast Brazil.* Stanford, CA: Stanford University Press.

Reid, G. (1982). *A Nest of Hornets: The Massacre of the Fraser Family at Hornet Bank Station, Central Queensland, 1857, and Related Events.* Melbourne: Oxford University Press.

Reinert, E. S. (2008). *How Rich Countries Got Rich ... And Why Poor Countries Stay Poor.* London: Constable.

Research Triangle Park. (2016). Wikipedia. https://en.wikipedia.org/wiki/Research_Triangle_Park

Reyes, A. (2007). *Language, Identity and Stereotype among Southeast Asian American Youth: The Other Asian.* Mahwah, NJ: Lawrence Erlbaum Associates.

Ricks, D. A. (1996). Perspectives: Translation Blunders in International Business. *Journal of Language for International Business,* 7(2), 50–55.

Rist, R. C. (2015). On Understanding the Process of Schooling: The Contributions of Labeling Theory. In J. H. Ballantine and J. Z. Spade (Eds), *Schools and Society: A Sociological Approach to Education* (pp. 47–56). London: Sage.

Ritzer, G. (2007). *The Globalization of Nothing.* London: Sage.

Ritzer, G. (2014). *The McDonaldization of Society* (8th edn). Thousand Oaks, CA: Sage

Roberman, S. (2015a). Not to Be Hungry Is Not Enough: An Insight into Contours of Inclusion and Exclusion in Affluent Western Societies. *Sociological Forum,* 30(3), 743–763. doi: 10.1111/socf.12190

Roberman, S. (2015b). *Sweet Burdens: Welfare and Communality among Russian Jews in Germany.* Albany, NY: SUNY Press.

Roberts, C., Moss, B., Wass, V., Sarangi, S. and Jones, R. (2005). Misunderstandings: A Qualitative Study of Primary Care Consultations in Multilingual Settings, and Educational Implications. *Medical Education,* 39, 465–475.

Rohingya Migrants Claim Thai Abuses. (2009, 24 January). *Al Jazeera English.* Retrieved from https://www.youtube.com/watch?v=9p-WyHJb_T4

Römer, R. (1976). *Die Sprache der Anzeigenwerbung* [*The Language of Print Advertising*] (5th edn). Düsseldorf: Pädagogischer Verlag Schwann.

Romero, J. L. (1944). *Bases para una morfología de los contactos de cultura.* Buenos Aires: Institución Cultural Española.

Rosenthal, R. and Jacobson, L. (1968). *Pygmalion in the Classroom.* New York: Holt, Rinehart & Winston.

Rubin, D. L. (1992). Nonlanguage Factors Affecting Undergraduates' Judgements of Nonnative English-Speaking Teaching Assistants. *Research in Higher Education,* 33(4), 511–531.

Rubin, D. L. and Smith, K. A. (1990). Effects of Accent, Ethnicity, and Lecture Topic on Undergraduates' Perceptions of Non-Native English Speaking Teaching Assistants. *International Journal of Intercultural Relations,* 14, 337–353.

Said, E. W. (1978). *Orientalism: Western Conceptions of the Orient.* London: Routledge & Kegan Paul.

Sánchez, I. G. and Orellana, M. F. (2006). The Construction of Moral and Social Identity in Immigrant Children's Narratives-in-Translation. *Linguistics and Education*, *17*(3), 209–239. doi: http://dx.doi.org/10.1016/j.linged.2006.07.001

Sapir, E. and Mandelbaum, D. G. (1985). *Selected Writings of Edward Sapir in Language, Culture and Personality* (2nd edn). Berkeley, CA: University of California Press.

Sarangi, S. (2009). Culture. In G. Senft, J.-O. Östman and J. Verschueren (Eds), *Culture and Language Use* (pp. 81–104). Amsterdam: John Benjamins.

Schmitt, L. E. (1970). *Kurzer Grundriß der Germanischen Philologie bis 1500* [*Introduction to Germanic Philology up to 1500*]. Berlin: Walter de Gruyter.

Scollon, R., Scollon, S. W. and Jones, R. H. (2012). *Intercultural Communication: A Discourse Approach* (3rd edn). Malden, MA and Oxford: Wiley & Sons.

Sedaris, D. (2000). *Me Talk Pretty One Day*. London: Abacus.

Sehlin MacNeil, K. (2016). On Equal Terms?: Exploring Traditional Owners' Views Regarding Radioactive Waste Dumps on Adnyamathanha Country. *Journal of Australian Indigenous Issues*, *19*(3), 95–111.

Shardakova, M. and Pavlenko, A. (2004). Identity Options in Russian Textbooks. *Journal of Language, Identity & Education*, *3*(1), 25–46.

Shcherbatova, S. and Plessentin, U. (2013, 18 November). Zuwanderung und Selbstfindung: Die Jüdischen Gemeinden im Wiedervereinten Deutschland. *Heinrich Böll Stiftung: Migrationspolitisches Portal*. Retrieved from https://heimatkunde.boell. de/2013/11/18/zuwanderung-und-selbstfindung-die-j%C3%BCdischen-gemeinden-im-wiedervereinten-deutschland

Smith-Khan, L. (2017). Negotiating Narratives, Accessing Asylum: Evaluating Language Policy as Multi-Level Practice, Beliefs and Management. *Multilingua*, *36*(1), 31–57.

Spolsky, B. (2004). *Language Policy*. Cambridge: Cambridge University Press.

Spolsky, B. (2017). 'Shikl, What Did You Do for Yiddish Today?' An Appreciation of Activist Scholarship. *International Journal of the Sociology of Language*, *243*, 29–38. doi: 10.1515/ijsl-2016-0044

Steinbeck, J. (1939). *The Grapes of Wrath*. New York: Penguin.

Stevenson, R. L. (1885). A Child's Garden of Verses.

Street, B. V. (1993). Culture is a Verb. In D. Graddol, L. Thompson and M. Byram (Eds), *Language and Culture: Papers from the Annual Meeting of the British Association of Applied Linguistics Held at Trevelyan College, University of Durham, September 1991* (pp. 23–43). Clevedon: Multilingual Matters.

Strömmer, M. (2016). Affordances and Constraints: Second Language Learning in Cleaning Work. *Multilingua*, *35*(6), 697–721.

Subramanian, A. (2000). Indians in North Carolina: Race, Class, and Culture in the Making of Immigrant Identity. *Comparative Studies of South Asia, Africa and the Middle East*, *20*(1), 105–114.

Takahashi, H. (2014). Syriac as a Vehicle for Transmission of Knowledge across Borders of Empires. *Horizons*, *5*(1), 29–52.

Takahashi, K. (2010). Insult and Injury in Ueno Park. Retrieved from http://www.languageonthemove.com/recent-posts/insult-and-injury-in-ueno-park

Takahashi, K. (2013). *Language Learning, Gender and Desire: Japanese Women on the Move*. Clevedon: Multilingual Matters.

Tan, A. (1989). *The Joy Luck Club*. New York: Ballantine.

Tannen, D. (1986). *That's Not What I Meant! How Conversational Style Makes or Breaks Relationships*. New York: Ballantine Books.

Taylor, T. (2006). Wild, Wild East. *CNN Traveller*, March–April 2006, 50–54.

Tetteh, V. W. (2015). *Language, Education and Settlement: A Sociolinguistic Ethnography on, with, and for Africans in Australia* (PhD). Macquarie University. Retrieved from http://www.languageonthemove.com/wp-content/uploads/2015/07/Final-PhD-thesis_ Vera-Williams-Tetteh.pdf

Theobald, P. and Donato, R. (1990). Children of the Harvest: The Schooling of Dust Bowl and Mexican Migrants During the Depression Era. *Peabody Journal of Education, 67*(4), 29–45.

Thompson, C. (2007, 5 June). Can McDonald's Alter the Dictionary? *Time.* http:// content.time.com/time/business/article/0,8599,1628391,00.html

Thurlow, C. and Jaworski, A. (2010). *Tourism Discourse: Language and Global Mobility.* Basingstoke: Palgrave Macmillan.

Thurlow, C., Jaworski, A. and Ylänne-McEwen, V. (2005). 'Half-Hearted Tokens of Transparent Love'? 'Ethnic' Postcards and the Visual Mediation of Host-Tourist Communication. *Tourism, Culture and Communication, 5*(2), 93–104.

Tilbury, F. (2007). 'I Feel I Am a Bird without Wings': Discourses of Sadness and Loss among East Africans in Western Australia. *Identities-Global Studies in Culture and Power, 14*(4), 433–458. doi: 10.1080/10702890701578464

Topçu, Ö., Bota, A. and Pham, K. (2012). *Wir Neuen Deutschen: Wer Wir Sind, Was Wir Wollen [Us New Germans: Who We Are, What We Want].* Hamburg: Rowohlt.

Tsonga. (2016). *Ethnologue.* Retrieved from https://www.ethnologue.com/language/tso

Turnbull, S. (2002). *Almost French: A New Life in Paris.* Sydney: Bantam Books.

Tusting, K., Crawshaw, R. and Callen, B. (2002). 'I Know, 'Cos I Was There': How Residence Abroad Students Use Personal Experience to Legitimate Cultural Generalizations. *Discourse and Society, 13*(5), 651–672.

Tylor, E. B. (1920). *Primitive Culture: Researches into the Development of Mythology, Philosophy, Religion, Language, Art, and Custom* (6th edn, Vol. 1). London: John Murray.

Uchida, A. (1998). The Orientalization of Asian Women in America. *Women's Studies International Forum, 21*(2), 161–174.

Universal Declaration of Human Rights (1948).

Ustinova, I. P. and Bhatia, T. K. (2005). Convergence of English in Russian TV Commercials. *World Englishes, 24*(4), 495–508. doi: 10.1111/j.0883-2919.2005.00433.x

Vaara, E. (1999). Cultural Differences and Post-Merger Problems: Misconceptions and Cognitive Simplifications. *Nordiske Organisasjonsstudier, 1*(1), 59–88.

Vaara, E. (2000). Constructions of Cultural Differences in Postmerger Change Processes: A Sensemaking Perspective on Finnish-Swedish Cases. *M@n@gement, 3*(3), 81–101.

Vaara, E., Tienari, J., Piekkari, R. and Säntti, R. (2005). Language and the Circuits of Power in a Merging Multinational Corporation. *Journal of Management Studies, 42*(3), 595–623.

Vandermeeren, S. (1998). *Fremdsprachen in Europäischen Unternehmen. Untersuchungen zu Bestand und Bedarf im Geschäftsalltag mit Empfehlungen für Sprachenpolitik und Sprachunterricht [Foreign Languages in European Companies: Studies in the Language Use and Language Needs in Business with Recommendations for Language Policy and Language Teaching].* Waldsteinberg: Heidrun Popp.

Vathi, Z., Duci, V. and Dhembo, E. (2016). Homeland (Dis)Integrations: Educational Experience, Children and Return Migration to Albania. *International Migration, 54*(3), 159–172. doi: 10.1111/imig.12230

Vesterhus, S. A. (1991). Anglicisms in German Car Documents. *Language International, 3*(3), 10–15.

Villeneuve, D. (2016). Arrival. Retrieved from http://www.imdb.com/title/tt2543164/

Visson, L. (1998). *Wedded Strangers: The Challenges of Russian-American Marriages*. New York: Hippocrene.

Wei-Yu Chen, C. (2006). The Mixing of English in Magazine Advertisements in Taiwan. *World Englishes, 25*(3–4), 467–478. doi: 10.1111/j.1467-971X.2006.00467.x

Weichselbaumer, D. (2016). *Discrimination against Female Migrants Wearing Headscarves*. Bonn: IZA.

Westermann, F. (2016, 16 September). The Man Stuffed and Displayed Like a Wild Animal. *BBC News*. Retrieved from http://www.bbc.com/news/magazine-37344210

Who are the Kurds? (1999). *Washington Post*. Retrieved from http://www.washingtonpost.com/wp-srv/inatl/daily/feb99/kurdprofile.htm

Who are the Rohingya Refugees? (2016, 8 December). *Amnesty International*. Retrieved from https://www.amnesty.org.au/who-are-the-rohingya-refugees/

Widdicombe, S. (1998). Identity as an Analysts' and a Participants' Resource. In C. Antaki and S. Widdicombe (Eds), *Identities in Talk* (pp. 191–206). London: Sage.

Williams, E. (2014). *Bridges and Barriers: Language in African Education and Development*. London: Routledge.

Williams, J. (1998). *Don't they Know it's Friday? Cross-Cultural Considerations for Business and Life in the Gulf*. London: Motivate Publishing.

Williams, R. (1982). *Culture and Society: Coleridge to Orwell* (2nd edn). London: The Hogarth Press.

Williams, R. (1983). *Keywords: A Vocabulary of Culture and Society* (2nd edn). London: Fontana Press.

World Confederation of Organizations of the Teaching Profession. (1959). *Teaching Mutual Appreciation of Eastern and Western Cultural Values*. Washington, DC: World Confederation of Organizations of the Teaching Profession.

Wortham, S. E. F. (2003). Linguistic Anthropology of Education: An Introduction. In S. E. F. Wortham and B. Rymes (Eds), *Linguistic Anthropology of Education* (pp. 1–29). Westport, CT and London: Praeger.

Wustmann, G. (1903). *Allerhand Sprachdummheiten* [*All Manner of Linguistic Stupidities*] (3rd edn). Leipzig: Grunow.

Yalanta and Oak Valley Communities and Mattingley, C. (2009). *Maralinga: The Anangu Story*. Sydney: Allen & Unwin.

Yang, J. C. (1999). *The Xenophobe's Guide to the Chinese* (2nd edn). London: Oval Books.

Yano, C. R. (2013). *Pink Globalization: Hello Kitty's Trek across the Pacific*. Durham, NC: Duke University Press.

Zentella, A. C. (1997). The Hispanophobia of the Official English Movement in the US. *International Journal of the Sociology of Language, 127*, 71–86. doi: 10.1515/ijsl.1997.127.71

Zhang, J. (2011). *Language Policy and Planning for the 2008 Beijing Olympics: An Investigation of the Discursive Construction of an Olympic City and a Global Population* (PhD). Macquarie University, Sydney.

Index

9 781474 412919